Discovering Fiction

STUDENT'S BOOK 2

Discovering Fiction

A Reader *of* American Short Stories

STUDENT'S BOOK 2

■ Judith Kay

■ Rosemary Gelshenen

CAMBRIDGE
UNIVERSITY PRESS

PUBLISHED BY THE PRESS SYNDICATE OF THE UNIVERSITY OF CAMBRIDGE
The Pitt Building, Trumpington Street, Cambridge, United Kingdom

CAMBRIDGE UNIVERSITY PRESS
The Edinburgh Building, Cambridge CB2 2RU, UK
40 West 20th Street, New York, NY 10011–4211, USA
10 Stamford Road, Oakleigh, VIC 3166, Australia
Ruiz de Alarcón 13, 28014 Madrid, Spain
Dock House, The Waterfront, Cape Town 8001, South Africa

http://www.cambridge.org

First published as *America Writes* by St. Martin's Press, Inc. 1997
Reprinted 1998
Third printing 2000
First printed as *Discovering Fiction* Student's Book 2 by Cambridge University Press 2001

Printed in the United States of America

Typeface Adobe Garamond   *System* QuarkXPress®   [AH]

A catalog record for this book is available from the British Library

Library of Congress Cataloging in Publication data available

ISBN   0 521 00559 0   Student's Book 1
ISBN   0 521 00235 4   Instructor's Manual 1
ISBN   0 521 00351 2   Student's Book 2
ISBN   0 521 65448 3   Instructor's Manual 2

Art direction, book design, and layout services: Adventure House, NYC

Illustrations: Dan Brown: *A Day's Wait, The Last Leaf, The Lottery, My Father Sits in the Dark, The Circus;* Miles
Hyman: *The Quickening, The Ambitious Guest, All Summer in a Day, Too Soon a Woman, Talking to the Dead;* Lori
Mitchell: *Thank You, Ma'm, Désirée's Baby, A Rice Sandwich;* Rick Powell: *The One Day War, A Visit to Grandmother,
The Warriors;* Alexis Seabrook: *The Corn Planting, The Third Level.*

See acknowledgments on p. 281, which is an extension of this copyright page.

■　　■　　■

To our parents, who would have been proud.
To our families and friends, who encouraged us.
To our students, who inspired us.

■　　■　　■

About the Authors

JUDITH KAY has extensive experience teaching writing, communication skills, and grammar. She now teaches an academic composition class at Broward Community College in Broward County, Florida. Previously, she taught at Marymount Manhattan College in New York City, where she and Rosemary Gelshenen were colleagues. In addition, Kay has taught seminars in writing, and she and Gelshenen have collaborated on teaching curriculum and presented workshops at regional and international meetings of Teachers of English to Speakers of Other Languages (TESOL).

Kay has a master's degree in TESOL from Hunter College and is a member of Phi Beta Kappa. She is a writer of short stories and a poet.

ROSEMARY GELSHENEN teaches literature, creative writing, and grammar in New York City at both Marymount Manhattan College and New York University. Formerly, she taught English at Norman Thomas High School and was a teacher trainer for the New York City Board of Education. Her awards include the Veritas Medal for Excellence in Education (1986) and New York City Teacher of the Year (1983). She also received two Impact II grants for innovative methods of teaching.

Gelshenen's articles on teaching methods have appeared in numerous publications. She is the author of *Instant English Literature*, (1994), a lighthearted approach to the lives and works of nineteenth century English novelists.

Contents

APPENDIX   275

To the Student

As our students progress in their study of English, we have found that they often ask us to recommend stories and novels. For this book, we chose outstanding short stories by American authors – stories that we particularly like and that our students, over the years, have enjoyed reading and discussing, and that we hope you will enjoy, too.

At this point in your study of English, you have a good command of the language: you understand a great deal; you speak easily and comfortably; and you write well-structured English sentences. However, even though you've come a long way, there are probably certain aspects of English that continue to cause problems.

No matter how well you read and write English, sometimes you're still not sure which prepositions to use and when to use an article. Irregular verbs continue to "bug" you, and of course, there are all those idioms. To reinforce your study of English, this textbook will review some of the grammar you have already learned.

Any study of a language should also include an exploration of its culture. Whether you are observing the California landscape of William Saroyan's story, the midwestern farm in Sherwood Anderson's tale, or the city streets of Langston Hughes's writing, you are seeing America. Through these stories, you will develop some additional insights into American culture as it has spanned the past two hundred years.

Enter the world of literature with us now, and savor the richness of the words, images, and characters you will meet.

JUDITH KAY
ROSEMARY GELSHENEN

To the Instructor

After many years of teaching, we found no books that offered a combination of literature and grammatical review geared to meet the needs of the high-intermediate and advanced student. Though no book offers everything to the classroom instructor, we think our "offspring" comes close!

All the stories included in *Discovering Fiction* have been used successfully in our classes. The sections on "Vocabulary" and "Idioms and Expressions" enable students to read the stories on their own at home. We have chosen a cross section of outstanding stories both for their style and content, so that students will appreciate the breadth of American literature.

The grammar exercises that follow each selection are addressed to the high-intermediate and advanced student. These exercises are meant to serve as a grammar review and reinforcement. Hopefully, they will help students overcome those elusive trouble areas – prepositions, articles, irregular verbs, and so forth. We have not arranged the grammar in order of difficulty. Therefore, you may assign the stories according to the needs of your students.

Suggestions for writing and discussion are also included in each chapter. We find that our students respond best to assignments that touch on their personal experiences – for example, writing about their own fears after reading Hemingway's "A Day's Wait." Many of the stories lend themselves to dramatization. This is an excellent way to encourage shy students to participate in class activities.

We hope the variety of selections will enable you to expand the literary horizons of your students. Many students have read Mark Twain and Ernest Hemingway, but few have been exposed to Langston Hughes, Ray Bradbury, or Shirley Jackson. These short stories are often a springboard to reading other stories and novels by the same authors. What better gift can we give our students than to encourage them to read?

We would like to think the following reviewers for their participation in the project: Richard C. Burnson, University of Wisconsin-Madison; Tess Ferree, Columbia University; Denis A. Hall, New Hampshire College; and Howard Sage, New York University.

JUDITH KAY
ROSEMARY GELSHENEN

Instructions for Using This Book

The following discussion will give you a general overview of the various sections in the book. We also mention some suggestions for using the book in the classroom.

At the beginning of each chapter, the Think Before You Read questions create interest in the story and stimulate discussion before the actual reading. Sometimes, this section requires students to read the first paragraph of the story to answer certain questions.

Next, a Literary Term is defined, and there is a section on Idioms and Expressions. These sections also help to prepare students for the story that follows. The story may be read in class, either individually or in small groups with students taking turns. The longer stories may be assigned for homework or started in class and finished at home.

Before reading each story, students should read the biographical information about the author. We have included interesting information about each author's life as well as historical references to the period in which the author lived.

We ask our students to read the stories first without stopping to "look up" words. During a second reading of the story, they can underline or highlight any words that stump them. Amazingly, they often do know the words' meanings although they may not be able to clearly define them. Students are surprised that context clues and their previous knowledge of English vobabulary have helped them.

Comprehension questions follow each selection. Many of these questions refer to specific details in the story and require students to read carefully. This section may be given for homework as a written assignment, or discussed in pairs or in small groups.

Although the Vocabulary section is featured after the story, you may prefer to discuss it with your students beforehand. We encourage students to try to decipher the meaning of a word from its context in a sentence. Too often, we believe, our students become very reliant on dictionaries, computers, and instructors for definitions. The vocabulary exercises are varied so that students don't become bored with the same pattern.

The Grammar section following each story allows students to review a "problem area." This section, which focuses on an element of English that causes difficulties for most students, should be discussed in class, and the exercises should be reviewed even if they are assigned for homework.

In Sharing Ideas, you have an ideal opportunity to encourage discussions among students. These questions deal with the story and with other general issues that interest all of us. Once again, this section may be assigned to partners, small groups, or the whole class.

The final section after each story deals with Writing. There is a variety of creative ideas as well as more academic assignments. Depending on your students, you may give them free choice or assign specific writing questions.

Special review sections offer the opportunity to Take a Closer Look. Here, in Analyzing and Comparing, students are asked to interrelate the stories and further explore the part's theme. There is also a Freewriting activity. Other review features include Words Frequently Confused, Spelling, and a Review Test.

The Appendix at the end of the text includes a list of Common Errors, a glossary of Literary Terms (with many examples), and a list of Irregular Verbs.

Discovering Fiction

STUDENT'S BOOK 2

A Life Lesson

WE ALL learn in different ways. When we think of learning, we usually think of teachers and school. However, a great deal of our learning takes place outside the classroom. Life is the greatest teacher of all, and our experiences often change our lives forever.

■ In the following stories, the main characters undergo important changes through a single incident or a chance meeting, as occurs in "Thank You, Ma'm." As you finish each story in this part, ask yourself, How did the characters learn a lesson? and Have I ever experienced a similar situation? You might be surprised to find that you have learned a lesson just from reading these stories.

■ *Chapter 3*

THE CORN PLANTING
– Sherwood Anderson

■ *Chapter 4*

THE QUICKENING
– Lisa Interollo

Chapter 1

A Day's Wait ERNEST HEMINGWAY

A PRE-READING

1. Think Before You Read

Answer the following questions before you read the story:

1. What do you know about Ernest Hemingway's life and writings?
2. Which of his novels or short stories have you read?
3. What do you think the title of the story means?
4. What makes parents more or less sensitive to their children's fears?
5. Are parents always sensitive to their children's fears?
6. Why do children sometimes hide their fears from their parents?

2. Literary Term: Point of View

Eyewitnesses to accidents or crimes often describe what they saw in very different ways. People see situations from their own perspectives. In "A Day's Wait," Hemingway chose to write the narrative from the father's **point of view** (the "I" of the story). Imagine the events of the story from a different character's point of view.

3. Idioms and Expressions

Note the following idioms and expressions that appear in the story:

got a headache had a pain in one's head	**made a note** wrote something down
	take it easy relax
took the boy's temperature used a thermometer to measure fever	**we make** we create

B | THE STORY

ABOUT THE AUTHOR

Ernest Hemingway (1899–1961) is a well-known writer whose works are read all over the world. Like Mark Twain, he is regarded as a representative American writer.

Born in a suburb of Chicago, Hemingway began writing in high school, and after graduation he worked as a reporter. During World War I, Hemingway tried to join the army but was turned down because of his age. Instead, he volunteered as an ambulance driver for the Red Cross. In Italy, he was injured by a mortar shell and sent home. He was only eighteen years old.

Hemingway's life was an adventurous one in which he challenged nature and the dangers of war. He fought in the Spanish Civil War, was a correspondent in World War II, and ran with the bulls in Pamplona. He was an amateur boxer, avid hunter, and record-holding deep-sea fisherman.

Hemingway lived in Paris, the Florida Keys, and Cuba before settling in Idaho. After a period of failing health, he committed suicide by shooting himself. His father had also killed himself with a gun.

The story "A Day's Wait" exemplifies Hemingway's style: The sentences are clearly and sparsely written; the dialogues are short and to the point. Hemingway's heroes appear to be strong and unemotional, but they are also sensitive. Under the macho, brave exterior is a scared little child. Thus, the character becomes more human and believable.

A Day's Wait

HE CAME into the room to shut the windows while we were still in bed and I saw he looked ill. He was shivering, his face was white, and he walked slowly as though it ached to move.

"What's the matter, Schatz?"

"I've got a headache."

"You better go back to bed."

"No. I'm all right."

"You go to bed. I'll see you when I'm dressed."

But when I came downstairs he was dressed, sitting by the fire, looking a very sick and miserable boy of nine years. When I put my hand on his forehead I knew he had a fever.

"You go up to bed," I said, "you're sick."

"I'm all right," he said.

When the doctor came he took the boy's temperature.

"What is it?" I asked him.

"One hundred and two."

Downstairs, the doctor left three different medicines in different colored capsules with instructions for giving them. One was to bring down the fever, another a purgative, the third to overcome an acid condition. The germs of influenza can only exist in an acid condition, he explained. He seemed to know all about influenza and said there was nothing to worry about if the fever did not go above one hundred and four degrees. This was a light epidemic of flu and there was no danger if you avoided pneumonia.

Back in the room I wrote the boy's temperature down and made a note of the time to give the various capsules.

"Do you want me to read to you?"

"All right. If you want to," said the boy. His face was very white and there were dark areas under his eyes. He lay still in the bed and seemed very detached from what was going on.

I read aloud from Howard Pyle's *Book of Pirates;* but I could see he was not following what I was reading.

"How do you feel, Schatz?" I asked him.

"Just the same, so far," he said.

I sat at the foot of the bed and read to myself while I waited for it to be time to give another capsule. It would have been natural for him to go to sleep, but when I looked up he was looking at the foot of the bed, looking very strangely.

"Why don't you try to go to sleep? I'll wake you up for the medicine."

"I'd rather stay awake."

After a while he said to me, "You don't have to stay in here with me, Papa, if it bothers you."

"It doesn't bother me."

"No, I mean you don't have to stay if it's going to bother you."

I thought perhaps he was a little lightheaded and after giving him the prescribed capsules at eleven o'clock I went out for a while.

It was a bright, cold day, the ground covered with a sleet that had frozen so that it seemed as if all the bare trees, the bushes, the cut brush and all the grass and the bare ground had been varnished with ice. I took the young Irish setter for a little walk up the road and along a frozen creek, but it was difficult to stand or walk on the glassy surface and the red dog slipped and slithered and I fell twice, hard, once dropping my gun and having it slide away over the ice.

We flushed a covey of quail under a high clay bank with overhanging brush and I killed two as they went out of sight over the top of the bank. Some of the covey lit in trees, but most of them scattered into brush piles and it was necessary to jump on the ice-coated mounds of brush several times before they would flush. Coming out while you were poised unsteadily on the icy, springy brush they made difficult shooting and I killed two, missed five, and started back pleased to have found a covey close to the house and happy there were so many left to find another day.

At the house they said the boy had refused to let anyone come into the room.

"You can't come in," he said. "You mustn't get what I have."

I went up to him and found him in exactly the position I had left him, white-faced, but with the tops of his cheeks flushed by the fever, staring still, as he stared, at the foot of the bed.

■ ■ ■

". . . what time do you think I'm going to die?" he asked.

■ ■ ■

I took his temperature.

"What is it?"

"Something like a hundred," I said. It was one hundred and two and four tenths.

"It was a hundred and two," he said.

"Who said so?"

"The doctor."

"Your temperature is all right," I said. "It's nothing to worry about."

"I don't worry," he said, "but I can't keep from thinking."

"Don't think," I said. "Just take it easy."

"I'm taking it easy," he said and looked straight ahead. He was evidently holding tight onto himself about something.

"Take this with water."

"Do you think it will do any good?"

"Of course it will."

I sat down and opened the Pirate book and commenced to read, but I could see he was not following, so I stopped.

"About what time do you think I'm going to die?" he asked.

"What?"

"About how long will it be before I die?"

"You aren't going to die. What's the matter with you?"

"Oh, yes, I am. I heard him say a hundred and two."

"People don't die with a fever of one hundred and two. That's a silly way to talk."

"I know they do. At school in France the boys told me you can't live with forty-four degrees. I've got a hundred and two."

165 He had been waiting to die all day, ever since nine o'clock in the morning.

"You poor Schatz," I said. "Poor old Schatz. It's like miles and kilometers. You aren't going to die. That's a 170 different thermometer. On that thermometer thirty-seven is normal. On this kind it's ninety-eight."

"Are you sure?"

"Absolutely," I said. "It's like miles and kilometers. You know, like how 175 many kilometers we make when we do seventy miles in the car?"

"Oh," he said.

But his gaze at the foot of the bed relaxed slowly. The hold over himself 180 relaxed too, finally, and the next day it was very slack and he cried very easily at little things that were of no importance.

C | AFTER READING

1. *Comprehension*

Answer these questions to determine how well you understood the story.

1. In what season does the story take place?
2. How does the father know his son is sick?
3. Why doesn't the boy pay attention to the book his father is reading to him?
4. Where does the father go while his son is resting in bed?
5. What is the boy waiting for?
6. How much time passes from the beginning of the story until the end?
7. Why does the boy cry easily the next day?

2. *Vocabulary*

The following vocabulary words appear in Hemingway's story. Write the appropriate word(s) in each sentence.

flushed	detached	quail	varnished
capsule	lightheaded	poised	shivering
covey	sleet	bank	
commenced	pirates	prescribed	

1. The man, drenched by the rain, stood _____ in his wet clothes.

2. The little boy was too worried about his temperature to listen to stories of _____ and hidden treasure.

3. She felt _____ from the hot weather and lack of water.

4. Schatz's doctor _____ the medicine in _____ form.

5. The weather forecaster predicted a winter storm with snow and _____.

6. They _____ the antique furniture to protect it.

7. A _____ of _____ sat hidden in the bushes.

8. The hunter _____ his prey out of the woods.

9. The diver stood _____ at the edge of the diving board.

10. She sat apart from the other students feeling _____ and lonely.

11. At the signal from the instructor, the students _____ to take the exam.

12. An old, gnarled tree stood on the _____ of the river.

3. Grammar: Articles

The English articles include *a*, *an*, and *the*. *The* is the **definite** article; it is used with nouns that refer to something or someone definite or specific. *A* and *an* are **indefinite** articles; they are used with nouns that refer to something or someone that is not specific or known about.

The indefinite articles *a* and *an* are used with singular nouns only. The definite article *the* can be used with a singular or plural noun.

Sometimes, singular nouns sound plural, for example, *news, family, orchestra,* and *army*. It is important to remember that such nouns still take a singular verb, so that subject and verb agree.

Look at the following sentences:

> The **news** of his rescue **is** a relief.
> The **family** next door **is coming** for dinner.
> The **orchestra rehearses** every day.
> An **army needs** equipment.

Intangible or abstract nouns Nouns such as *love, life, hope, beauty,* and *hate* do not use any article when they are referred to in a general sense. For example,

> INCORRECT: The life is unpredictable.
> CORRECT: **Life** is unpredictable.

Using articles When we refer to a noun the first time, we use *a* or *an*. Thereafter, since the identity of the noun is established, we use the definite article *the.* For example,

There is **a** large elm tree in the park. **The** tree is more than a hundred years old.

◼ *Application*
Write the correct articles in these sentences. For some sentences, there is more than one correct article.

1. I read _____ book *The Color Purple* before I saw _____ movie.

2. The house has _____ beautiful garden. Would you like to sit in _____ garden?

3. _____ police found _____ kidnapped child.

4. He bought _____ expensive car, and he washes _____ car every week.

5. _____ bank was closed because it was _____ holiday.

6. I didn't have _____ stamp, so I couldn't mail _____ letter.

7. She asked _____ waiter to bring her _____ menu.

8. Did you submit _____ application for _____ credit card?

4. Grammar: Prepositions

Prepositions, which occur frequently in English, act as bridges or connections between their objects and other words in a sentence. A preposition always has an object – a noun or pronoun. The preposition plus its object is called a **prepositional phrase.** Prepositional phrases may occur anywhere in a sentence. At the beginning of a sentence, the prepositional phrase is usually followed by a comma. Here are some examples of prepositional phrases:

The story **of her recovery** is an inspiration.
We saw the clouds **above the mountain.**
After the summer, we will visit France.

Using prepositions The following are some frequently used prepositions:

about	below	in	through
above	by	into	to
after	down	of	under
among	during	off	up
around	for	on	with
at	from	over	without

The prepositions *in* and *on* are often confused. When we are discussing time, *on* refers to a specific date. These, for example, are correct:

I was born **on** April 5, 1950.
I was born **in** April; or I was born **in** 1950.

■ Application

Write the correct prepositions in the sentences below. For some sentences, there is more than one correct preposition.

1. The man _____ the car looked suspicious.

2. He gave some money _____ the beggar.

3. _____ the meeting, we went _____ the cafeteria

   _____ lunch.

4. As he stepped _____ the street, he heard the screeching sound

   _____ brakes.

5. He was heartbroken _____ her betrayal, but he hoped he would

   fall _____ love again.

6. They jogged _____ the park _____ the rain.

7. We celebrate Independence Day _____ July 4.

8. Are you taking a trip _____ January?

Often, a preposition consists of a group of words. The following are typical examples:

in front of	because of	by means of	according to
next to	in place of	in order to	in spite of

■ *Application*

Use the preceding prepositions (groups of words) in the following sentences:

1. We played the game _____ the rules.

2. _____ his disability, he graduated with honors.

3. He used chopsticks _____ a fork.

4. It was hard to see the stage because the man _____ me wore

   a hat.

5. He turned up the volume _____ hear the music better.

6. _____ a hidden camera, the police were able to trap the

   terrorist.

7. _____ the blizzard, travelers were stranded at the airport.

8. He enjoyed sitting _____ the window and watching the children

   play.

   Note: The omission of prepositions is a common error. If you read your sentences aloud, often you will hear the mistake and correct it yourself. Trust your ear for the language!

■ *Application*

For this exercise you need to combine the various things you have just learned. Use appropriate articles and prepositions to complete the following sentences:

1. He came _____ _____ room to shut _____ windows while we were still in bed.

2. When I put my hand _____ his forehead, I knew he had _____ fever.

3. Downstairs, _____ doctor left three different medicines _____ different colored capsules _____ instructions _____ giving them.

4. Back _____ _____ room, I wrote _____ boy's temperature down and made _____ note _____ _____ time to give _____ various capsules.

5. It was _____ bright, cold day, _____ ground covered _____ _____ sleet.

6. I took _____ young Irish setter _____ _____ little walk _____ _____ road.

7. People don't die _____ _____ fever _____ one hundred and two.

8. _____ school _____ France, _____ boys told me you can't live _____ forty-four degrees.

D | THINKING ABOUT THE STORY

1. Sharing Ideas

Discuss the following questions with a partner, in a small group, or with the whole class:

1. Describe the relationship between the boy and his father. Are they close? How do they communicate? Is there a mother in this family? Where is she?
2. Why doesn't Schatz tell his father that he is afraid?
3. How does the father sense Schatz's fear?
4. How does Hemingway portray the boy and the father?
5. Choose another title for the story.

2. Writing

Read the writing ideas that follow. Your instructor may make specific assignments, or ask you to choose one of these.

1. Pretend you are Schatz. Write a paragraph about what is going on in your mind as you lie in bed thinking about your illness. Use the present tense.
2. Describe a fear of death you may have had as a child. Were you ever injured or in a hospital when you were young?
3. How did you feel after reading the story? How did you relate to the boy and the father? Write about these feelings.
4. Create a conversation between the father and the doctor the next day.
5. Compare the characters of Schatz and his father.
6. Rewrite the story from the doctor's point of view.

Chapter 2
Thank You, Ma'm LANGSTON HUGHES

A PRE-READING

1. Think Before You Read

Read the first paragraph of the story once and think of it as describing the opening scene of a play. Then answer the following questions:

1. Who are the characters in this scene?
2. What is happening?
3. Where and when is the action taking place?
4. Why does the action take place?
5. Do you think a chance encounter between people can sometimes change their lives? Think about chance or fate as you read this story.

2. Literary Term: Dialect

A **dialect** consists of words or phrases that reflect the regional variety of a language. An author or playwright will often use a regional dialect to make the dialogue more authentic. Initially, a dialect may be difficult to understand; it is similar to watching a foreign film with subtitles. However, the language will become more comfortable as you continue reading, and the rhythm of the dialect will be as natural as if you were one of the characters.

The following examples of dialect occur in the story:

ain't aren't		**I didn't aim to** I didn't intend to	
gonna going to		**sit you down** sit down	
could of could have		**I were** I was	
late as it be late as it is		**fix us** prepare for us	

3. Idioms and Expressions

Note the following idioms and expressions that appear in the story:

I got a great mind to I should	**took care** was careful
get through with finish	**set the table** put out plates, glasses,
make a dash for it run away	and so forth

B | THE STORY

ABOUT THE AUTHOR

Langston Hughes (1902–1967) had a varied career that took him far away from his birthplace in Joplin, Missouri. His early love for reading books was encouraged by his mother, who often took him to the library. His mother also wrote poetry and gave dramatic readings. Her work required her to travel extensively.

After his parents separated, his father moved to Mexico and Hughes went to live with his maternal grandmother. She, too, had an influence on his future career. She was a good storyteller, and she often told him about the days of slavery. The maternal influence and the sense of deep pride in his people (then referred to as Negroes) are evident in all of Hughes's writing.

At nineteen, Langston enrolled at Columbia University but left after a year. He traveled throughout Europe and Africa and worked at many jobs, including being a deckhand on a ship and a dishwasher in a Parisian nightclub. Money was always a problem, but he persevered and remained optimistic. Whether he was struggling as a student at Columbia or working as a waiter in Washington, D.C., he continued writing poetry that praised his race for its beauty and humanity.

In the 1960s, Hughes chronicled the civil rights movement in the United States. He wrote about the sit-ins, the marches, the church bombings, the hatred, and the hope. His poem "I Dream a World" begins:

> I dream a world where man
> No other man will scorn
> Where love will bless the earth
> And peace its paths adorn.

Hughes died in 1967. His plays, poems, and stories are the legacy he left to the American people, who he hoped one day could live in racial harmony.

Thank You, Ma'm

SHE WAS a large woman with a large purse that had everything in it but a hammer and nails. It had a long strap, and she carried it slung across her
5 shoulder. It was about eleven o'clock at night, dark, and she was walking alone, when a boy ran up behind her and tried to snatch her purse. The strap broke with the sudden single tug the boy gave
10 it from behind. But the boy's weight and the weight of the purse combined caused him to lose his balance. Instead of taking off full blast as he had hoped, the boy fell on his back on the sidewalk
15 and his legs flew up. The large woman simply turned around and kicked him right square in his blue-jeaned sitter. Then she reached down, picked the boy up by his shirt front, and shook him
20 until his teeth rattled.

After that the woman said, "Pick up my pocketbook, boy, and give it here."

She still held him tightly. But she bent down enough to permit him to stoop and pick up her purse. Then she 25 said, "Now ain't you ashamed of yourself?"

Firmly gripped by his shirt front, the boy said, "Yes'm."

The woman said, "What did you 30 want to do it for?"

The boy said, "I didn't aim to."

By that time two or three people passed, stopped, turned to look, and some stood watching. 35

"If I turn you loose, will you run?" asked the woman.

"Yes'm," said the boy.

"Then I won't turn you loose," said the woman. She did not release him. 40

"Lady, I'm sorry," whispered the boy.

"Um-hum! Your face is dirty. I got a great mind to wash your face for you. Ain't you got nobody home to tell you to wash your face?"

"No'm," said the boy.

"Then it will get washed this evening," said the large woman, starting up the street, dragging the frightened boy behind her.

He looked as if he were fourteen or fifteen, frail and willow-wild in tennis shoes and blue jeans.

The woman said, "You ought to be my son. I would teach you right from wrong. Least I can do right now is to wash your face. Are you hungry?"

"No'm," said the being-dragged boy. "I just want you to turn me loose."

"Was I bothering you when I turned that corner?" asked the woman.

"No'm."

"But you put yourself in contact with me," said the woman. "If you think that contact is not going to last awhile, you got another thought coming. When I get through with you, sir, you are going to remember Mrs. Luella Bates Washington Jones."

Sweat popped out on the boy's face and he began to struggle. Mrs. Jones stopped, jerked him around in front of her, put a half-nelson about his neck, and continued to drag him up the street. When she got to her door, she dragged the boy inside, down a hall, and into a large kitchenette-furnished room at the rear of the house. She switched on the light and left the door open. The boy could hear other roomers laughing and talking in the large house. Some of their doors were open, too, so he knew he and the woman were not alone. The woman still had him by the neck in the middle of her room.

She said, "What is your name?"

"Roger," answered the boy.

"Then, Roger, you go to that sink and wash your face," said the woman, whereupon she turned him loose – at last. Roger looked at the door – looked at the woman – looked at the door – and went to the sink.

"Let the water run until it gets warm," she said. "Here's a clean towel."

"You gonna take me to jail?" asked the boy, bending over the sink.

"Not with that face, I would not take you nowhere," said the woman. "Here I am trying to get home to cook me a bite to eat, and you snatch my pocketbook! Maybe you ain't been to your supper either, late as it be. Have you?"

"There's nobody home at my house," said the boy.

"Then we'll eat," said the woman. "I believe you're hungry – or been hungry – to try to snatch my pocketbook!"

"I want a pair of blue suede shoes," said the boy.

"Well, you didn't have to snatch my pocketbook to get some suede shoes," said Mrs. Luella Bates Washington Jones. "You could of asked me."

"Ma'm?"

The water dripping from his face, the boy looked at her. There was a long pause. A very long pause. After he had dried his face and not knowing what else to do, dried it again, the boy turned around, wondering what next.

The door was open. He would make a dash for it down the hall. He would run, run, run!

The woman was sitting on the day bed. After a while, she said, "I were young once and I wanted things I could not get."

There was another long pause. The boy's mouth opened. Then he frowned, not knowing he frowned.

The woman said, "Um-hum! You thought I was going to say but, didn't you? You thought I was going to say, but I didn't snatch people's pocketbooks. Well, I wasn't going to say that." Pause. Silence. "I have done things, too, which I would not tell you, son – neither tell God, if He didn't already know. Everybody's got something in common. Sit you down while I fix us something to eat. You might run that comb through your hair so you will look presentable."

In another corner of the room behind a screen was a gas plate and an icebox. Mrs. Jones got up and went behind the screen. The woman did not watch the boy to see if he was going to run now, nor did she watch her purse, which she left behind her on the day bed. But the boy took care to sit on the far side of the room, away from the purse, where he thought she could easily see him out of the corner of her eye if she wanted to. He did not trust the woman to trust him. And he did not trust the woman not to trust him. And he did not want to be mistrusted now.

"Do you need somebody to go to the store," asked the boy, "maybe to get some milk or something?"

"Don't believe I do," said the woman, "unless you just want sweet milk yourself. I was going to make cocoa out of this canned milk I got here."

She heated some lima beans and ham she had in the icebox, made the cocoa, and set the table. The woman did not ask the boy anything about where he lived, or his folks, or anything else that would embarrass him. Instead, as they ate, she told him about her job in a hotel beauty shop that stayed open late, what the work was like, and how all kinds of women came in and out, blondes, redheads and Spanish. Then she cut him half of her ten-cent cake.

"Eat some more, son," she said.

When they finished eating, she got up and said, "Now here, take this ten dollars and buy yourself some blue suede shoes. And, next time, do not make the mistake of latching onto my pocketbook nor nobody else's – because shoes got by devilish ways will burn your feet. I got to get my rest now. But from here on in, son, I hope you will behave yourself."

She led the way down the hall to the front door and opened it. "Good night! Behave yourself, boy!" she said, looking into the street as he went down the steps.

The boy wanted to say something other than "Thank you, ma'm," to Mrs. Luella Bates Washington Jones, but although his lips moved, he couldn't even say that, as he turned at the foot of the barren stoop and looked up at the large woman in the door. Then she shut the door.

1. Comprehension

Answer these questions to determine how well you understood the story.

1. How old do you think Mrs. Jones is?
2. How does she feel about Roger? Is she angry at him? Does she like him?
3. At what point in the story does Mrs. Jones show that she cares about Roger?
4. Describe Roger's physical appearance.
5. Describe his behavior.
6. How does Mrs. Jones treat Roger initially? How does her behavior change?
7. Find examples of sentences that show Mrs. Jones understands Roger very well.

2. Vocabulary

Each of the numbered vocabulary words appears in Hughes's story. Look at the four definitions for each word and circle the correct one.

1. tug
   a. force
   b. steal
   c. pull
   d. shoot

2. permit
   a. allow
   b. push
   c. keep
   d. worry

3. stoop
   a. forget
   b. bend over
   c. run away
   d. fool

4. frail
   a. strong
   b. athletic
   c. tall
   d. delicate

5. bothering
   a. whispering
   b. stealing
   c. annoying
   d. meeting

6. sweat
   a. perspiration
   b. dessert
   c. cake
   d. blasphemy

7. snatch
   - a. trick
   - b. grab
   - c. watch
   - d. follow

8. frowned
   - a. grimaced
   - b. smiled
   - c. discovered
   - d. laughed

3. *Grammar: Verb Tenses*

Tenses indicate time. In English, we use six tenses – three simple and three perfect. The simple tenses are past, present, and future. The perfect tenses are past perfect, present perfect, and future perfect.

Simple tenses   The simple tenses are more specific about when an action or state of being occurs. For example,

> PAST: They **ran** in the marathon.
> PRESENT: They **run** in the marathon every year.
> FUTURE: They **will run** in the marathon next year.

Perfect tenses   The perfect tenses show the time an action or state of being begins and is completed (perfected).

In the **present perfect tense,** a situation exists up to now (the present). The construction would be: *has* (third person singular) or *have* + the *past participle.* For example,

He **has run** in five previous marathons.   (up to now)
They **have run** in many marathons.   (up to the present time)

In the **past perfect tense,** the situation was completed by the time another past event occurred. The past perfect can be thought of as a previous past. When a sentence describes two past events, the past perfect tense indicates what happened first. The construction would be: *had* + the *past participle.* For example,

He **had run** in several marathons before he finished in first place.

The **future perfect tense** describes an action or state of being that we are predicting for a time in the future. The construction would be: *will have* + the *past participle.* For example,

By next year, they **will have run** in ten marathons.

Using the present perfect with for *and* since   When you use *since* and *for* to indicate that a passage of time has elapsed, use the perfect tenses. Remember: Use *since* when you mention an exact date (day, month, or year), and use *for* when you show a period of time. For example,

He **has lived** in Hong Kong *since* 1997.   (exact year)
He **has lived** in Hong Kong *for* ten years.   (He still lives in Hong Kong.)

■ *Application*
Write the correct present perfect verb form in the following sentences:

1. We _____ (study) for the exam for a week.

2. Since last week, he _____ (write) five pages of his novel.

3. She _____ (fall) many times since she started Rollerblading.

4. For many weeks, the jury _____ (hear) testimony.

5. Since last year, Carl _____ (feel) happy at work.

6. Michelle _____ (sleep) late since she was a teenager.

4. Grammar: Irregular Verbs

Most verbs in English change to the past tense by adding *-ed* or *-d* (if the verb already ends in an *e*). However, there are more than one hundred irregular verbs, and these verbs do not follow this rule. The simple past and past participle forms of irregular verbs are listed in the Appendix on pages 278–280.

■ *Application*
Some of the most troublesome irregular verbs are dealt with in the exercise that follows. For each sentence, write the verb(s) in the simple past or one of the perfect tenses. Read the sentences aloud.

1. It _____ (begin) to rain before we arrived at the stadium.

2. The children _____ (begin) to sing a song after the teacher _____ (begin) playing the piano.

3. He _____ (bear) the burden of supporting his family for many years.

4. The wild dog _____ (bite) the hunter. It was the first time the dog _____ (bite) anyone.

5. He _____ (buy) a corsage for his girlfriend. It was the first time he _____ (buy) her flowers.

6. The voters _____ (choose) a new president on Election Day.

7. The morning dew _____ (cling) to the rose petals.

8. The two lions _____ (creep) slowly toward their prey.

9. As they watched the sunset, they _____ (drink) their tea and _____ (dream) of former days.

10. After the apples _____ (fall) from the trees, we _____ (find) them on the ground.

11. Her grandfather _____ (teach) her many things before she _____ (leave) for college.

12. The lake _____ (freeze) two weeks ago, and we _____ (slide) on it as we walked.

13. She was pleased to see that her nephew _____ (grow) into a fine adult.

14. We _____ (hear) the loud music blasting from their car stereo.

15. The scout _____ (lead) the way through the woods. He _____ (be) their guide many times before.

16. The thief _____ (hide) the jewels, and the police never found out where he _____ (put) them.

■ *Application*
Irregular verbs in the story
These sentences are taken from Hughes's story. Fill in the past tense forms of the verbs in parentheses.

1. The strap _____ (break) with the sudden, single tug.

2. The boy _____ (fall) on his back, and his legs _____ (fly) up.

3. She _____ (shake) him until his teeth rattled.

4. She still _____ (hold) him tightly.

5. Then she _____ (say), "Now ain't you ashamed of yourself?"

6. He _____ (begin) to struggle.

7. He _____ (think) she could easily see him.

8. As they _____ (eat), she told him about her job.

9. All kinds of women _____ (come) into the beauty shop.

10. She _____ (cut) him half of her ten-cent cake.

11. When they finished eating, she _____ (stand) up.

12. She _____ (lead) the way down the hall.

■ *Application*
Using past participles as adjectives The past participle form of a verb may be used as an adjective. In sentences 4, 6, 10, 13, and 16 of the irregular verbs application on pages 22 and 23, change the first verb in parentheses into the past participle form and combine it with the noun it modifies. For example,

the **frozen** lake
the **stolen** money

5. *Grammar: Negative Verb Forms*

To change the meaning of a sentence to the negative, we use an auxiliary verb plus the main verb. Remember: The auxiliary shows the tense and the main verb stays in its simple form.

> INCORRECT: I didn't went shopping.
> He didn't swam.
> CORRECT: I **didn't go shopping.**
> He **didn't swim.**

When changing the present perfect or past perfect to the negative form, *has* becomes *hasn't* (*has not*); *have* becomes *haven't* (*have not*); and *had* becomes *hadn't* (*had not*). Then add the past participle, as shown in the following examples:

I **haven't gone shopping.**
He **hasn't swum.**

■ *Application*

Look at sentences 1, 4, 5, and 14 of the irregular verbs application on pages 22 and 23. Change each sentence to a negative by using a form of *do* or *have* plus *not*. For example, sentence 1 would read:

It **hadn't begun** to rain before we arrived at the stadium.

6. Editing

Edit the following essay. Correct any errors in grammar, spelling, or punctuation.

I think mrs Jones teached the boy a good lesson she could of reported him to

Police but instead she decided she would taught him a lesson herself. The boy who

was lucky she was a good-hearted person done wrong when he stealed her purse. I

bet he didn't espect this old lady to be strong enuf to knock him over and drag him

to her house and he was afraid to run away and also he liked her. She cared more

for him then his own family. The boy was lucky to meet someone like mrs jones.

D | THINKING ABOUT THE STORY

1. Sharing Ideas

Discuss the following questions with a partner, in a small group, or with the whole class:

1. How does Mrs. Jones react when Roger tries to steal her purse?
2. Is her reaction believable? Why or why not?
3. When they arrive at the boarding house, what do you think Roger is thinking or planning to do?
4. Does Mrs. Jones like the boy? Why?
5. How do you think Roger's encounter with Mrs. Jones alters his life?
6. Why does Hughes title the story, "Thank You, Ma'm"?

2. *Writing*

Read the writing ideas that follow. Your instructor may make specific assignments, or ask you to choose one of these.

1. Continue the story, assuming that the characters meet again. Write a dialogue between Roger and Mrs. Jones. Describe their second encounter – a week later, a month later, or a year later.
2. Describe Mrs. Jones and the way she treats Roger. Describe Roger and the way he responds to Mrs. Jones.
3. Write a different ending to the story. For example, Mrs. Jones calls the police, or Roger runs away.
4. Have you ever had a purse or wallet stolen from you? How did you feel? Write about the experience.
5. Juvenile crime can be a problem in the United States. Compare the situation with that in your country.
6. Who should be responsible for the moral education of a child? Parents? Society? Schools? Write about your opinion and give reasons for it.

A Life Lesson

Chapter 3
The Corn Planting
SHERWOOD ANDERSON

A | PRE-READING

1. Think Before You Read

Answer the following questions before you read the story:

1. Have you ever read a book or seen a movie that depicts life on a farm?
2. What sacrifices do farmers make in order to feed their livestock and plant their crops?
3. What are some of the problems that couples must face if they get married late in life?
4. Do you think these marriages are more or less successful than the marriages of young people? Why?

2. Literary Term: Symbolism

Why do people salute the flag of their country? After all, it is just a piece of cloth with a design and some special colors. People honor their flag because it represents what their country means to them. It is a symbol, for example, of freedom or equality or whatever else people love about their country. In literature, the term **symbol** means the use of expressions that represent or recall certain ideas. As you read this story, think of how the planting of corn symbolizes the emotions of the main characters.

3. Idioms and Expressions

In "The Corn Planting," the expression "make a go of it" describes the success of the main characters' marriage. Other idioms from the story include:

when it came to scratch when it came right down to it	**stuck close** stayed in one place, didn't move to another location
It was a thing to curl your hair an experience to frighten a person	**was always at them** insisting, constantly trying to persuade them
in command of themselves in a calm state	**got his notion** understood
stands out is noticeable, distinctive	

B THE STORY

ABOUT THE AUTHOR

Sherwood Anderson (1876–1941), born in Camden, Ohio, is often called "the mid-American Chekhov." He inherited his gift of narrative fiction from his father, a roaming, improvident storyteller of unlikely tales.

Anderson had little formal schooling, but he learned from life's experiences. He served in the U.S. Army in Cuba during the Spanish-American War. Later, he worked in a factory until his brother Karl, a well-known painter, got him a job as a copywriter in Chicago. He made his reputation with the publication of his first novel, *Winesburg, Ohio,* which is partly autobiographical.

Despite his fame, Anderson led a life of confusion and indecision. He drifted from city to city and from wife to wife. He was married four times and seemed incapable of settling down. Nonetheless, Anderson understood human nature and possessed a remarkable ability to portray the vulnerability of ordinary people. This is evident in his short story "The Corn Planting."

The Corn Planting

THE FARMERS WHO COME to our town to trade are a part of the town life. Saturday is the big day. Often the children come to the high school in town.

It is so with Hatch Hutchenson. Although his farm, some three miles from town, is small, it is known to be one of the best-kept and best-worked places in all our section. Hatch is a little gnarled old figure of a man. His place is on the Scratch Gravel Road and there are plenty of poorly kept places out that way.

Hatch's place stands out. The little frame house is always kept painted, the trees in his orchard are whitened with lime halfway up the trunks, and the barn and sheds are in repair, and his fields are always clean-looking.

Hatch is nearly seventy. He got a rather late start in life. His father, who owned the same farm, was a Civil War man and came home badly wounded, so that, although he lived a long time after the war, he couldn't work much. Hatch was the only son and stayed at home, working the place until his father died. Then, when he was nearing fifty, he married a schoolteacher of forty, and they had a son. The schoolteacher was a small one like Hatch. After they married, they both stuck close to the land. They seemed to fit into their farm life as certain people fit into the clothes they wear. I have noticed something about people who make a go of marriage. They grow more and more alike. They even grow to look alike.

Their one son, Will Hutchenson, was a small but remarkably strong boy. He came to our high school in town and pitched on our town baseball team. He was a fellow always cheerful, bright and alert, and a great favorite with all of us.

For one thing, he began as a young boy to make amusing little drawings. It was a talent. He made drawings of fish and pigs and cows and they looked like people you knew. I never did know, before, that people could look so much like cows and horses and pigs and fish.

When he had finished in the town high school, Will went to Chicago, where his mother had a cousin living, and he became a student in the Art Institute out there. Another young fellow from our town was also in Chicago. He really went two years before Will did. His name is Hal Weyman, and he was a student at the University of Chicago. After he graduated, he came home and got a job as principal of our high school.

Hal and Will Hutchenson hadn't been close friends before, Hal being several years older than Will, but in Chicago they got together, went together to see plays, and, as Hal later told me, they had a good many long talks.

I got it from Hal that, in Chicago, as at home here when he was a young boy, Will was immediately popular. He was good-looking, so the girls in the art school liked him, and he had a straightforwardness that made him popular with all the young fellows.

Hal told me that Will was out to some party nearly every night, and right away he began to sell some of his amusing little drawings and to make money. The drawings were used in advertisements, and he was well paid.

He even began to send some money home. You see, after Hal came back here, he used to go quite often out to the Hutchenson place to see Will's father and mother. He would walk or drive out there in the afternoon or on summer evenings and sit with them. The talk was always of Will.

Hal said it was touching how much the father and mother depended on their one son, how much they talked about him and dreamed of his future. They had never been people who went about much with the town folks or even with their neighbors. They were of the sort who work all the time, from early morning till late in the evenings, and on moonlight nights, Hal said, and after the little old wife had got the supper, they often went out into the fields and worked again.

You see, by this time old Hatch was nearing seventy and his wife would have been ten years younger. Hal said that whenever he went out to the farm they quit work and came to sit with him. They might be in one of the fields, working together, but when they saw him in the road, they came running. They had got a letter from Will. He wrote every week.

The little old mother would come running following the father. "We got another letter, Mr. Weyman," Hatch would cry, and then his wife, quite breathless, would say the same thing, "Mr. Weyman, we got a letter."

The letter would be brought out at once and read aloud. Hal said the letters were always delicious. Will larded them with little sketches. There were humorous drawings of people he had seen or been with, rivers of automobiles on Michigan Avenue in Chicago, a policeman at a street crossing, young stenographers hurrying into office buildings. Neither of the old people had ever been to the city and they were curious and eager. They wanted the drawings explained, and Hal said they were like two children wanting to know every little detail Hal could remember about their son's life in the big city. He was always at them to come there on a visit and they would spend hours talking of that.

"Of course," Hatch said, "we couldn't go."

"How could we?" he said. He had been on that one little farm since he was a boy. When he was a young fellow, his father was an invalid and so Hatch had to run things. A farm, if you run it right, is very exacting. You have to fight weeds all the time. There are the farm animals to take care of. "Who would milk our cows?" Hatch said. The idea of anyone but him or his wife touching one of the Hutchenson cows seemed to hurt him. While he was alive, he didn't want anyone else plowing one of his fields, tending his corn, looking after things about the barn. He felt that way about his farm.

It was a thing you couldn't explain, Hal said. He seemed to understand the two old people.

It was a spring night, past midnight, when Hal came to my house and told me the news. In our town we have a night telegraph operator at the railroad station and Hal got a wire. It was really addressed to Hatch Hutchenson, but the operator brought it to Hal. Will Hutchenson was dead, had been killed. It turned out later that he was at a party with some other young fellows and there might have been some drinking. Anyway, the car was wrecked, and Will Hutchenson was killed. The operator wanted Hal to go out and take the message to Hatch and his wife, and Hal wanted me to go along.

I offered to take my car, but Hal said no. "Let's walk out," he said. He wanted to put off the moment, I could see that. So we did walk. It was early spring, and I remember every moment of the silent walk we took, the little leaves just coming on the trees, the little streams we crossed, how the moonlight made the water seem alive. We loitered and loitered, not talking, hating to go on.

Then we got out there, and Hal went to the front door of the farmhouse while I stayed in the road. I heard a dog bark, away off somewhere. I heard a child crying in some distant house. I think that Hal, after he got to the front door of the house, must have stood there for ten minutes, hating to knock.

Then he did knock, and the sound his fist made on the door seemed terrible. It seemed like guns going off. Old Hatch came to the door, and I heard Hal tell him. I know what happened. Hal had been trying, all the way out from town, to think up words to tell the old couple in some gentle way, but when it came to the scratch, he couldn't. He blurted everything right out, right into old Hatch's face.

That was all. Old Hatch didn't say a word. The door was opened, he stood there in the moonlight, wearing a funny long white nightgown, Hal told him, and the door went shut again with a bang, and Hal was left standing there.

He stood for a time, and then came back out into the road to me. "Well," he said, and "Well," I said. We stood in the road looking and listening. There wasn't a sound from the house.

And then – it might have been ten minutes or it might have been a half-hour – we stood silently, listening and watching, not knowing what to do – we couldn't go away – "I guess they are trying to get so they can believe it," Hal whispered to me. I got his notion all right. The two old people must have thought of their son Will always only in terms of life, never of death.

We stood watching and listening, and then, suddenly, after a long time, Hal touched me on the arm. "Look," he whispered. There were two white-clad figures going from the house to the barn. It turned out, you see, that old Hatch had been plowing that day. He had finished plowing and harrowing a field near the barn.

The two figures went into the barn and presently came out. They went into the field, and Hal and I crept across the farmyard to the barn and got to where we could see what was going on without being seen.

It was an incredible thing. The old man had got a hand corn-planter out of the barn and his wife had got a bag of seed corn, and there, in the moonlight, that night, after they got that news, they were planting corn.

It was a thing to curl your hair – it was so ghostly. They were both in their nightgowns. They would do a row across the field, coming quite close to us as we stood in the shadow of the barn, and then, at the end of each row, they would kneel side by side by the fence and stay silent for a time. The whole thing went on in silence. It was the first time in my life I ever understood something, and I am far from sure now that I can put down what I understood and felt that night – I mean something about the connection between certain people and the earth – a kind of silent cry, down into the earth, of these two old people, putting corn down into the earth. It was as though they were putting death down into the ground that life might grow again – something like that.

They must have been asking something of the earth, too. But what's the use? What they were up to in connection with the life in their field and the lost life in their son is something you can't very well make clear in words. All I know is that Hal and I stood the sight as long as we could, and then we crept away and went back to town, but Hatch Hutchenson and his wife must have got what they were after that night, because Hal told me that when he went out in the morning to see them and to make the arrangements for bringing their dead son home, they were both curiously quiet and Hal thought in command of themselves. Hal said he thought they had got something. "They have their farm and they have still got Will's letters to read," Hal said.

C AFTER READING

1. Comprehension

Answer these questions to determine how well you understood the story.

1. Why did Hatch marry late in life?
2. What sentence describes the relationship between Hatch and his wife?
3. The reader never meets Will Hutchenson, but what do we learn about him from the narrator? Do you think you would have liked him?
4. Why don't the Hutchensons go to Chicago to visit their son?
5. How do the Hutchensons react to the tragedy of their son's death?
6. What sentence in the story explains the symbolism of the planting of the corn?

2. Vocabulary

Each of the numbered vocabulary words appears in Anderson's story. Look at the four definitions for each word and circle the correct one.

1. gnarled
   a. twisted
   b. disabled
   c. diminutive
   d. strong

2. larded
   a. shortened
   b. lengthened
   c. enriched
   d. illustrated

3. invalid
   a. aged man
   b. incompetent
   c. unpleasant person
   d. sickly person

4. exacting
   a. precise
   b. demanding
   c. inappropriate
   d. expensive

5. loitered
   a. delayed
   b. hastened
   c. debated
   d. left

6. blurted
   a. spoke abruptly
   b. hesitated
   c. wiped out
   d. blocked

7. notion
   a. gesture
   b. hint
   c. idea
   d. resolution

8. incredible
   a. unusual
   b. sad
   c. believable
   d. unbelievable

3. Grammar: Adverbs of Time and Degree

Like the word *often,* many of the adverbs in this story are adverbs of **time,** such as *always, immediately,* and *still.* Others are adverbs of **degree,** such as *rather, remarkably, quite, nearly,* and *never.*

■ *Application*

Using the adverbs just listed, insert the appropriate adverb in each space in the following paragraph:

The Hutchensons were _____ old when their son Will was born.

Hatch was _____ fifty when he married. Although Will was a small

child, he was _____ strong. When he grew up, he went to live in

Chicago, where he became _____ popular. The Hutchensons

_____ visited their son in Chicago because they

_____ had to take care of the farm. They _____

received letters from Will, which they _____ read. They even read

the letters to Hal Weyman. After they received news of Will's death, they planted

corn in the field. They worked all night and were _____ planting

when Hal and his friend went back to town.

4. Grammar: Adverb Placement

While doing the preceding exercise, did you notice the placement of the adverbs? Knowing where to put an adverb can sometimes be a problem. If an adverb modifies a verb, you may place the adverb in any one of the following positions:

1. Before the verb: The Hutchensons **immediately** read their son's letters.
2. After the verb: Hal went **silently** to the Hutchenson farm to break the news.
3. At the end of the sentence: The Hutchensons read their son's letters **immediately.**
4. At the beginning of a sentence: **Occasionally,** the Hutchensons read Will's letters to Hal.

You may **not,** however, place an adverb between a verb and its direct object:

INCORRECT: The Hutchensons read immediately the letters.
CORRECT: The Hutchensons **immediately read the letters.**

In sentences with *auxiliary + verb,* you should place the adverb **between** the two verbs:

Will had **always** been the pride of his parents.
You may **never** see such a sight again.

Now try this exercise. Rewrite each of the following sentences, placing the adverb in parentheses in the preferred position in the sentence. For example,

You can do that simple assignment if you try.   (surely)
You can **surely** do that simple assignment if you try.

1. Maria goes out without her family. (rarely)

_____

2. They have helped us whenever we had a problem. (always)

_____

3. We have seen him at the office before noon. (seldom)

_____

4. My sister walks to school. (never)

_____

5. She takes the bus. (always)

_____

6. Let's go out. It has stopped raining. (finally)

_____

7. You must wrap that package. It contains fragile china. (carefully)

_____

8. Carlo drove to the airport to meet his friend. (quickly)

_____

9. The lecturer spoke about his past experiences. (humorously)

_____

10. We chose a restaurant without looking at the prices. The one we chose was

too expensive. (foolishly)

_____

_____

1. Sharing Ideas

Discuss the following questions with a partner, in a small group, or with the whole class:

1. Based on your own experience or observation, discuss why you agree or disagree with this statement from the story: "I have noticed something about people who make a go of marriage. They grow more and more alike. They even grow to look alike."
2. In many stories we, as readers, have to read between the lines. What doesn't the author tell us about Will's life in Chicago? What do you think Will did in Chicago that he didn't tell his parents about in his letters?
3. Discuss whether or not you would like Will if you ever met him.
4. What advice would you give the Hutchensons in dealing with their grief?

2. Writing

Read the writing ideas that follow. Your instructor may make specific assignments, or ask you to choose one of these.

1. "The Corn Planting" is written by an objective narrator. Suppose the Hutchensons were to tell their own story. Rewrite it from the viewpoint of Hatch and his wife.
2. Write Will Hutchenson's last letter to his parents.
3. Create a dialogue between two of Will's Chicago friends in which they discuss Will's death.
4. Write Hal Weyman's journal as he returned from Will's funeral.
5. Write an essay contrasting the various ways people in your native country deal with grief.
6. Choose any other story you have read in which symbolism has a major role. Write a short summary of that story and explain how symbolism is used in it.

Chapter 4
The Quickening LISA INTEROLLO

A | PRE-READING

1. Think Before You Read

Answer the following questions before you read the story:

1. Have you ever been tempted to take something that didn't belong to you?
2. Why do some teenagers steal?
3. How do your culture, religion, and family view the act of petty theft?
4. What are some of the things you have done because of peer pressure?
5. What does the word *quickening* mean to you?

2. Literary Term: Sense Impressions

Sometimes, written descriptions are so vivid that we can see, smell, or taste the objects the author is describing. These descriptions are called **sense impressions.** For example, in the story you are about to read, the author describes the inside of a variety store as "swimming-pool green." Be aware of any other expressions that may appeal to one of your five senses.

3. Idioms and Expressions

In this story you will encounter the following idioms and expressions, all of which refer to stealing:

> **shoplifting**
> **a haul**
> **ripped off**

You may wish to look up other idioms before you begin to read. For instance, do you know what it means if someone looks daffy, gets into a jam, or is told to cut it out?

B | THE STORY

ABOUT THE AUTHOR

Lisa Interollo is a writer of both fiction and nonfiction. "The Quickening," her first published story, was a winner in *Redbook's* Fourth Young Writers' Contest in 1985. The story reflects an intimate knowledge of New York City, where she was born, raised, and currently lives. The author graduated from the Columbia University School of Journalism, where she began her nonfiction career. Many of her articles have appeared in *Cosmopolitan, Newsday,* and other leading publications.

Interollo's fiction is characterized by a remarkably descriptive ability, which is evidenced in "The Quickening."

The Quickening

THE INSIDE OF Woolworth's is swimming-pool green. I breathe in the smell of the store – hand soap, face powder, plastic, skillet grease – in short, anxious puffs. I am seven and moving along the first aisle searching for my sister Patty, four years older than I, who baby-sits me each afternoon with her friend Rebecca. They have trained me to shoplift, and I have caught on well, exceeding their expectations. The first aisle, lower than the others, reaches chest-high on me. There are eyebrow pencils and artificial nails and false eyelashes encased in clear, hard plastic. And lipsticks: True Red, Proposal Pink, Warm Toast. I hurry on to the next aisle, where I see that the store manager, a man in green, has caught my sister and Rebecca and is scolding them. I walk up to them, and he holds me gently by the shoulders, squatting down to look in my eyes. "You shouldn't play with these girls. They're very bad girls," he says. I nod, feeling he is somehow right about them, although I can't say why. My underpants are full of lipsticks.

Next, I remember Easter week and a storekeeper and my mother both staring down at me. "Turn out your pockets," my mother says, and her voice seems to come from a long way away. I pull on the pocket of my turquoise stretch pants, and out comes a long, multicolored, bunny-shaped balloon. Even though I put it there just moments earlier, I feel surprised, almost mesmerized, by seeing it, as if I were watching a magician drawing scarves out of his sleeve. As we leave the store, my mother says, "I'm never coming shopping with you again."

My mother is always tired. She has varicose veins, migraines, three children, and a job at the Social Security office – all of which exhaust her. All except my brother, that is, who is one year younger than me and seems younger. "Boys mature slower," my mother repeats defensively, explaining why he never matches the grades I made the previous year at school. George has curly brown hair, bright dark eyes, and a beguiling smile. His shoulder blades jut out beneath his T-shirt, since he has a tendency to eat a few forkfuls of dinner, then push his plate away with a bored sigh. We all eat his favorite foods because he won't eat at all if they aren't served. My sister and I, both more robust, call him Runty. We don't see our father much. On weekdays, he rarely comes home before we're in bed. On those days, we carry our dinner plates into the shadowy living room and watch TV. But when he is home, he likes us to eat together at the kitchen table. These meals tend to have a cramped, tense quality; George, especially, hates missing programs, and the rest of us are not in the habit of making table conversation. Afterward, we all scatter while my father heads for the living room, drifting cautiously around as if it were the waiting room of a doctor's office and any moment might bring an unpleasant diagnosis. His shyness makes me nervous. Sometimes – though I know better now – I used to think he was mad at me. "Oh, no, of course not," my mother would reassure me impatiently. "You know how he is."

When I am twelve, I take a test and win a partial scholarship to Kingston, a small private school for girls on Fifth Avenue, far from our apartment. My brother and sister stay in nearby parochial schools, where most of our friends in the neighborhood go. Occasionally, I stand in the gym at recess, remembering my old school – how it had no cafeteria and long folding metal tables had to be set up each day at eleven on the varnished planks of the gymnasium floor and how steaming meatballs were served on big round metal plates and the room smelled of sneakers and sweat. The boiler hissed; voices roared.

At Kingston, our behavior reflects not only on us but on the school itself. Charity is stressed. Not the petty sort of charity that consists of giving a few pennies here and there. That, in fact, is frowned upon as insignificant, meaningless. A grander, vaguer, philosophical charity is encouraged. We certainly don't fritter away time praying for indulgences; we think about issues. Our religion classes are called Philosophy/Theology, or simply P.T. And to stress their importance, they are taught by the principal herself, Mrs. Medford, a handsome woman whose well-groomed hand any parent or alumna might shake and be reassured. In one P.T. class, Mrs. Medford explains this subtler form of charity by saying, "I obviously don't expect you girls to go and give your allowances away on 115th Street and Amsterdam Avenue."

I feel my face heating up like a warm bath. Amsterdam and 115th: That's near where I live, that's where the post office is; that's not a bad neighborhood. I decide to tell her, to raise my hand and say, "That isn't a bad neighborhood. The people there wouldn't *want* your money." But she moves along to another subject. When the class is dismissed, four girls gather around her with questions about the exam. I linger on the outskirts for a minute, then turn and leave the room.

In the eighth grade, everyone is exchanging turquoise friendship rings. I trade mine with Andrea Spencer – a tall, quiet girl with flame-colored hair. Andrea doesn't make trouble, and all the teachers like her for this but also because her family were killed when their BMW missed a turn near Ajaccio. Now she lives with an aunt in an apartment with long dark corridors near the school. During the summers, she visits relatives from her father's side in England. She went on a camping trip with them once, she told me, and her cousin Kevin – who's our age – got inside her sleeping bag for five minutes. Sometimes when I'm in bed with the lights out, listening to the late subways creep along the el, I think about being in England for the summer and having no parents or brother or sister anywhere and meeting the unknown, daring Kevin.

The next year, Susan Doherty comes into our class from a school that doesn't go past eighth grade. Susan, whose black bangs tickle her eyes, has more classes with Andrea than I do; once I overhear her telling Andy, "You're so beautiful, you should try to become a model." At lunchtime, the three of us walk one block to a delicatessen to buy Tab. My eyes sweep around quickly, and I slip a yellow package of chewing gum into my pocket. Outside, Andy and Susan have already started strolling toward school. I catch up with them, breathing harder than I should. "Look what I got," I say, punctuating the sentence with a wire-thin, conspiratorial smile. "You didn't!" Susan shrieks instantly. I smile again, and we all chew gum.

I steal frequently after that, and Susan joins me, although Andy never will. She waits outside. One snowy day in February in the same delicatessen, Susan and I each drop round red Gouda cheeses into our woven shoulder bags, which everyone at school is using. We exchange glances, each taking another cheese and then another. No one notices. The store is noisy, smoky, and warm, the fogged windows blocking a view of the street. When we get outside, Andy's face has turned red and blotchy, and she looks angry. Susan and I are keyed up. We insist on heading over to the park despite the cold. Andy refuses and turns back toward school, but we go on alone against a freezing wind. On Fifth Avenue, we stop at a bench to unload the cheeses. My numb fingers stumble over the red cellophane. I bite through the red wax, spit it out, and bite into the cheese. Susan takes another cheese and does the same. The cold is appalling, the street almost silent. I take another cheese, abandoning the first. Bite, spit, bite. Swallowing hurts: I take another bite. "Let's get rid of these cheeses," Susan says in almost a whisper. Standing on the bench, the wind searing my thighs, I hurl the cheeses, one after another, into the empty park. They sail over the wall in sharp arcs, sinking into the new-fallen snow. In class that afternoon, my mind keeps going back to those wasted cheeses. I compose a riddle for Susan, neatly writing it on a part of a sheet of loose-leaf paper. It reads: "What did the man say to the judge after he stabbed someone with a knife? Answer: I used the knife for evil, but it was meant for Gouda . . . ho, ho, ho." I watch Susan unfold the note, study it, and then – finally! – get it. Her suppressed laugh sounds like air rushing out of a balloon.

Susan and I don't talk about stealing, we just do it, more and more. Soon, I recognize every feeling – and every gradation of every feeling – that arises in the process of taking something. An inexplicably pretty object sets everything in motion. From the moment my eyes settle on it – whatever it is – I know I'm going to go for it. This first impulse is unpleasant, because unyielding: There is no backing down. It is followed by a quickening: of the pulse, the heart, the senses. These last play tricks. Voices become more acute but seem to come from far away. Colors – all colors – turn distractingly rich. Afterward: relief, release, a rush of pleasure, a certain increasing grayness, which disappears instantly once another inexplicably pretty object is spotted.

Boutiques, bookstores, gift shops, pharmacies – all these we frequent when a change in school policy allows students to leave the school during free periods to "explore the cultural offerings of the city." Our hauls become larger, our methods brazen.

In a sprawling unisex clothing store, a young salesman with a downy mustache shows me to a fitting room. Whenever I glance at him, he's looking at me with dark, flashing eyes. He doesn't count the hangers but checks to see that every dress has one. I hear Susan outside talking to him, saying she doesn't need clothes. "Do you have a boyfriend?" he asks. I pull the curtain open. Four dresses and four hangers. "Walk fast," I say outside, ignoring her "Did you get anything?" We round the corner onto Eighty-ninth Street. The dress is in my purse. The hanger inches lower and lower down my back, finally clattering onto the sidewalk. Her laugh: air escaping from a balloon. I scoop the hanger up fast. I break it in half, the thick plastic raking my hand as it splits with a cracking sound. I throw it into a narrow alley. I begin laughing hard. My hand is bleeding.

"See this shirt," I say to my mother, holding a turquoise silk blouse. "I got it on sale." She is lying on her bed reading *The Fan Club*. I try it on for her. The color makes my skin glow as if I were immersed in a motel swimming pool on a sunny day.

"It's nice," she says, fingering the sleeve, "soft."

"Eight dollars," I say, "reduced from twenty-five." She doesn't ask where I bought it.

"Where did you get this?" asks Mr. Donnelly when I give him a heavy picture book with color plates, entitled *The Life of Mozart*. He's a tall, thin young man with pockmarked cheeks and ironic, smiling eyes. Susan often says that with his talent, he could have been a lot more than a music teacher in a girls' school.

"I ripped it off from Stanley's," I say.

"Stanley's," he repeats slowly. "That guy's a friend of mine. I have a charge account there."

"So? Take it back if you don't like it. Tell him *you* took it."

My voice is firm. For him, things are perplexingly complicated, much too complicated to act on. He muses to our class all the time about questions that have never been satisfactorily answered: Did Süssmayr finish the Requiem in D minor as Mozart had

> "Walk fast," I say outside. . . . The dress is in my purse.

intended? Could Chopin have triumphed in "larger" areas of composition? Dilemma was his charm, also his undoing. "He's obviously thrown his life away," Susan often says decisively. And I don't know whether to agree or disagree, so I say nothing.

It is spring and junior year. The season has arrived unfairly early, in February, and signs of it are everywhere: that smell of rain and wet turf, even on blocks far from the park; that pitiless, diffused light. The season's aching promise disturbs me. What is the future? Senior year, college, the rest of life. I imagine you have to be thin, blond, and confident to meet spring on equal terms.

"Want to go for a walk?" Susan asks on this certain February morning and I know what that means and I go along. The street is crowded with shoppers, workmen, and women pushing pudgy toddlers along in strollers. A redhead in the distance looks just like Andy – no longer a regular companion of ours – but as she comes closer, she becomes a stranger.

We stop before an old-fashioned drugstore with a display of trusses in the window. The store is dark and cool inside, with a comforting medicinal smell. The long aisles are lined with shampoos, lotions, bubble baths, and intriguing tonics. In a large glass display case, hairbrushes and tortoiseshell combs are pinned onto red velvet like rare butterflies mounted in a museum.

"Can I help you girls?" asks the old man at the counter, poking his head out from behind a giant cash register. He looks daffy. He has wispy flyaway white hair and a matching flyaway goatee. His voice cavorts high and low as he talks, each syllable a surprise. I'd never trust this guy to fill a prescription.

"I'd like a bottle of contact-lens wetting solution," says Susan. This is always kept behind the counter for some reason. He putters off to get it, and Susan turns to me, pitching her eyes upward. While she waits, I turn into one of the aisles. A few other customers glide noiselessly, almost reverently, along as if they were in a house of worship and the shampoo bottles were sacred statues. Susan joins me in a moment. We walk to the end of the aisle, where there is a rotating rack with packages of foam curlers, aluminum clips, eyebrow pencils, and other objects hanging from it. She turns the rack, and it, too, moves without a sound, without creaking. We stand close together with my shoulder bag, an open pouch, dangling between us.

Susan says in a low, apologetic voice, "I have no purse." Unwillingly, my senses sharpen. I track the movements of the noiseless, gliding customers, the fey pharmacist, and his assistant, a large, bespectacled saleswoman. The gentle, almost imperceptible tug on my shoulder is Susan dropping something in my bag.

Suddenly, something begins to go wrong. It happens rapidly, with points merging in awful combination, control slinking helplessly away. I stand fast, paralyzed, flooded with a strange visceral recognition of what is approaching. It starts innocently: The large, no-nonsense saleswoman moves up the aisle parallel to us on her rounds. There, she is corralled by a reedy, elderly woman wearing a purple turban who demands, in a snobby, self-amused drawl, to know why the store has stopped carrying a certain brand of laxative that she has been purchasing here "for the past two hundred years." This is funny, and the saleswoman's glance veers – unpredictably, really – to see if anyone is overhearing and sharing the joke. She spots us. If she weren't standing exactly where a sliver of space joins the two aisles – the point where the shelves leave off and the rotating rack begins – there would be no problem. But she is, and that is all it takes. Very quickly she sees – or senses with absolute certainty – that something is amiss, that Susan's hand is in my bag.

Her mood changes palpably. She begins moving toward us, dodging the turbaned customer.

"Get those things out," I hiss to Susan, looking straight ahead.

Tug. Tug.

"Get those things out."

"They're out."

"Get them out."

"They're out."

I don't know what she put in or whether to believe her or whether she found everything – half the time, I can't even find my wallet in that bag. There is no time to check, though; the saleswoman has reached us, her face sweaty and severe.

"What are you girls doing?" she demands.

"Just looking," I hear myself answer in a curiously detached voice. Inwardly, I am in a state of emergency. There is a heavy pressure on my chest, as if a pine tree had fallen across it, pinning me down.

"What do you have in that bag?" she asks, her eyes straining to see inside it, sure of what she saw, yet doubting it, mainly because of my steady voice. There is a pause. My eyes falter downward, but I quickly pull them up to meet hers: shrewd and medium-brown behind wire-rimmed lenses.

"Were you stealing something?" she asks directly.

"No!" I sound shocked, slightly offended. She doesn't fall for it but doesn't know what to do, either. By now, the other customers have formed a silent, threatening ring around us. The pharmacist breaks through the ring, his face working as if he were maneuvering a bicycle through heavy, unyielding traffic. The saleswoman is appreciative of this supportive audience but also flustered by it. She plows on with a determination to triumph that I admire in spite of myself.

"If I ever catch you girls stealing in here again . . ." Her voice trails off in search of the appropriate threat.

"We're going," I say breathlessly, falling short of the intended huffiness, then adding irrelevantly, "we have a class."

The saleswoman's eyes settle on the Kingston emblem on my blazer.

"I'm going with you," she announces suddenly. "I think we should all have a talk with your principal. I don't know what you girls are doing out roaming the streets at this hour, anyway."

An approving murmur runs through the ring. A moment later, the three of us are marching along the street toward the school, an unlikely, stony-faced tribe. The absurdity of the situation bothers me, despite my nervousness. I consider running, but that would be an outright admission of guilt. Anyway, she could just come to the school and identify us. And prove what? Nothing. Worse still, she might come bounding after us and make a scene, which would be mortifying. I don't even dare check my purse. She is walking behind me, watching me.

Mrs. Medford is in conference with Mr. Donnelly when we arrive. I see Donnelly – his head bobbing earnestly as he talks – through the glass partition dividing the principal's office from the reception area, and my queasiness swells. How many times had I hoped to bump into him accidentally in the halls, skimmed my eyes over the crowd to give chance a nudge? I rarely spotted him. But there he is now, at the worst possible moment. The saleswoman is telling Medford's assistant the matter is "urgent."

We are shown in. Mr. Donnelly rests his ironic eyes on the three of us. The saleswoman introduces herself to Medford – who responds with a cold, polite nod – and begins to explain what happened: She caught us stealing something in her store, makeup or something – but someone put something in my bag – and then when asked about it, we denied it, quite rudely, and she doesn't even know what we're doing roaming the streets at this hour, anyway.

Her explanation is garbled. I feel bad for her. She, too, has lost her nerve before Medford's supercilious confidence. They are opposites, I see now. She is a commonsense right-and-wrong woman. Medford, you never know what she believes, but she is always well-dressed and soft-spoken and quietly impressive. And this is her office, her terrain, painted pale yellow and gray in understated cheeriness, not the dark, old-fashioned drugstore. And they don't like each other.

Medford smooths her gray hair. She leans forward in her chair, looking first at Susan, then me, then the saleswoman, with an intent, pondering gaze. She picks up a felt-tipped pen, taps its point twice on her desk, puts it down. She pauses, looks at us again, and says, "What do you girls have to say?"

"We didn't do anything," says Susan.

"No," I murmur. "I don't know what she's talking about."

Mr. Donnelly clears his throat.

"These girls are students of mine," he says slowly, looking significantly into the saleswoman's eyes with a kind, nearly pleading gaze. "They've been under a lot of pressure lately – they're preparing for the college boards. I'm sure they didn't mean to be rude to you. They've always been good – " he pauses – "forthright students."

Medford takes it up, on a haughtier note.

"Frankly, Miss – what did you say your name was?"

"Olafson."

"Miss Olafson, I'll have to stand by our girls in this case. They have very good records. And they are not out of the building illegally. We have a program here that permits that. It's been highly successful and was recently written up in an educational journal. I think you'll find, if you ask around, that this school has a very good reputation."

And as if to demonstrate this, she says to me, "Vicky, give me your bag."

I feel that pine tree again, bearing down hard on my chest. I press my legs together to keep them still and hand her my bag.

Woven out of thick Greek wool, the bag has a black, gray, and red geometric pattern. It looks out of place in Medford's hands. She would never own anything like it. She grips the rim of the bag with both hands, thumbs on top, and squints inside. Then her hand and wrist disappear into it. She takes out my wallet and puts it on her desk. She reaches in again: a copy of *The Great Gatsby*. Then a hairbrush. And a bus pass. My pen.

"That's it," she says, surveying the objects. "Everything."

Miss Olafson's lips move to the verge of speech. She hesitates, as if reconsidering. Her face looks moist and reddened. Then an outburst: "That can't be it," she says. "That just can't be it."

She reaches across the desk, grabs the bag, and plunges her hand inside, pressing it to the bottom. "That can't be . . . I saw . . ." Her eyes widen seriously as she touches bottom, as if

she has discovered something. She has – that there is nothing inside.

When she speaks again, her voice is different, faltering. "I . . . uh . . . we have a lot of problems with kids shoplifting. And I guess in this case, I may have overreacted."

"I quite understand," says Medford graciously. "That happens to all of us."

Our little gathering disperses. Susan gives me a we-have-a-lot-to-talk-about look and then runs downstairs to get books from her locker. I take a few slow steps next to Mr. Donnelly. Classes are going on; the halls are deserted.

"Well," he says, looking ahead down the corridor. "Aren't you going to say anything?"

"Like what?"

"You might tell me what happened – though I can pretty much guess. Or even thank me for helping to get you out of that jam."

"Thank you," I say curtly.

He laughs softly. We walk along in silence.

"You know," he says, after what seems a long while, "you're getting a bit old for this sort of thing. I wish you'd cut it out."

"Maybe that's what I planned to do," I say.

"I certainly hope so."

"Why?"

"I don't know," he says. "I guess it's because I like you and would hate to see you screw things up for yourself. Or other people, for that matter – I don't think you feel too good about dragging that woman in here."

"I didn't drag her. She followed us."

"Whatever," he shrugs. "I'm not

interested in quibbling. I just think you should consider putting your energy to some use. Other than stealing makeup."

665 "Like what?"

"You figure it out," he says quickly. "You're smart."

He stops talking, as if trying to catch and hold a thought that keeps slipping 670 forward and away from him like a minnow. I look at him, picturing how he might look on a hot summer beach: white and serious, with a book on his towel, watching the water, the bathers 675 shouting and raging in the water. I think of Susan's harsh pronouncement on his life and still can't – don't – endorse it. The bell rings. I make out one, two, voices behind us. Then 680 others coming from the opposite direction. The din builds.

"Look, I have a class," Mr. Donnelly says now, in a louder voice. "But I'll just say in passing that I think it takes 685 more guts to develop yourself than to . . ." The end of his sentence drowns in the growing wave of voices.

At three o'clock, I leave the school building without books or my coat. 690 The sun is gone, and it is February again. The wind throttles me. I close the top button on my shirt, draw my blazer closer, and begin to walk, thinking with faint guilt, "I won't wait 695 for Susan today, I'll call her later." I walk fast, though without destination: to Lexington, then downtown, not toward home. Ten, twenty blocks, and I am less cold; thirty, and the 700 housewives carrying groceries have become working women and men with briefcases. Under the eerie, bright fluorescent light of a counter restaurant, I stop and order coffee. The first black draft scalds my throat. I cup 705 my hands around the thick ceramic mug and wait, then look up and into the mirror facing me: I am there with long, strong brown hair, wild now around my shoulders; a round face, 710 still babyish but possessing a flushed prettiness; eyes dark and direct – honest (yes!) and alive-looking, with a certain liquidy sparkle.

Outside, I buy the *Times*. I rarely 715 read the newspaper. But I feel good casually pressing the coins into the vendor's palm. Who knows? There may be something of interest in it, I think, folding the paper into the offending 720 shoulder bag, satisfied to find that it doesn't fit completely, that it sticks out.

I walk on, and as I walk, I feel a certain exhilaration grow inside me, a familiar quickening of the pulse, the 725 heart, the senses. The lavender of a nearby store awning is distractingly rich. The singsong wail of a passing siren sounds at once acute and oddly distant, as if coming from farther away. 730 Unsettled, I resist the old sensation, unbeckoned this time. But as it stays on, it reveals itself as different, a harmless euphoria, gentler and less frantic than the one I have known: The 735 wanting is gone.

The man and woman walking ahead of me wind their arms around each other's waist and dip, as one, through a restaurant door. On the avenue, a 740 crowded blue bus sighs to a stop. A lovely, cold evening: I think I'll walk home.

1. Comprehension

Answer these questions to determine how well you understood the story.

1. Who set Vicky on her life of crime?
2. Describe Vicky's home life.
3. Contrast Vicky's former school with Kingston.
4. Why does Mrs. Medford's idea of charity make Vicky feel uncomfortable?
5. How do we know Andrea disapproved of Susan's and Vicky's stealing?
6. Describe Mrs. Medford's meeting with Miss Olafson.
7. What examples do you find of the principal's snobbishness?
8. What sentence best describes the advice Mr. Donnelly gave Vicky?

2. Vocabulary

The following words appear in Interollo's story. From the way each word is used (from its **context**), you may be able to determine its meaning. If not, look up certain words in the dictionary. Place the appropriate word in each of the following sentences. Use each word only once.

mesmerize	supercilious	mortifying	palpable
beguiling	defensively	eerie	garbled
cavort	ironic	robust	quibble
irrelevant	imperceptible	dilemma	

1. One must be in _____ health in order to run the marathon.

2. Vicky's mother always protected her son, acting _____ whenever he was criticized.

3. Young horses often _____ to show their playfulness.

4. That charming young man bewitches us with his _____ personality.

5. We don't understand John. His behavior is always illogical and his speech is _____.

6. Vicky's denial was a(n) _____ lie, since she did steal the merchandise.

7. Her question was _____ because it had nothing to do with the subject we were discussing.

8. Effective speakers have the ability to _____ their audiences by their forceful personalities.

9. Mrs. Medford's snobbishness and _____ manner put Miss Olafson at a disadvantage.

10. Although the owl is a harmless bird, its _____ sound can be frightening.

11. Don't worry about that spot on your shirt. It's so small, it's almost

    _____.

12. It was _____ that Beethoven, who wrote such beautiful symphonies, could never hear them because he was deaf.

13. It was _____ to Vicky when Mrs. Medford looked through her cheaply made canvas bag.

14. People who _____ about unimportant matters or small sums of money can be called *nitpickers.*

15. Impoverished students often have to face the _____ of taking out loans to continue their studies or of giving up their education entirely.

3. *Grammar: Using Adjectives and Adverbs*

Adjectives describe only nouns and pronouns. They often directly modify a person, place, or thing, such as **artificial** nails, a **snowy** day, **warm** toast. But some adjectives are separated from the noun or pronoun they describe. For example: The store is **dark** and **cool** inside. These are called **predicate adjectives** because they follow the verb *to be,* which is a nonaction verb. It is important to remember that you cannot use an adjective to describe an action verb; adverbs do that. (See the grammar exercises accompanying "The Corn Planting," pp. 33–35.)

Study the following chart. You will notice that besides the verb *to be,* other nonaction verbs are *look, sound, feel, taste,* and *smell* (verbs referring to the five senses).

Adjectives With Nonaction Verbs	Adverbs With Action Verbs
She **is** beautiful. The dinner **tastes** good. The cake **looks** good. The meat **smells** bad. I don't **feel** well today.	She **sings** beautifully. Marie **cooks** well. He **paints** well. Jack **writes** badly.

■ *Application*

As a review, try these sentences. In each instance, underline your choice of adjective or adverb. Note: *Well* is an adjective when it means *health;* otherwise, *well* is an adverb.

1. My friends always speak (good, well) of you.
2. My stereo sounds (good, well), but my sister's sounds (bad, badly).
3. Don't feel (bad, badly) about that mistake.
4. He drives too (slow, slowly).
5. Robert hasn't felt (good, well) since he got the flu.
6. We were (careful, carefully) about choosing a new car.
7. We have (careful, carefully) chosen our new home.
8. It is not (good, well) to drive too (quick, quickly).
9. The flower smells (sweet, sweetly).
10. Many people don't think (clear, clearly) in an emergency.

It is important to remember that adjectives may **never** modify adverbs. Therefore, it is wrong to say: That ring is **real** pretty. *Pretty* is an adjective, modifying *ring. Real* is also an adjective. It may not describe how pretty the ring is. The correct sentence is: That ring is **really** (or **very**) pretty.

4. Grammar: Using Adjectives to Create Word Pictures

Authors use adjectives to create descriptive word pictures, making scenes and characters more vivid to the reader. Look at the following sentences from the story. Then, underline the adjectives in each sentence and circle the noun or pronoun each adjective describes.

I breathe in the smell of the store – hand soap, face powder, plastic, skillet grease – in short, anxious puffs.

I pull on the pocket of my turquoise stretch pants, and out comes a long, multicolored, bunny-shaped balloon.

My mother is always tired.

George has curly brown hair, bright dark eyes, and a beguiling smile.

■ *Application*
Create eight sentences of your own, using adjectives to describe a person you know, a place you have visited, or an object that has intrigued you.

1. _____

2. _____

3. _____

4. _____

5. _____

6. _____

7. _____

8. _____

5. Grammar: Using Hyphenated Adjectives

Interollo uses a number of hyphenated words as adjectives, for example, *chest-high*.

■ *Application*
Find five more hyphenated expressions in the story and tell what each one describes. Then write sentences using the following words:

golden-brown	well-prepared	self-conscious	poorly-paid
even-tempered	sky-blue	up-to-date	newly-painted

1. _____

2. _____

3. _____

4. _____

5. _____

Now, make up at least six hyphenated adjectives of your own.

1. _____   4. _____

2. _____   5. _____

3. _____   6. _____

6. Editing

Read the following paragraph. Underline and correct any errors in the use of adjectives or adverbs.

Vicky felt awful badly when Mr. Donnelly, her favorite teacher, knew she was

stealing. He gave her real good advice when he suggested that she was too old to

keep up a life of petty theft. Vicky's mother never felt good, so she didn't notice

that both her daughters moved careful along the aisles of Woolworth's stealing

anything they could snatch quick. When Miss Olafson caught the girls stealing,

she took them to the principal, who dressed nice and spoke distinct. She treated

Miss Olafson bad because Miss Olafson was a poor paid employee and not

dressed well.

D THINKING ABOUT THE STORY

1. Sharing Ideas

Discuss the following questions with a partner, in a small group, or with the whole class:

1. Why did Vicky become a shoplifter?
2. How is her mother partly responsible for her dishonesty? Her sister? Mrs. Medford?
3. Contrast Andrea Spencer and Susan Doherty in circumstances and character.

4. How did Mr. Donnelly affect Vicky's decision at the end of the story?

5. Explain how the purchase of the *Times* symbolizes Vicky's reformation.

6. What is the meaning of the title as it relates to the plot of the story? Did your definition of the word *quickening* change as a result of reading the story? Explain.

2. Writing

Read the writing ideas that follow. Your instructor may make specific assignments, or ask you to choose one of these.

1. List at least five sense impressions you have found in the story. Then write a paragraph using your own sense impressions. The paragraph should describe a person, place, or thing you have observed or experienced.

2. Pretend to be Vicky, the main character of the story. Write a letter to Mr. Donnelly telling him how he has turned your life around.

3. Describe a teacher who affected your life either positively or negatively.

4. Imagine that Vicky meets Susan a year later. Write a dialogue between the two former friends.

Summing Up

A TAKE A CLOSER LOOK

1. Analyzing and Comparing

In each of the following sections, you are asked to think about and compare two of the stories in Part One.

"A Day's Wait" and "Thank You, Ma'm"

■ Compare Hemingway's Schatz to Hughes's Roger. In what ways are the two boys alike? How are they different?

■ How do the adults in both stories treat the boys?

■ What do the adults gain from their experiences with the boys?

"The Corn Planting" and "The Quickening"

■ Describe the contrast in the settings of both stories. Cite specific images from the text.

■ Despite the tragedy in their lives, do you feel the Hutchensons will achieve a sense of peace?

■ How does Vicky achieve a sense of peace in her young life? Is there hope for her?

"The Quickening" and "Thank You, Ma'm"

■ Compare Roger and Vicky. How are they similar? Different?

■ How would Vicky react to Mrs. Jones?

2. Freewriting

Fear is a theme in each of the stories in Part One. For fifteen minutes, write about fear as it occurs in the stories. What kinds of fears do the characters have? How do they deal with them? Which character do you understand best? Why?

When you have finished writing, exchange papers with a classmate and discuss your reactions.

B   WORDS FREQUENTLY CONFUSED

Some people confuse English words that have similar pronunciations (homonyms) but different meanings, such as *too, to, two;* and *there, their, they're.* Other words are sometimes misused because they closely resemble one another in either spelling or meaning. For example,

thought (noun or verb)
though (conjunction)
Though he never called her, he often **thought** about her.

In Part One, there are many words that could be confused if not properly understood. Study the following list. Then, choose ten pairs of words from the list and write sentences clearly showing the different meanings. You may use your dictionary.

From "A Day's Wait"

bear   noun: a large furry animal (such as a polar bear)

bare   adjective: unclothed, untrimmed (a bare arm or an empty refrigerator)

attach   verb: to connect to (Attach the plug to the appliance.)

detach   verb: to remove from (detach the plug)

die   verb: to expire (The butterfly may die.)

dead   adjective or noun: no longer living (The butterfly is dead.)

read (pronounced *reed*) verb: to look at and understand a book or paper (to read the novel)

read (pronounced *red*) past tense of preceding verb (I read the novel yesterday.)

stare   verb: to look intently at someone or something (to stare at your friend)

stair   noun: a step (to sit on the stair)

heard   verb: past tense of *hear* (I heard the noise.)

herd   noun: a group of cattle (a herd of cows or sheep)

From "Thank You, Ma'm"

sat   verb: past tense of *sit* (sat on the steps)

set   verb: to place or put (to set the table)

weigh   verb: to determine the heaviness of an object (to weigh the meat on a scale)

weight   noun: the measure (the weight of the meat)

woman   singular noun: one female (a woman working)

women   plural noun: two or more females (several women working)

teach   verb: to instruct (to teach a class)

learn   verb: to absorb instruction (The students learn.)

From "The Corn Planting"

know   verb: to be acquainted with (to know a friend well)

known   past participle (We have known many people.) *Known* can also be used as an adjective, as in *well-known.*

close   verb: to shut (to close the door)

clothes   noun, always plural: garments (Her clothes are clean.)

quiet   adjective: silent (a quiet boy)

quite   adverb: to a considerable extent (The restaurant was quite nice.)

quit   verb: to leave a situation (to quit a job)

From "The Quickening"

through   preposition: a passage (Cars often go through a tunnel.)

thorough   adjective: complete (making a thorough search)

tired   adjective: exhausted (You may become tired at the end of the day.)

tried   verb, past tense of *try:* attempted (tried to look away)

cute   adjective: small, delightfully pretty (Children and puppies are often cute.)

acute   adjective: sharp (an acute mind)

anxious   adjective: nervously anticipating something (anxious about tomorrow's test)

eager   adjective: happily anticipating something (eager to take a vacation)

expect   verb: to consider something probable (I expect to receive a letter.)

except   preposition: leave out (You invited everyone except Susan.)

1. *Forming the Past Tense of Regular Verbs*

In "The Quickening" it seems that Vicky's mother *cared* only for her son. It never *occurred* to her that Vicky was shoplifting. Does it seem strange to you that we double the *r* in *occur* to form the past tense but not the *r* in *care?* The following are patterns that may help you remember the spelling of past tense regular verbs.

1. The verb *care* is a one-syllable word that ends in the vowel *e*. As in *hope* or *date*, the past tense is formed by adding the letter *d* to the root word: *cared, hoped, dated.*

2. *Occur* is a two-syllable word, and the accent (or stress) is on the second syllable. For all two-syllable words with second-syllable accents, we double the final consonant to form the past tense: *occur, occurred; prefer, preferred.*

3. If, however, the accent is on the first syllable, the past tense is formed by simply adding *-ed*, such as in *listen, listened; offer, offered.*

4. For one-syllable words, we double the final letter to add *-ed* if the last letter is preceded by one vowel: *stop, stopped; top, topped.*

5. If a one-syllable word contains two vowels preceding the final letter, the past is formed just by adding *-ed*, as in *rain, rained; stain, stained.*

6. What about one-syllable words that end in two consonants, such as *walk* or *talk?* Just add *-ed.*

To see if you understand the patterns, practice by forming the past tense of the following:

Words That End in *e*

cope   _____
spare   _____
dine   _____

One-Syllable Words With One Vowel Preceding
the Final Consonant

rob   _____
sob   _____
plan   _____

One-Syllable Words With Two Vowels Preceding the Final Consonant

stain _____
fool _____
wait _____

Two-Syllable Words That Stress the First Syllable

offer _____
happen _____
open _____

Two-Syllable Words That Stress the Second Syllable

control _____
regret _____
admit _____

Words That End in Two Consonants

start _____
fold _____
warn _____

A Life Lesson

Some of the following sentences are correct; in others, there are errors in the use of articles, prepositions, verb tense, adjectives, and adverbs. If you think the sentence is correct, write the letter *C* in the space below each sentence. If the sentence is incorrect, underline the error(s) and rewrite the sentence correctly. For example,

> INCORRECT: She should have saw the car coming.
> CORRECT: She should have **seen** the car coming.

1. The life isn't always easy, especially when we are studying a new language.

   _____

2. We could have went to a better restaurant.

   _____

3. Since I arrived to United States, I will enjoy many new experiences.

   _____

4. Because we are learning English, we have read a number of short stories.

   _____

5. It is necessary to drive careful, especially on highways.

   _____

6. Mrs. Medford had known rarely any poor people.

   _____

7. I have seen seldom him in the supermarket.

   _____

8. Everything at the wedding had went smooth.

   _____

9. Schatz thought he would soon die in his bed.

   _____

10. The Hutchensons visited never their son in Chicago.

_____

11. My birthday is in June 25.

_____

12. I want to buy a pens.

_____

13. Roger was poor child in a story "Thank You, Ma'm."

_____

14. The flower smells sweet.

_____

15. You don't look good. Are you tired?

_____

16. She plays the piano well but she sings bad.

_____

17. Last summer we had swam almost every day.

_____

18. My father, who is a reporter, has known many famous people.

_____

19. Mrs. Jones asked Roger, "Aren't you ashamed with yourself?"

_____

20. She grabbed him on the neck and dragged him in the street.

_____

21. Vicky stole small items to department stores.

_____

22. Students like to read stories about a adventurous heroes.

_____

23. Mrs. Medford always dressed nice.

_____

24. Vicky was impressed on what Mr. Donnelly told her.

_____

25. The story "The Quickening" is set at New York City.

_____

Part Two

The Unexpected Twist

LIFE IS full of surprises. How many times have you been amazed by the turn of events in your own life and the lives of your acquaintances? You were sure, for example, that your best friend would marry the girl next door, only to learn that he eloped with someone he just met. Or, you're deep into that mystery novel; you think you can name the murderer. Then you get to the end of the story. You're astounded to find out that the least suspicious character is really the guilty one.

This literary device, used by most writers of suspense novels, is called the "unexpected twist" or the "surprise ending." O. Henry, the famous American author, never failed to shock his readers by his totally unpredictable endings, as you'll discover in "The Last Leaf." If you read the following stories carefully, you'll find some hints that the authors give to indicate that a surprise is coming. Look for these clues.

Chapter 7

THE LOTTERY
– Shirley Jackson

Chapter 8

THE ONE DAY WAR
– Judith Soloway

Chapter 5

The Last Leaf
O. HENRY
(WILLIAM SYDNEY PORTER)

A | PRE-READING

1. Think Before You Read

Answer the following questions before you read the story:

1. Greenwich Village is a section in the lower part of New York City where many aspiring artists have lived. What else do you know about "the Village"? What is it famous for now?
2. In your opinion, what constitutes a masterpiece?
3. Have you ever read a story in which a person made a great sacrifice either for a career or for another human being?
4. In the fourth paragraph of the story, the author describes pneumonia as though the disease were a person. This device is called **personification.** As you read, see if you can find other examples of personification.

5. You will also see references to items that are no longer used very often. People generally used a *chafing dish* to warm up food, whereas now we have the microwave. Do you know what *bishop's sleeves* are? Have you heard of *ragtime*?

2. Literary Term: Surprise Ending

The **surprise ending** is, as the term indicates, an ending that is totally unexpected. O. Henry is so famous for this type of ending that it is often called "the O. Henry ending." Other short-story writers have followed his example, especially American authors like Shirley Jackson and Edith Wharton.

Prepare yourself for a shock when you get to the conclusion of "The Last Leaf."

3. Idioms and Expressions

Note the following idioms and expressions that appear in the story:

fair game something easy to conquer	**fibbertigibbet** flighty, frivolous person
dunderhead stupid person	**make up her mind** make a decision

B THE STORY

ABOUT THE AUTHOR

William Sydney Porter (1862–1910) lived a tragic but adventurous life. He was born in Greensboro, North Carolina, where he worked as a pharmacist. Then he drifted off to Texas, where he met and eloped with his future wife. After their marriage, Porter worked as a bank teller but was accused of embezzling funds. Fearful of being convicted of a crime he said he did not commit, he fled to Central America. There he met other fugitives, worked on ranches as a cowboy, and gathered material that he later used in his short stories. Learning that his wife was seriously ill, Porter returned to the United States to stand trial. He was found guilty and sentenced to five years in prison. While in jail, Porter wrote and published twelve short stories under the pen name O. Henry. There are many versions of why he adopted that name. The most popular one is that he overheard the wife of the warden, whose first name was Henry, call out to her husband, "Oh, Henry."

While he was in prison, O. Henry's wife died. On his release, the bereaved husband decided to begin a new life in New York and settled in Greenwich Village. O. Henry enjoyed life in the city and became a famous writer. His short stories are noted for their surprise endings, as you will see when you read "The Last Leaf," which is part of a collection called *The Trimmed Lamp*, published in 1907.

The Last Leaf

IN A LITTLE DISTRICT west of Washington Square the streets have run crazy and broken themselves into small strips called "places." These "places" make strange angles and curves. One street crosses itself a time or two. An artist once discovered a valuable possibility in this street. Suppose a collector with a bill for paints, paper and canvas should, in traversing this route, suddenly meet himself coming back, without a cent having been paid on account!

So, to quaint old Greenwich Village the art people soon came prowling, hunting for north windows and eighteenth-century gables and Dutch attics and low rents. Then they imported some pewter mugs and a chafing dish or two from Sixth Avenue, and became a "colony."

At the top of a squatty, three-story brick Sue and Johnsy had their studio. "Johnsy" was familiar for Joanna. One was from Maine; the other from California. They had met at the *table d'hôte* of an Eighth Street "Delmonico's," and found their tastes in art, chicory salad and bishop sleeves so congenial that the joint studio resulted.

That was in May. In November a cold, unseen stranger, whom the doctors called Pneumonia, stalked about the colony, touching one here and there with his icy fingers. Over on the east side this ravager strode boldly, smiting his victims by scores, but his feet trod slowly through the maze of the narrow and moss-grown "places."

Mr. Pneumonia was not what you would call a chivalric old gentleman. A mite of a little woman with blood thinned by California zephyrs was hardly fair game for the red-fisted, short-breathed old duffer. But Johnsy he smote; and she lay, scarcely moving, on her painted iron bedstead, looking through the small Dutch window-panes at the blank side of the next brick house.

One morning the busy doctor invited Sue into the hallway with a shaggy, gray eyebrow.

"She has one chance in – let us say, ten," he said, as he shook down the mercury in his clinical thermometer. "And that chance is for her to want to live. This way people have of lining-up on the side of the undertaker makes the entire pharmacopœia look silly. Your little lady has made up her mind that she's not going to get well. Has she anything on her mind?

"She – she wanted to paint the Bay of Naples some day," said Sue.

"Paint? – bosh! Has she anything on her mind worth thinking about twice – a man, for instance?"

"A man?" said Sue, with a jew's-harp twang in her voice. "Is a man worth – but, no, doctor; there is nothing of the kind."

"Well, it is the weakness, then," said the doctor. "I will do all that science, so far as it may filter through my efforts, can accomplish. But whenever my patient begins to count the carriages in her funeral procession I subtract 50 per cent from the curative power of medicines. If you will get her to ask one question about the new winter styles in cloak sleeves I will promise you a one-in-five chance for her, instead of one in ten."

After the doctor had gone Sue went into the workroom and cried a Japanese napkin to a pulp. Then she swaggered into Johnsy's room with her drawing board, whistling ragtime.

Johnsy, lay, scarcely making a ripple under the bedclothes, with her face toward the window. Sue stopped whistling, thinking she was asleep.

She arranged her board and began a pen-and-ink drawing to illustrate a magazine story. Young artists must pave their way to Art by drawing pictures for magazine stories that young authors write to pave their way to Literature.

As Sue was sketching a pair of elegant horseshow riding trousers and a monocle on the figure of the hero, an Idaho cowboy, she heard a low sound, several times repeated. She went quickly to the bedside.

Johnsy's eyes were open wide. She was looking out the window and counting – counting backward.

"Twelve," she said, and a little later "eleven"; and then "ten," and "nine"; and then "eight" and "seven," almost together.

Sue looked solicitously out of the window. What was there to count? There was only a bare, dreary yard to be seen, and the blank side of the brick house twenty feet away. An old, old ivy vine, gnarled and decayed at the roots, climbed half way up the brick wall. The cold breath of autumn had stricken its leaves from the vine until its skeleton branches clung, almost bare, to the crumbling bricks.

"What is it, dear?" asked Sue.

"Six," said Johnsy, in almost a whisper. "They're falling faster now. Three days ago there were almost a hundred. It made my head ache to count them. But now it's easy. There goes another one. There are only five left now."

"Five what, dear? Tell your Sudie."

"Leaves. On the ivy vine. When the last one falls I must go, too. I've known that for three days. Didn't the doctor tell you?"

"Oh, I never heard of such nonsense," complained Sue, with magnificent scorn. "What have old ivy leaves to do with your getting well? And you used to love that vine, so, you naughty girl. Don't be a goosey. Why, the doctor told me this morning that your chances for getting well real soon were – let's see exactly what he said – he said the chances were ten to one! Why, that's almost as good a chance as we have in New York when we ride on the street cars or walk past a new building. Try to take some broth now, and let Sudie go back to her drawing, so she can sell the editor man with it, and buy port wine for her sick child, and pork chops for her greedy self."

"You needn't get any more wine," said Johnsy, keeping her eyes fixed out the window. "There goes another. No, I don't want any broth. That leaves just four. I want to see the last one fall before it gets dark. Then I'll go, too."

"Johnsy, dear," said Sue, bending over her, "will you promise me to keep your eyes closed, and not look out the window until I am done working? I must hand those drawings in by tomorrow. I need the light, or I would draw the shade down."

"Couldn't you draw in the other room?" asked Johnsy, coldly.

"I'd rather be here by you," said Sue. "Besides, I don't want you to keep looking at those silly ivy leaves."

"Tell me as soon as you have finished," said Johnsy, closing her eyes, and lying white and still as a fallen statue, "because I want to see the last one fall. I'm tired of waiting. I'm tired of thinking. I want to turn loose my hold on everything, and go sailing down, down, just like one of those poor, tired leaves."

"Try to sleep," said Sue. "I must call Behrman up to be my model for the old hermit miner. I'll not be gone a minute. Don't try to move 'til I come back."

Old Behrman was a painter who lived on the ground floor beneath them. He was past sixty and had a Michael Angelo's Moses beard curling down from the head of a satyr along the body of an imp. Behrman was a failure in art. Forty years he had wielded the brush without getting near enough to touch the hem of his Mistress's robe. He had been always about to paint a masterpiece, but had never yet begun it. For several years he had painted nothing except now and then a daub in the line of commerce or advertising. He earned a little by serving as a model to those young artists in the colony who could not pay the price of a professional. He drank gin to excess, and still talked of his coming masterpiece. For the rest he was a fierce little old man, who scoffed terribly at softness in any one, and who regarded himself as especial mastiff-in-waiting to protect the two young artists in the studio above.

Sue found Behrman smelling strongly of juniper berries in his dimly lighted den below. In one corner was a blank canvas on an easel that had been waiting there for twenty-five years to receive the first line of the masterpiece. She told him of Johnsy's fancy, and how she feared she would, indeed, light and fragile as a leaf herself, float away, when her slight hold upon the world grew weaker.

Old Behrman, with his red eyes plainly streaming, shouted his contempt and derision for such idiotic imaginings.

"Vass!" he cried. "Is dere people in de world mit der foolishness to die because leafs dey drop off from a confounded vine? I haf not heard of such a thing. No, I will not bose as a model for your fool hermit-dunderhead. Vy do you allow dot silly pusiness to come in der brain of her? Ach, dot poor leetle Miss Yohnsy."

"She is very ill and weak," said Sue, "and the fever has left her mind morbid and full of strange fancies. Very well, Mr. Behrman, if you do not care to pose for me, you needn't. But I think you are a horrid old – old flibbertigibbet."

"You are just like a woman!" yelled Behrman. "Who said I will not bose? Go on. I come mit you. For half an hour I haf peen trying to say dot I am ready to bose. Gott! dis is not any blace in which one so goot as Miss Yohnsy shall lie sick. Some day I vill baint a masterpiece, and ve shall all go away. Gott! yes."

Johnsy was sleeping when they went upstairs. Sue pulled the shade down to the window-sill, and motioned Behrman into the other room. In there they peered out the window fearfully at the ivy vine. Then they looked at each other for a moment without speaking. A persistent, cold rain was falling, mingled with snow. Behrman, in his old blue shirt, took his seat as the hermit miner on an upturned kettle for a rock.

When Sue awoke from an hour's sleep the next morning she found Johnsy with dull, wide-open eyes staring at the drawn green shade.

"Pull it up; I want to see," she ordered, in a whisper.

Wearily Sue obeyed.

But, lo! after the beating rain and fierce gusts of wind that had endured through the livelong night, there yet stood out against the brick wall one ivy leaf. It was the last on the vine. Still dark green near its stem, but with its serrated edges tinted with the yellow of dissolution and decay, it hung bravely from a branch some twenty feet above the ground.

"It is the last one," said Johnsy. "I thought it would surely fall during the night. I heard the wind. It will fall today, and I shall die at the same time."

"Dear, dear!" said Sue, leaning her worn face down to the pillow, "think of me, if you won't think of yourself. What would I do?"

But Johnsy did not answer. The lonesomest thing in all the world is a soul when it is making ready to go on its mysterious, far journey. The fancy seemed to possess her more strongly as one by one the ties that bound her to friendship and to earth were loosed.

The day wore away, and even through the twilight they could see the lone ivy leaf clinging to its stem against the wall. And then, with the coming of the night the north wind was again loosed, while the rain still beat against the windows and pattered down from the low Dutch eaves.

When it was light enough Johnsy, the merciless, commanded that the shade be raised.

The ivy leaf was still there.

Johnsy lay for a long time looking at it. And then she called to Sue, who was stirring her chicken broth over the gas stove.

"I've been a bad girl, Sudie," said Johnsy. "Something has made that last leaf stay there to show me how wicked I was. It is a sin to want to die. You may bring me a little broth now, and some milk with a little port in it, and — no; bring me a hand-mirror first, and then pack some pillows about me, and I will sit up and watch you cook."

An hour later she said:

"Sudie, some day I hope to paint the Bay of Naples."

The doctor came in the afternoon, and Sue had an excuse to go into the hallway as he left.

"Even chances," said the doctor, taking Sue's thin, shaking hand in his. "With good nursing you'll win. And now I must see another case I have downstairs. Behrman, his name is – some kind of an artist, I believe. Pneumonia, too. He is an old, weak man, and the attack is acute. There is no hope for him; but he goes to the hospital today to be made more comfortable."

The next day the doctor said to Sue: "She's out of danger. You've won. Nutrition and care now – that's all."

And that afternoon Sue came to the bed where Johnsy lay, contentedly knitting a very blue and very useless woollen shoulder scarf, and put one arm around her, pillows and all.

"I have something to tell you, white mouse," she said. "Mr. Behrman died of pneumonia today in the hospital. He was ill only two days. The janitor found him on the morning of the first day in his room downstairs helpless with pain. His shoes and clothing were wet through and icy cold. They couldn't imagine where he had been on such a dreadful night. And then they found a lantern, still lighted, and a ladder that had been dragged from its place, and some scattered brushes, and a palette with green and yellow colors mixed on it, and – look out the window, dear, at the last ivy leaf on the wall. Didn't you wonder why it never fluttered or moved when the wind blew? Ah, darling, it's Behrman's masterpiece – he painted it there the night that the last leaf fell."

C AFTER READING

1. Comprehension

Answer these questions to determine how well you understood the story.

1. The story is set in New York's Greenwich Village, at one time famous for its art colony. How do we know that the author is familiar with his setting?
2. Why does Johnsy feel she is fated to die?
3. Describe Mr. Behrman.
4. What was Mr. Behrman's masterpiece?
5. At what point in the story do you begin to think that Mr. Behrman will help Johnsy?
6. What was the ending of "The Last Leaf"? How did you feel when you reached the end of the story?

2. Vocabulary

In the following sentences, the **bold** words have been selected from "The Last Leaf." From the way the words are used in the sentences, try to guess their meanings. If you have trouble, consult your dictionary. Write a synonym for each word in the space provided at the end of the sentence.

1. The hiker had to **traverse** many paths before he found a stream to wash his face and hands. _walk across_

2. That **quaint** little house is a contrast to all the modern buildings surrounding it. _Charming / old fashion_

3. Cats often **prowl** all night, looking for food. _Wandar / Roam_

4. When we go to a party, we expect to meet **congenial** people. _Friendly / sociable_

5. Frankenstein's monster was a **ravager** who roamed the countryside, causing widespread damage. _one of destroy with violence._

6. An epidemic often **smites** children and old people. _Attack / Strike_

7. In medieval times, knights were expected to be **chivalric.** _Gentlemanly_

8. The conceited football player **swaggered** off the field after having made the winning touchdown. _Walked in a boast manner._

9. Sue's care of Johnsy showed how **solicitous** she was for her friend's welfare. _Concerned_

10. People who are afraid of being robbed sometimes have a **mastiff** to protect them. _A big guard dog_

11. Johnsy had a **morbid** conviction that she would die when the last leaf fell from the vine. _b Gloomy_

12. Years ago, many immigrants came to America thinking that the streets were **paved** with gold. _Linen / Covered_

13. A saw, like a leaf, has edges that are **serrated.** _Notched / Uneven_

14. Parents should never **scoff** at their children's ambitions even if they seem ridiculous. _Ridicule_

15. Most women like to look **elegant** when attending a dinner party. _Stylish_

3. Grammar: Infinitives and Gerunds

In "The Last Leaf," O. Henry uses many infinitives and gerunds. Here are some examples from the story:

Infinitives	Gerunds
want **to see**	tired **of waiting**
try **to sleep**	go **sailing**
hope **to plant**	without **speaking**

Infinitives are formed by using *to* + the present tense of a verb, for example, *to run*. Never form an infinitive by adding *to* to the past tense.

INCORRECT: to walked
CORRECT: **to walk**

Gerunds are formed by placing -*ing* at the end of a verb, for example, *running*.

Infinitives and gerunds are called **verbals** because they look like verbs but function as other parts of speech. Infinitives function as nouns, adjectives, or adverbs. Gerunds function as nouns. Certain verbs must be followed by infinitives – not gerunds. You cannot say, for example: I want *seeing* that film. You must say: I want *to see* that film.

Here are some other verbs that require infinitives:

hope	pretend	need	seem
decide	refuse	offer	
agree	expect	promise	

Other verbs are always followed by gerunds, such as *go* (go swimming) and the verbs listed here:

avoid	delay	consider	discuss
mind	quit	dislike	
finish	enjoy	keep	

Do not say, for example: I enjoy **to dance.** Use the gerund: I enjoy **dancing.**
Note: Although you must use a gerund with *dislike,* you may use either a gerund
or an infinitive with *like.* You may say: I like **to dance** or I like **dancing.**

■ *Application*
Now try this exercise by using the correct form of the verbal (infinitive or
gerund).

1. I lost my bracelet. Will you keep _____ (look) for it?

2. Johnsy wanted _____ (paint) the Bay of Naples.

3. Do you mind _____ (turn) off the TV?

4. Both Sue and Johnsy enjoyed _____ (live) in Greenwich
   Village.

5. Mr. Behrman offered _____ (help) the sick Johnsy.

6. I dislike _____ (stay) out late on weeknights.

7. Many restaurants won't allow customers _____ (smoke).

8. I need _____ (buy) a new chair for my living room.

9. Mr. Behrman hoped some day _____ (produce) a masterpiece.

10. In fact, he expected _____ (do) it very soon.

11. It seems _____ (be) cloudy every day.

12. When you finish _____ (work), let's go out to the movies.

13. We decided _____ (stay) home for the Thanksgiving holidays.

14. That way we can avoid _____ (travel) in the heavy traffic.

15. I promise _____ (go) on a diet soon.

16. Sue refused _____ (believe) that Johnsy would die.

17. Shall we consider _____ (hire) an artist to illustrate our book?

18. Why do you delay _____ (make) a decision?

19. Let's agree _____ (wait) until tomorrow before telling her the bad news.

20. Mr. Behrman promised _____ (pose) for Sue's picture.

4. Editing

As a review, correct the misuse of infinitives and gerunds in the following paragraph:

I have always enjoyed to read stories with a surprise ending. I dislike to know what will happen before I finish to read the ending. I need having an unexpected twist, and I refuse selecting any more stories by authors who decide giving the reader too many hints. O. Henry was a master who delayed to tell the outcome of the plot until the very last sentence. I hope finding other authors like O. Henry.

D | THINKING ABOUT THE STORY

1. Sharing Ideas

Discuss the following questions with a partner, in a small group, or with the whole class:

1. Do you know of any cases in life or in literature in which a person lost the will to live? Do you think a desire to survive can overcome even a fatal illness?
2. Discuss the friendship between Sue and Johnsy. Give examples that prove Sue's loyalty.
3. In what way is the setting important to the story? Suppose Johnsy had become ill in the spring or the summer?
4. How does the ending prove that Mr. Behrman was a great artist?
5. What other examples in the story indicate Mr. Behrman's deep feeling for Sue and Johnsy?

2. Writing

Read the writing ideas that follow. Your instructor may make specific assignments, or ask you to choose one of these.

1. In the fourth paragraph of the story, O. Henry describes pneumonia as though the disease were a person. Write a paragraph in which you also use

personification. You might wish to describe a season, an old house, flowers, falling leaves, or something else.

2. Write a dialogue between Johnsy and Sue a year later, on the anniversary of Mr. Behrman's death.

3. Write an original story with a surprise ending.

4. Retell a story from your native country that contains the theme of someone making a sacrifice for another.

5. Compare Johnsy's attitude toward her chances for survival with Schatz's in "A Day's Wait." Cite specific examples from each story.

Chapter 6

The Ambitious Guest NATHANIEL HAWTHORNE

A PRE-READING

1. Think Before You Read

Answer the following questions before you read the story:

1. Look at a map of the New England states and locate the White Mountains. What state are they in? What problems do you think you would encounter if you were to live there in the winter? Would there be any advantages?
2. Consult your dictionary for the meaning of the following geographical terms: *notch, slide,* and *flume.*
3. In what ways is nature sometimes a threat to human existence?

2. Literary Term: Foreshadowing

In the mystery stories you have seen in movies or on television, has there ever been an opening scene in which there is a big thunderstorm and the wind howls and the doors on a lonely house rattle? You know from this type of scene that something frightening is going to happen. This is called **foreshadowing,** since the author is giving the reader hints as to what will soon take place. There are many indications in "The Ambitious Guest" that some force of nature is going to affect the characters. Be aware of foreshadowing as you read the story.

3. Idioms and Expressions

Note the following idioms and expressions that appear in the story:

hard by nearby	**pour out his heart** express one's deep emotions
nonsensical foolish	**hark** to listen attentively
gathered round their hearth sat around the fireplace	**set my mind a wandering** influenced me to think about many things; to daydream
heart's ease a comfortable feeling	**sepulchre** a grave
steal a kiss kiss someone without permission	
pair of bellows instruments to increase the draft of a fire	

B | THE STORY

ABOUT THE AUTHOR

Nathaniel Hawthorne (1804–1864), one of the principal authors of the early New England period, was descended from well-known ancestors. His grandfather was a famous sea captain in the American Revolution, and another relative had been a judge at the Salem witch trials. Perhaps that is why many of Hawthorne's stories reflect the manners, superstitions, and customs of life in a Puritan culture. People in Hawthorne's day believed in magic spells and the power of witches and the devil. Lawbreakers were often publicly flogged, or put in stocks and ducking stools to be ridiculed by passersby. Hawthorne's most famous novel, *The Scarlet Letter,* tells the tale of Hester Prynne, who was forced to wear on her dress the letter *A* for adultery because she bore an illegitimate child.

It was years, however, before Hawthorne became a recognized author. Although he embarked on a literary career upon graduating from Bowdoin College, his early efforts were unsuccessful. Finally, he found a publisher for his collection of short stories entitled *Twice Told Tales*. The success of this book brought him into the literary circle of Elizabeth Peabody, teacher, author, and publisher, whose bookstore became the meeting place for writers and philosophers. There he met Peabody's sister, Sophia, whom he married in 1842.

Although Hawthorne wrote two highly successful novels, *The House of the Seven Gables* and *The Scarlet Letter*, he found that he could not make a living as an author. He entered politics, and through his friend, President Franklin Pierce, he became the U.S. consul at Liverpool, England. Through this post, he was able to save enough money to return to his literary career.

Many of Hawthorne's short stories deal with the force of destiny, as you will see when you read "The Ambitious Guest."

The Ambitious Guest

ONE SEPTEMBER NIGHT a family had gathered round their hearth, and piled it high with the driftwood of mountain streams, the
5 dry cones of the pine, and the splintered ruins of great trees that had come crashing down the precipice. Up the chimney roared the fire, and brightened the room with its broad
10 blaze. The faces of the father and mother had a sober gladness; the children laughed; the eldest daughter was the image of Happiness at seventeen; and the aged grandmother,
15 who sat knitting in the warmest place, was the image of Happiness grown old. They had found the "herb, heart's-ease," in the bleakest spot of all New England. This family were situated in
20 the Notch of the White Hills, where the wind was sharp throughout the year, and pitilessly cold in the winter, – giving their cottage all its fresh inclemency before it descended on the valley of the Saco. They dwelt in a cold 25 spot and a dangerous one; for a mountain towered above their heads, so steep, that the stones would often rumble down its sides and startle them at midnight. 30

The daughter had just uttered some simple jest that filled them all with mirth, when the wind came through the Notch and seemed to pause before their cottage – rattling the door, with a 35 sound of wailing and lamentation, before it passed into the valley. For a moment it saddened them, though there was nothing unusual in the tones. But the family were glad again when 40 they perceived that the latch was lifted by some traveler, whose footsteps had been unheard amid the dreary blast which heralded his approach, and wailed as he was entering, and went moaning away from the door.

Though they dwelt in such a solitude, these people held daily converse with the world. The romantic pass of the Notch is a great artery, through which the life-blood of internal commerce is continually throbbing between Maine, on one side, and the Green Mountains and the shores of the St. Lawrence, on the other. The stage-coach always drew up before the door of the cottage. The wayfarer, with no companion but his staff, paused here to exchange a word, that the sense of loneliness might not utterly overcome him ere he could pass through the cleft of the mountain, or reach the first house in the valley. And here the teamster, on his way to Portland market, would put up for the night; and, if a bachelor, might sit an hour beyond the usual bedtime, and steal a kiss from the mountain maid at parting. It was one of those primitive taverns where the traveller pays only for food and lodging, but meets with a homely kindness beyond all price. When the footsteps were heard, therefore, between the outer door and the inner one, the whole family rose up, grandmother, children, and all, as if about to welcome some one who belonged to them, and whose fate was linked with theirs.

The door was opened by a young man. His face at first wore the melancholy expression, almost despondency, of one who travels a wild and bleak road, at nightfall and alone, but soon brightened up when he saw the kindly warmth of his reception. He felt his heart spring forward to meet them all, from the old woman, who wiped a chair with her apron, to the little child that held out its arms to him. One glance and smile placed the stranger on a footing of innocent familiarity with the eldest daughter.

"Ah, this fire is the right thing!" cried he; "especially when there is such a pleasant circle round it. I am quite benumbed; for the Notch is just like the pipe of a great pair of bellows; it has blown a terrible blast in my face all the way from Bartlett."

"Then you are going towards Vermont?" said the master of the house, as he helped to take a light knapsack off the young man's shoulders.

"Yes; to Burlington, and far enough beyond," replied he. "I meant to have been at Ethan Crawford's tonight; but a pedestrian lingers along such a road as this. It is no matter; for, when I saw this good fire, and all your cheerful faces, I felt as if you had kindled it on purpose for me, and were waiting my arrival. So I shall sit down among you, and make myself at home."

The frank-hearted stranger had just drawn his chair to the fire when something like a heavy footstep was heard without, rushing down the steep side of the mountain, as with long and rapid strides, and taking such a leap in passing the cottage as to strike the opposite precipice. The family held their breath, because they knew the

125 sound, and their guest held his by
instinct.

"The old mountain has thrown a
stone at us, for fear we should forget
him," said the landlord, recovering
130 himself. "He sometimes nods his head
and threatens to come down; but we
are old neighbors, and agree together
pretty well upon the whole. Besides we
have a sure place of refuge hard by if he
135 should be coming in good earnest."

Let us now suppose the stranger to
have finished his supper of bear's meal;
and, by his natural felicity of manner,
to have placed himself on a footing of
140 kindness with the whole family, so that
they talked as freely together as if he
belonged to their mountain brood. He
was of a proud, yet gentle spirit –
haughty and reserved among the rich
145 and great; but ever ready to stoop his
head to the lowly cottage door, and be
like a brother or a son at the poor man's
fireside. In the household of the Notch
he found warmth and simplicity of
150 feeling, the pervading intelligence of
New England, and a poetry of native
growth, which they had gathered when
they little thought of it from the
mountain peaks and chasms, and at the
155 very threshold of their romantic and
dangerous abode. He had travelled far
and alone; his whole life, indeed, had
been a solitary path; for, with the lofty
caution of his nature, he had kept
160 himself apart from those who might
otherwise have been his companions.
The family, too, though so kind and
hospitable, had that consciousness of
unity among themselves, and
165 separation from the world at large,
which, in every domestic circle, should

still keep a holy place where no
stranger may intrude. But this evening
a prophetic sympathy impelled the
refined and educated youth to pour out 170
his heart before the simple
mountaineers, and constrained them
to answer him with the same free
confidence. And thus it should have
been. Is not the kindred of a common 175
fate a closer tie than that of birth?

The secret of the young man's
character was a high and abstracted
ambition. He could have borne to live
an undistinguished life, but not to be 180
forgotten in the grave. Yearning desire
had been transformed to hope; and
hope, long cherished, had become like
certainty, that, obscurely as he
journeyed now, a glory was to beam on 185
all his pathway, – though not, perhaps,
while he was treading it. But when
posterity should gaze back into the
gloom of what was now the present,
they would trace the brightness of his 190
footsteps, brightening as meaner
glories faded, and confess that a gifted
one had passed from his cradle to his
tomb with none to recognize him.

"As yet," cried the stranger – his 195
cheek glowing and his eye flashing
with enthusiasm – "as yet, I have done
nothing. Were I to vanish from the
earth tomorrow, none would know so
much of me as you: that a nameless 200
youth came up at nightfall from the
valley of the Saco, and opened his heart
to you in the evening, and passed
through the Notch by sunrise, and was
seen no more. Not a soul would ask, 205
'Who was he? Whither did the
wanderer go?' But I cannot die till I
have achieved my destiny. Then, let

The Unexpected Twist

Death come! I shall have built my monument!"

There was a continual flow of natural emotion, gushing forth amid abstracted reverie, which enabled the family to understand this young man's sentiments, though so foreign from their own. With quick sensibility of the ludicrous, he blushed at the ardor into which he had been betrayed.

"You laugh at me," said he, taking the eldest daughter's hand, and laughing himself. "You think my ambition as nonsensical as if I were to freeze myself to death on the top of Mount Washington, only that people might spy at me from the country round about. And, truly, that would be a noble pedestal for a man's statue!"

"It is better to sit here by this fire," answered the girl, blushing, "and be comfortable and contented, though nobody thinks about us."

"I suppose," said her father, after a fit of musing, "there is something natural in what the young man says; and if my mind had been turned that way, I might have felt just the same. It is strange, wife, how his talk has set my head running on things that are pretty certain never to come to pass."

"Perhaps they may," observed the wife. "Is the man thinking what he will do when he is a widower?"

"No, no!" cried he, repelling the idea with reproachful kindness. "When I think of your death, Esther, I think of mine, too. But I was wishing we had a good farm in Bartlett, or Bethlehem, or Littleton, or some other township round the White Mountains; but not where they could tumble on our heads.

I should want to stand well with my neighbors and be called Squire, and sent to General Court for a term or two; for a plain, honest man may do as much good there as a lawyer. And when I should be grown quite an old man, and you an old woman, so as not to be long apart, I might die happy enough in my bed, and leave you all crying around me. A slate gravestone would suit me as well as a marble one – with just my name and age, and a verse of a hymn, and something to let people know that I lived an honest man and died a Christian."

"There now!" exclaimed the stranger; "it is our nature to desire a monument, be it slate or marble, or a pillar of granite, or a glorious memory in the universal heart of man."

"We're in a strange way, tonight," said the wife, with tears in her eyes. "They say it's a sign of something, when folks' minds go a wandering so. Hark to the children!"

They listened accordingly. The younger children had been put to bed in another room, but with an open door between, so that they could be heard talking busily among themselves. One and all seemed to have caught the infection from the fireside circle, and were outvying each other in wild wishes, and childish projects of what they would do when they came to be men and women. At length a little boy, instead of addressing his brothers and sisters, called out to his mother.

"I'll tell you what I wish, mother," cried he. "I want you and father and grandma'm, and all of us, and the stranger too, to start right away, and go and take a drink out of the basin of the Flume!"

Nobody could help laughing at the child's notion of leaving a warm bed, and dragging them from a cheerful fire, to visit the basin of the Flume, – a brook, which tumbles over the precipice, deep within the Notch. The boy had hardly spoken when a wagon rattled along the road, and stopped a moment before the door. It appeared to contain two or three men, who were cheering their hearts with the rough chorus of a song, which resounded, in broken notes, between the cliffs, while the singers hesitated whether to continue their journey or put up here for the night.

"Father," said the girl, "they are calling you by name."

But the good man doubted whether they had really called him, and was unwilling to show himself too solicitous of gain by inviting people to patronize his house. He therefore did not hurry to the door; and the lash being soon applied, the travellers plunged into the Notch, still singing and laughing, though their music and mirth came back drearily from the heart of the mountain.

"There, mother!" cried the boy, again. "They'd have given us a ride to the Flume."

Again they laughed at the child's pertinacious fancy for a night ramble. But it happened that a light cloud passed over the daughter's spirit; she looked gravely into the fire, and drew a breath that was almost a sigh. It forced its way, in spite of a little struggle to repress it. Then starting and blushing, she looked quickly round the circle, as if they had caught a glimpse into her bosom. The stranger asked what she had been thinking of.

"Nothing," answered she, with a downcast smile. "Only I felt lonesome just then."

"Oh, I have always had a gift of feeling what is in other people's hearts," said he, half seriously. "Shall I tell the secrets of yours? For I know what to think when a young girl shivers by a warm hearth, and complains of lonesomeness at her mother's side. Shall I put these feelings into words?"

"They would not be a girl's feelings any longer if they could be put into words," replied the mountain nymph, laughing, but avoiding his eye.

All this was said apart. Perhaps a germ of love was springing in their hearts, so pure that it might blossom in Paradise, since it could not be matured on earth; for women worship such gentle dignity as his; and the proud, contemplative, yet kindly soul is oftenest captivated by simplicity like hers. But while they spoke softly, and he was watching the happy sadness, the lightsome shadows, the shy yearnings of a maiden's nature, the wind through the Notch took a deeper and drearier sound. It seemed, as the fanciful stranger said, like the choral strain of the spirits of the blast, who in old Indian times had their dwelling among these mountains, and made their heights and recesses a sacred region. There was a wail along the road, as if a funeral were passing. To chase away the gloom, the family threw pine branches on their fire, till the dry leaves crackled and the flame arose, discovering once again a scene of peace and humble happiness. The light hovered about them fondly, and caressed them all. There were the little faces of the children, peeping from their bed apart, and here the father's frame of strength, the mother's subdued and careful mien, the high-browed youth, the budding girl, and the good old grandam, still knitting in the warmest place. The aged woman looked up from her task, and, with fingers ever busy, was the next to speak.

"Old folks have their notions," said she, "as well as young ones. You've been wishing and planning; and letting your heads run on one thing and another, till you've set my mind a wandering too. Now what should an old woman wish for, when she can go but a step or two before she comes to her grave? Children, it will haunt me night and day till I tell you."

"What is it, mother?" cried the husband and wife at once.

Then the old woman, with an air of mystery which drew the circle closer round the fire, informed them that she had provided her grave-clothes some years before, – a nice linen shroud, a cap with a muslin ruff, and everything of a finer sort than she had worn since her wedding day. But this evening an old superstition had strangely recurred to her. It used to be said, in her younger days, that if anything were amiss with a corpse, if only the ruff were not smooth, or the cap did not set right, the corpse in the coffin and beneath the clods would strive to put up its cold hands and arrange it. The bare thought made her nervous.

"Don't talk so, grandmother!" said the girl, shuddering.

"Now," – continued the old woman, with singular earnestness, yet smiling strangely at her own folly, – "I want one of you, my children – when your mother is dressed and in the coffin – I want one of you to hold a looking-glass over my face. Who knows but I may take a glimpse at myself, and see whether all's right?"

"Old and young, we dream of graves and monuments," murmured the stranger youth. "I wonder how mariners feel when the ship is sinking, and they, unknown and undistinguished, are to be buried together in the ocean – that wide and nameless sepulchre?"

For a moment, the old woman's ghastly conception so engrossed the minds of her hearers that a sound abroad in the night, rising like the roar of a blast, had grown broad, deep, and terrible, before the fated group were conscious of it. The house and all within it trembled; the foundations of the earth seemed to be shaken, as if this awful sound were the peal of the last trump. Young and old exchanged one wild glance, and remained an instant, pale, affrighted, without utterance, or power to move. Then the same shriek burst simultaneously from all their lips.

"The Slide! The Slide!"

The simplest words must intimate, but not portray, the unutterable horror of the catastrophe. The victims rushed from their cottage, and sought refuge in what they deemed a safer spot –

where, in contemplation of such an emergency, a sort of barrier had been reared. Alas! they had quitted their security, and fled right into the pathway of destruction. Down came the whole side of the mountain, in a cataract of ruin. Just before it reached the house, the stream broke into two branches – shivered not a window there, but overwhelmed the whole vicinity, blocked up the road, and annihilated everything in its dreadful course. Long ere the thunder of the great Slide had ceased to roar among the mountains, the mortal agony had been endured, and the victims were at peace. Their bodies were never found.

The next morning, the light smoke was seen stealing from the cottage chimney up the mountain side. Within, the fire was yet smouldering on the hearth, and the chairs in a circle round it, as if the inhabitants had but gone forth to view the devastation of the Slide, and would shortly return, to thank Heaven for their miraculous escape. All had left separate tokens, by which those who had known the family were made to shed a tear for each. Who has not heard their name? The story has been told far and wide, and will forever be a legend of these mountains. Poets have sung their fate.

There were circumstances which led some to suppose that a stranger had been received into the cottage on this awful night, and had shared the catastrophe of all its inmates. Others denied that there were sufficient grounds for such a conjecture. Woe for the high-souled youth, with his dream of Earthly Immortality! His name and person utterly unknown; his history, his way of life, his plans, a mystery never to be solved, his death and his existence equally a doubt! Whose was the agony of that death moment?

C AFTER READING

1. Comprehension

Answer these questions to determine how well you understood the story.

1. In the first paragraph of the story, why is the word *happiness* capitalized to describe the seventeen-year-old daughter and the aged grandmother?
2. What is the first evidence of foreshadowing in the story?
3. What words tell you the setting (time and place)?
4. Select words that contribute to the atmosphere of mystery and fear.
5. What mistake did the family make when they felt the house tremble?
6. What was the guest's ambition? How did he fail to fulfill his dream?

2. *Vocabulary*

Each of the numbered vocabulary words appears in Hawthorne's story. Look at the four definitions for each word and circle the correct one.

1. despondency
   a. ambition
   b. depression
   c. dependency
   d. determination

2. precipice
   a. edge
   b. valley
   c. mountain
   d. bottom

3. inclemency
   a. good weather
   b. bad weather
   c. lacking kindness
   d. pleasing in appearance

4. rumble
   a. fail
   b. make a noise
   c. moan
   d. break

5. mirth
   a. laughter
   b. sadness
   c. confusion
   d. fear

6. lamentation
   a. happiness
   b. fright
   c. abuse
   d. mournful sound

7. solitude
   a. companionship
   b. social life
   c. isolation
   d. sorrow

8. primitive
   a. modern
   b. undeveloped
   c. in good condition
   d. well-located

9. yearning
   a. regret
   b. longing
   c. certainty
   d. embarrassment

The Ambitious Guest

10. pertinacious
   a. inquisitive
   b. impolite
   c. persistent
   d. particular

3. *Grammar: Comparative and Superlative Adjectives*

The story you have just read contains many adjectives that describe the scenery, the weather, and the characters. Adjectives have what we call the **comparative** degree – they compare two persons, places, or things. For example, the wind at Crawford Notch, where the family lived, was *sharper* than the wind in other parts of New England. Life was certainly *harder*. Notice that the comparative degree is indicated by adding the letters *-er* to the adjective: The brother was **younger** than his sister, and she was **prettier** than her cousin. If an adjective ends in *y*, as in *pretty, lovely,* or *funny,* you must change the *y* to *i* and add *-er*. Notice also that after using an adjective in the comparative degree, we use the word *than*.

All the adjectives we have just put into the comparative degree contain one or two syllables, and they are short words. Suppose, however, an adjective is longer, or it ends in the letters *ful*. It's hard to say "carefuller" or "seriouser," so we place the word *more* in front of the adjective to form the comparative. Note the following examples:

Loretta is **more beautiful** than Jane.
Ted is **more serious** than his brothers.

If an adjective contains three or more syllables, we always place the word *more* in front of it to form the comparative degree. An example for the word *comfortable* would be: My chair is **more comfortable** than yours.

It is important to remember that when you form the comparative degree of an adjective, you must **not** use a double comparison: Loretta is not more prettier than Jane; she is **prettier.**

There is also a **superlative** degree of adjectives, which is used when we want to compare more than two persons, places, or things. Crawford Notch is described as the *bleakest* spot in all New England. *Bleak* is a short word with only one syllable. Therefore, we just add the superlative suffix, *-est*. The stranger in the story is ambitious. He probably was the *most* ambitious guest the family ever entertained. *Ambitious* is a longer word with more than two syllables, so we cannot add *est* to form the superlative. Instead, we say *most ambitious*.

The adjectives *good* and *bad* have irregular comparative and superlative forms. These forms are shown here.

	Comparative	Superlative
good	better	best
bad	worse	worst

Look at the following examples:

Kate feels **better** than she did last week.
Of the three books, I like this one **best.**
She's the **worst** dancer on the floor.
This storm is **worse** than the one we had last year.

■ *Application*
Complete these sentences by inserting the correct degree of adjective in each space. For example,

David is **smarter** than Ted. (smart)

1. This shirt is too small. I need something _____ (large).

2. The family lived in the _____ (dangerous) location of all the mountain people.

3. The path the stranger took was _____ (narrow) than he thought it would be.

4. When I saw James, he was even _____ (melancholy) than he was last year.

5. This restaurant is the _____ (expensive) one in the area.

6. In the winter, mountainous areas are the _____ (lonely) places in the world.

7. Nobody is _____ (honest) than John.

8. The weather in New England is always _____ (cold) than that of the Middle Atlantic states.

9. Her handwriting is _____ (neat) than mine.

10. Of the three homes, yours is the _____ (beautiful).

11. You are the _____ (happy) person I know.

The Ambitious Guest

12. Dick is a _____ (good) athlete than his brother.

13. Last winter was bad, but this one, I think, will be even _____

    (bad).

14. That movie was the _____ (bad) one I've ever seen.

15. I just read that book you recommended. It was even _____

    (good) than the last one you lent me.

4. Grammar: Placement of Adjectives

As you learned in the exercises accompanying "The Corn Planting," the proper placement of adverbs is important. The same is true of adjectives. In what order do we place a series of adjectives?

We know, for example, that the guest in Hawthorne's story is a young man. The word *young* is a fact, but what is your opinion of him? Is he romantic, intelligent, conceited? If you decide that he is romantic, do you place the word *romantic* before or after *young?* The rule is: **Opinion adjectives precede fact adjectives.** Therefore, we would say that the guest is a romantic young man, not a young romantic man.

Here are some other opinion and fact adjectives:

Opinion	Fact
beautiful	slender
poorly-dressed	old
happy	fat
elegant	young

Sometimes, we have more than one fact adjective. Suppose, for example, you want to describe the nice coat the stranger is wearing. You have the following facts: woolen, brown, heavy, new, made in France. This is the order in which you would place these adjectives:

1. *opinion:* nice
2. *how big:* heavy
3. *how old:* new
4. *what color:* brown
5. *where made:* France
6. *what material:* woolen

So, the stranger was wearing a nice, heavy, new, brown, French woolen coat.

■ *Application*

Try this exercise. Place the adjectives in the correct order to modify each noun in the first column.

Noun	Adjectives
beach	long, sandy, white, lovely _____
necklace	Egyptian, antique, silver, beautiful _____
day	sunny, warm, spring, pleasant _____
table	wooden, early American, round, kitchen _____
dog	red, setter, friendly, big _____
teacher	middle-aged, tall, dark, efficient _____
notebook	thick, lined, blue, useful _____
hat	large, pretty, straw, flowered _____
novel	old, big, English, interesting _____

■ *Application*

Now write ten sentences using opinion and fact adjectives to describe some of the items in your home.

1. _____

2. _____

3. _____

4. _____

5. _____

6. _____

7. _____

8. _____

9. _____

10. _____

D | THINKING ABOUT THE STORY

1. Sharing Ideas

Discuss the following questions with a partner, in a small group, or with the whole class:

1. Describe the stranger. Why does the author call him the "ambitious" guest?
2. Give two examples of irony from this story.
3. What is the story's message or theme?
4. Discuss whether or not the stranger would have been seriously interested in the daughter of the household if they had both lived.
5. Do you know any other stories that have unfulfilled dreams as part of the plot?
6. How is foreshadowing used in this story?

2. Writing

Read the writing ideas that follow. Your instructor may make specific assignments, or ask you to choose one of these.

1. In the course of the story, the stranger tells his host, "I cannot die until I have achieved my destiny." Pretend that the young man had survived the slide. Write his story, assuming it is ten years after his visit to the mountain family.
2. What do you think the stranger's last thoughts were as he realized his fate? Write about what he was thinking.
3. Hawthorne describes the remote family inn with clarity and a suggestion of foreshadowing. Write a description of a place you have visited, seen, or imagined.
4. Read another story by Nathaniel Hawthorne and compare it in theme or style to "The Ambitious Guest." (Suggestion: "The Minister's Black Veil")
5. Read a story by any other author in which there is foreshadowing and write a summary of the story, explaining how the author foreshadows the ending. Many of Edgar Allan Poe's stories contain foreshadowing.

Chapter 7

The Lottery SHIRLEY JACKSON

A PRE-READING

1. Think Before You Read

Answer the following questions before you read the story:

1. What is a lottery?
2. Have you ever bought a lottery ticket? Why did you buy it?
3. Look at the story "The Quickening" and think about the discussion of sense impressions as you read this story.
4. Many writers use surprise endings in their stories. Why is such an ending effective?
5. Recall the foreshadowing in "The Ambitious Guest." How did Hawthorne make you think something bad was going to happen? Look for examples of foreshadowing as you read the following story.

2. Literary Term: Irony

Irony results from a difference between reality and appearance. We say there is irony in a situation when something that happens is the opposite of what we expect. For example, pretend you are in a gambling casino and have only one dollar left. You give your last dollar to a waiter as a tip. He puts it in a slot machine and wins the jackpot. It is ironic that you gave away your last dollar, which was a winner. Irony makes us aware of how unpredictable life can be.

3. Idioms and Expressions

Note the following idioms and expressions that appear in the story:

sat uneasily was a new experience, didn't feel right	**a good sport** someone who reacts well to a situation
give me a hand help me	**clean forgot** completely forgot something
get this over with finish doing something unpleasant	
A sudden hush fell on the crowd. It became quiet. People stopped talking.	

B | THE STORY

ABOUT THE AUTHOR

Shirley Jackson (1919–1965) was born in San Francisco, California, but spent her college years in the Northeast. After her marriage, she moved to Vermont and raised four children.

Jackson's writing ranges from humorous stories and novels, including a memoir of her life with her children called *Life among the Savages,* to psychological and horror stories such as "The Lottery." Some of her stories have been adapted into movies.

An important element in Jackson's style is her ability to use minor details and casual conversation to convey powerful images. Her language is carefully chosen to heighten the impact of the horror. What may appear ordinary and commonplace on the surface is intended to produce a memorable effect.

"The Lottery" was published in 1948 in *The New Yorker* magazine, and it created a lot of attention. Many readers and literary critics consider the story symbolic of World War II.

The Lottery

THE MORNING of June 27th was clear and sunny, with the fresh warmth of a full-summer day; the flowers were blossoming profusely and the grass was richly green. The people of the village began to gather in the square, between the post office and the bank, around ten o'clock; in some towns there were so many people that the lottery took two days and had to be started on June 26th, but in this village, where there were only about three hundred people, the whole lottery took less than two hours, so it could begin at ten o'clock in the morning and still be through in time to allow the villagers to get home for noon dinner.

The children assembled first, of course. School was recently over for the summer, and the feeling of liberty sat uneasily on most of them; they tended to gather together quietly for a while before they broke into boisterous play, and their talk was still of the classroom and the teacher, of books and reprimands. Bobby Martin had already stuffed his pockets full of stones, and the other boys soon followed his example, selecting the smoothest and roundest stones; Bobby and Harry Jones and Dickie Delacroix – the villagers pronounced this name "Dellacroy" – eventually made a great pile of stones in one corner of the square and guarded it against the raids of the other boys. The girls stood aside, talking among themselves, looking over their shoulders at the boys, and the very small children rolled in the dust or clung to the hands of their older brothers or sisters.

Soon the men began to gather, surveying their own children, speaking of planting and rain, tractors and taxes. They stood together, away from the pile of stones in the corner, and their jokes were quiet and they smiled rather than laughed. The women, wearing faded house dresses and sweaters, came shortly after their menfolk. They greeted one another and exchanged bits of gossip as they went to join their husbands. Soon the women, standing by their husbands, began to call to their children, and the children came reluctantly, having to be called four or five times. Bobby Martin ducked under his mother's grasping hand and ran, laughing, back to the pile of stones. His father spoke up sharply, and Bobby came quickly and took his place between his father and his oldest brother.

The lottery was conducted – as were the square dances, the teenage club, the Halloween program – by Mr. Summers, who had time and energy to devote to civic activities. He was a round-faced, jovial man and he ran the coal business, and people were sorry for him, because he had no children and his wife was a scold. When he arrived in the square, carrying the black wooden box, there was a murmur of conversation among the villagers and he waved and called, "Little late today, folks." The postmaster, Mr. Graves, followed him, carrying a three-legged stool, and the stool was put in the center of the square and Mr. Summers set the black box down on it. The villagers kept their distance, leaving a space between themselves and the stool, and when Mr. Summers said, "Some of you fellows want to give me a hand?" there was a hesitation before two men, Mr. Martin and his oldest son, Baxter, came forward to hold the box steady on the stool while Mr. Summers stirred up the papers inside it.

The original paraphernalia for the lottery had been lost long ago, and the black box now resting on the stool had been put into use even before Old Man Warner, the oldest man in town, was born. Mr. Summers spoke frequently to the villagers about making a new box, but no one liked to upset even as much tradition as was represented by the black box. There was a story that the present box had been made with some pieces of the box that had preceded it, the one that had been constructed when the first people settled down to make a village here. Every year, after the lottery, Mr. Summers began talking again about a new box, but every year the subject was allowed to fade off without anything's being done. The black box grew shabbier each year; by now it was no longer completely black but splintered badly along one side to show the original wood color, and in some places faded or stained.

Mr. Martin and his oldest son, Baxter, held the black box securely on the stool until Mr. Summers had stirred the papers thoroughly with his hand. Because so much of the ritual had been forgotten or discarded, Mr. Summers had been successful in having slips of paper substituted for the chips of wood that had been used for generations. Chips of wood, Mr. Summers had argued, had been all very well when the village was tiny, but now that the population was more than three hundred and likely to keep on growing, it was necessary to use something that would fit more easily into the black box. The night before the lottery, Mr. Summers and Mr. Graves made up the slips of paper and put them in the box, and it was then taken to the safe of Mr. Summers's coal company and locked up until Mr. Summers was ready to take it to the square next morning. The rest of the year, the box was put away, sometimes one place, sometimes another; it had spent one year in Mr. Graves's barn and another year underfoot in the post office, and sometimes it was set on a shelf in the Martin grocery and left there.

There was a great deal of fussing to be done before Mr. Summers declared the lottery open. There were lists to make up – heads of families, heads of households in each family, members of each household in each family. There was the proper swearing-in of Mr. Summers by the postmaster, as the official of the lottery; at one time, some people remembered, there had been a recital of some sort, performed by the official of the lottery, a perfunctory, tuneless chant that had been rattled off duly each year; some people believed that the official of the lottery used to stand just so when he said or sang it, others believed that he was supposed to walk among the people, but years and years ago this part of the ritual had been allowed to lapse. There had been, also, a ritual salute, which the official of the lottery had had to use in addressing each person who came up to draw from the box, but this also had changed with time, until now it was felt necessary only for the official to speak to each person approaching. Mr. Summers was very good at all this; in his clean white shirt and blue jeans, with one hand resting carelessly on the black box, he seemed very proper and important as he talked interminably to Mr. Graves and the Martins.

Just as Mr. Summers finally left off talking and turned to the assembled villagers, Mrs. Hutchinson came hurriedly along the path to the square, her sweater thrown over her shoulders, and slid into place in the back of the crowd. "Clean forgot what day it was," she said to Mrs. Delacroix, who stood next to her, and they both laughed softly. "Thought my old man was out back stacking wood," Mrs. Hutchinson went on, "and then I looked out the window and the kids were gone, and then I remembered it was the twenty-seventh and came a-running." She dried her hands on her apron, and Mrs. Delacroix said, "You're in time, though. They're still talking away up there."

Mrs. Hutchinson craned her neck to see through the crowd and found her husband and children standing near the front. She tapped Mrs. Delacroix on the arm as a farewell and began to make her way through the crowd. The people separated good-humoredly to let her through; two or three people said, in voices just loud enough to be heard across the crowd, "Here comes your Missus, Hutchinson," and "Bill, she made it after all." Mrs. Hutchinson reached her husband, and Mr. Summers, who had been waiting, said cheerfully, "Thought we were going to have to get on without you, Tessie." Mrs. Hutchinson said, grinning, "Wouldn't have me leave m'dishes in the sink, now would you, Joe?" and soft laughter ran through the crowd as the people stirred back into position after Mrs. Hutchinson's arrival.

"Well, now," Mr. Summers said soberly, "guess we better get started, get this over with, so's we can go back to work. Anybody ain't here?"

"Dunbar," several people said. "Dunbar, Dunbar."

Mr. Summers consulted his list. "Clyde Dunbar," he said. "That's right. He's broke his leg, hasn't he? Who's drawing for him?"

"Me, I guess," a woman said, and Mr. Summers turned to look at her. "Wife draws for her husband," Mr. Summers said. "Don't you have a grown boy to do it for you, Janey?" Although Mr. Summers and everyone else in the village knew the answer perfectly well, it was the business of the official of the lottery to ask such questions formally. Mr. Summers waited with an expression of polite interest while Mrs. Dunbar answered.

"Horace's not but sixteen yet," Mrs. Dunbar said regretfully. "Guess I gotta fill in for the old man this year."

"Right," Mr. Summers said. He made a note on the list he was holding. Then he asked, "Watson boy drawing this year?"

A tall boy in the crowd raised his hand. "Here," he said. "I'm drawing for m'mother and me." He blinked his eyes nervously and ducked his head as several voices in the crowd said things like "Good fellow, Jack," and "Glad to see your mother's got a man to do it."

"Well," Mr. Summers said, "guess that's everyone. Old Man Warner make it?"

"Here," a voice said and Mr. Summers nodded.

A sudden hush fell on the crowd as Mr. Summers cleared his throat and looked at the list. "All ready?" he called. "Now, I'll read the names – heads of families first – and the men come up and take a paper out of the box. Keep the paper folded in your hand without looking at it until everyone has had a turn. Everything clear?"

The people had done it so many times that they only half listened to the directions; most of them were quiet, wetting their lips, not looking around. Then Mr. Summers raised one hand high and said, "Adams." A man disengaged himself from the crowd and came forward. "Hi, Steve," Mr. Summers said, and Mr. Adams said, "Hi, Joe." They grinned at one another humorlessly and nervously. Then Mr. Adams reached into the black box and took out a folded paper. He held it firmly by one corner as he turned and went hastily back to his place in the crowd, where he stood a little apart from his family, not looking down at his hand.

"Allen," Mr. Summers said. "Anderson . . . Bentham."

"Seems like there's no time at all between lotteries any more," Mrs. Delacroix said to Mrs. Graves in the back row. "Seems like we got through with the last one only last week."

"Time sure goes fast," Mrs. Graves said.

"Clark . . . Delacroix."

"There goes my old man," Mrs. Delacroix said. She held her breath while her husband went forward.

"Dunbar," Mr. Summers said, and Mrs. Dunbar went steadily to the box while one of the women said, "Go on, Janey," and another said, "There she goes."

"We're next," Mrs. Graves said. She watched while Mr. Graves came around from the side of the box, greeted Mr. Summers gravely, and selected a slip of paper from the box. By now, all through the crowd there were men holding the small folded papers in their large hands, turning

A sudden hush fell on the crowd as Mr. Summers cleared his throat and looked at the list. "All ready?" he called.

them over and over nervously. Mrs. Dunbar and her two sons stood together, Mrs. Dunbar holding the slip of paper.

"Harburt . . . Hutchinson."

"Get up there, Bill," Mrs. Hutchinson said, and the people near her laughed.

"Jones."

"They do say," Mr. Adams said to Old Man Warner, who stood next to him, "that over in the north village they're talking of giving up the lottery."

Old Man Warner snorted. "Pack of crazy fools," he said. "Listening to the young folks, nothing's good enough for *them*. Next thing you know, they'll be wanting to go back to living in caves, nobody work any more, live *that* way for a while. Used to be a saying about 'Lottery in June, corn be heavy soon.' First thing you know, we'd all be eating stewed chickweed and acorns. There's *always* been a lottery," he added petulantly. "Bad enough to see young Joe Summers up there joking with everybody."

"Some places have already quit lotteries," Mrs. Adams said.

"Nothing but trouble in *that*," Old Man Warner said stoutly. "Pack of young fools."

"Martin." And Bobby Martin watched his father go forward. "Overdyke . . . Percy."

"I wish they'd hurry," Mrs. Dunbar said to her older son. "I wish they'd hurry."

"They're almost through," her son said.

"You get ready to run tell Dad," Mrs. Dunbar said.

Mr. Summers called his own name and then stepped forward precisely and selected a slip from the box. Then he called, "Warner."

"Seventy-seventh year I been in the lottery," Old Man Warner said as he went through the crowd. "Seventy-seventh time."

"Watson." The tall boy came awkwardly through the crowd. Someone said, "Don't be nervous, Jack," and Mr. Summers said, "Take your time, son."

"Zanini."

After that, there was a long pause, a breathless pause, until Mr. Summers, holding his slip of paper in the air, said, "All right, fellows." For a minute, no one moved, and then all the slips of paper were opened. Suddenly, all women began to speak at once, saying, "Who is it?" "Who's got it?" "Is it the Dunbars?" "Is it the Watsons?" Then the voices began to say, "It's Hutchinson. It's Bill." "Bill Hutchinson's got it."

"Go tell your father," Mrs. Dunbar said to her older son.

People began to look around to see the Hutchinsons. Bill Hutchinson was standing quiet, staring down at the paper in his hand. Suddenly, Tessie Hutchinson shouted to Mr. Summers, "You didn't give him time enough to take any paper he wanted. I saw you. It wasn't fair!"

"Be a good sport, Tessie," Mrs. Delacroix called, and Mrs. Graves said, "All of us took the same chance."

"Shut up, Tessie," Bill Hutchinson said.

"Well, everyone," Mr. Summers said,

"that was done pretty fast, and now we've got to be hurrying a little more to get done in time." He consulted his next list. "Bill," he said, "you draw for the Hutchinson family. You got any other households in the Hutchinsons?"

"There's Don and Eva," Mrs. Hutchinson yelled. "Make *them* take their chance!"

"Daughters draw with their husbands' families, Tessie," Mr. Summers said gently. "You know that as well as anyone else."

"It wasn't fair," Tessie said.

"I guess not, Joe," Bill Hutchinson said regretfully. "My daughter draws with her husband's family, that's only fair. And I've got no other family except the kids."

"Then, as far as drawing for families is concerned, it's you," Mr. Summers said in explanation, "and as far as drawing for households is concerned, that's you, too. Right?"

"Right," Bill Hutchinson said.

"How many kids, Bill?" Mr. Summers asked formally.

"Three," Bill Hutchinson said. "There's Bill, Jr., and Nancy, and little Dave. And Tessie and me."

"All right, then," Mr. Summers said. "Harry, you got their tickets back?"

Mr. Graves nodded and held up the slips of paper. "Put them in the box, then," Mr. Summers directed. "Take Bill's and put it in."

"I think we ought to start over," Mrs. Hutchinson said, as quietly as she could. "I tell you it wasn't *fair*. You didn't give him time enough to choose. *Everybody* saw that."

Mr. Graves had selected the five slips and put them in the box, and he dropped all the papers but those onto the ground, where the breeze caught them and lifted them off.

"Listen, everybody," Mrs. Hutchinson was saying to the people around her.

"Ready, Bill?" Mr. Summers said, "take the slips and keep them folded until each person has taken one. Harry, you help little Dave." Mr. Graves took the hand of the little boy, who came willingly with him up to the box. "Take a paper out of the box, Davy," Mr. Summers said. Davy put his hand into the box and laughed. "Take just *one* paper," Mr. Summers said. "Harry, you hold it for him." Mr. Graves took the child's hand and removed the folded paper from the tight fist and held it while Dave stood next to him and looked up at him wonderingly.

"Nancy next," Mr. Summers said. Nancy was twelve, and her school friends breathed heavily as she went forward, switching her skirt, and took a slip daintily from the box. "Bill, Jr.," Mr. Summers said, and Billy, his face red and his feet overlarge, nearly knocked the box over as he got a paper out. "Tessie," Mr. Summers said. She hesitated for a minute, looking around defiantly, and then set her lips and went up to the box. She snatched a paper out and held it behind her.

"Bill," Mr. Summers said, and Bill Hutchinson reached into the box and felt around, bringing his hand out at last with the slip of paper in it.

The crowd was quiet. A girl

whispered, "I hope it's not Nancy," and the sound of the whisper reached the edges of the crowd.

"It's not the way it used to be," Old Man Warner said clearly. "People ain't the way they used to be."

"All right," Mr. Summers said. "Open the papers. Harry, you open little Dave's."

Mr. Graves opened the slip of paper and there was a general sigh through the crowd as he held it up and everyone could see that it was blank. Nancy and Bill, Jr., opened theirs at the same time, and both beamed and laughed, turning around to the crowd and holding their slips of paper above their heads.

"Tessie," Mr. Summers said. There was a pause, and then Mr. Summers looked at Bill Hutchinson, and Bill unfolded his paper and showed it. It was blank.

"It's Tessie," Mr. Summers said, and his voice was hushed. "Show us her paper, Bill."

Bill Hutchinson went over to his wife and forced the slip of paper out of her hand. It had a black spot on it, the black spot Mr. Summers had made the night before with the heavy pencil in the coal-company office. Bill Hutchinson held it up, and there was a stir in the crowd.

"All right, folks," Mr. Summers said, "let's finish quickly."

Although the villagers had forgotten the ritual and lost the original black box, they still remembered to use stones. The pile of stones the boys had made earlier was ready; there were stones on the ground with the blowing scraps of paper that had come out of the box. Mrs. Delacroix selected a stone so large she had to pick it up with both hands and turned to Mrs. Dunbar. "Come on," she said. "Hurry up."

Mrs. Dunbar had small stones in both hands, and she said, gasping for breath, "I can't run at all. You'll have to go ahead and I'll catch up with you."

The children had stones already, and someone gave little Davy Hutchinson a few pebbles.

Tessie Hutchinson was in the center of a cleared space by now, and she held her hands out desperately as the villagers moved in on her. "It isn't fair," she said. A stone hit her on the side of the head.

Old Man Warner was saying, "Come on, come on, everyone." Steve Adams was in the front of the crowd of villagers, with Mrs. Graves beside him.

"It isn't fair, it isn't right," Mrs. Hutchinson screamed, and then they were upon her.

C | AFTER READING

1. Comprehension

Answer these questions to determine how well you understood the story.

1. At what time of year is the lottery held? What month?
2. Who is in charge of the lottery? Is anyone exempt from it?
3. Why isn't Mr. Dunbar present at the lottery drawing?
4. Why have some villages stopped having lotteries?
5. How does Old Man Warner feel about the lottery?
6. Who picks the paper with the black dot?
7. What is the lottery winner's prize?
8. Why does Mrs. Delacroix pick up a large stone?

2. Vocabulary

The following vocabulary words appear in Jackson's story. Write the appropriate word(s) in each sentence. Use each word only once.

profusely	reprimand	boisterous
murmur	scold	jovial
paraphernalia	splintered	soberly
perfunctory	interminably	craned
petulantly	hastily	snorted

1. They _____ their necks to see the president in the motorcade.

2. The hikers carried all their _____ for the trip in their

   backpacks.

3. The lecture seemed _____ long, and many people dozed off.

4. You could hear the low _____ among the waiting crowd.

5. We were embarrassed to see the teacher _____ him in front of

   the whole class. Teachers shouldn't _____ students in public.

6. The wooden table was old and _____ from constant use.

7. The children were _____ as they ran out to play.

8. Don't be so unfriendly; try to be more _____.

9. The runners perspired _____ after they finished the marathon.

10. Our professor's _____ remarks before the exam made us more nervous.

11. The stubborn little girl looked at her father _____.

12. The pigs _____ as they followed the farmer around their sty.

13. The lawyer was very serious as she _____ questioned the potential jurors.

14. Because he was late, he _____ packed his clothes and creased everything.

3. Grammar: Roots, Prefixes, and Suffixes

Expanding your vocabulary is an important part of becoming fluent in a language. It is helpful to know the meanings of roots, prefixes, and suffixes in order to "attack" new vocabulary.

Roots English is based on Latin, but many English words have been borrowed from the Greek, French, German, Italian, and Spanish languages.

■ *Application*
The following roots will help you define new words. In addition to the sample words given, think of other words and write them on the lines.

auto self	automobile, autocrat	_____
bio life	biology	_____
capit head	capital	_____
ced move	recede	_____
chron time	chronicle	_____
corp body	corporate	_____
cycle circle	recycle	_____
derm skin	epidermis	_____
dic, dict say, word	predict, dictionary	_____

duc, duct lead	conduct	
fac, fact make, do	facsimile	
flect bend	reflect	
geo earth	geography	
graph write, record	autograph	
homo same	homonym	
log, logy study	biology	
manu hand	manual	
micro small	microcosm	
mort death	mortal	
peri around	periscope	
phil love	Francophile	
phon sound	phonograph	
photo light	photograph	
port carry	portable	
psych mind	psychology	
scop see	telescope	
scrib, script write	prescription	
soph wise	philosopher	
spir breath	inspiration	
tele far	telephone	
terra earth	territory	
therm heat	thermal	
vene, vent come	convention	

The Unexpected Twist

Prefixes Often, the definition of a word can be determined by knowing the meaning of a prefix. Prefixes are common in English; the following prefixes are frequently used to change the meanings of words:

ambi both
dis not, apart from
im, ir, il, in not
inter between

mal, mis badly
pre before
re again

■ *Application*

For the following exercise, first enter the meaning of each word in the column on the left. Then, use the prefixes listed above to change the words. Enter the new words and their meanings in the column on the right. For example,

regular = normal
ir + regular = irregular = not normal

	Meaning of the Word	Word With a Prefix Added and Its Meaning
1. national	_____	_____
2. action	_____	_____
3. material	_____	_____
4. respect	_____	_____
5. existing	_____	_____
6. conception	_____	_____
7. legal	_____	_____
8. complete	_____	_____
9. adjust	_____	_____
10. establish	_____	_____
11. dexterous	_____	_____
12. literate	_____	_____

Here is a list of additional prefixes:

ante before   **de** away
anti against   **intro, intra** inside
bene well   **sub** under
bi two   **syn, sym** same
circum around   **trans** across
co, com, col together, with   **un** not

■ *Application*

For the exercise that follows, use the list of prefixes above but complete each entry as you did before.

	Meaning of the Word	Word With a Prefix Added and Its Meaning
1. cycle		
2. compose		
3. marine		
4. operate		
5. continental		
6. diction		
7. appreciative		
8. navigate		
9. room		
10. virus		
11. passionate		
12. phonic		
13. social		
14. thesis		

Suffixes Suffixes are added to the end of a root and, like prefixes, they change the meanings of words. For instance, the word *national* is made by adding *-al* to the root *nation*.

■ *Application*

The suffixes in the following exercise will help you define new words. In addition to the sample words given, think of other words and write them on the lines.

al pertaining to, of, belonging to national, natural _____

ary pertaining to elementary _____

er, or one who, that which actor, winner _____

ful full of careful _____

ible, able able to reliable _____

ion, tion state of, result of creation _____

ious, tious state of anxious _____

ist one who does artist _____

less without, not having hopeless _____

■ *Application*

By looking carefully at the following words, you should be able to discover their meanings. Pay attention to the roots, prefixes, and suffixes, and write a definition for each word.

autobiography _____

circumnavigation _____

synonymous _____

unicycle _____

perspiration _____

geology _____

manufacture _____

mortuary _____

reflection _____

1. Sharing Ideas

Discuss the following questions with a partner, in a small group, or with the whole class:

1. Does Jackson tell us when (the year) and where (the town) the story takes place? Why?
2. Why does the village have a lottery?
3. Describe the character Tessie Hutchinson.
4. How does Tessie's husband react to her protests of unfairness? How do her neighbors react?
5. When do you first realize that something bad is going to happen? What words and images are omens of the future horror?
6. Why does the author choose stones as the weapons?

2. Writing

Read the writing ideas that follow. Your instructor may make specific assignments, or ask you to choose one of these.

1. Many people feel that humans are inherently violent. How does this story illustrate the violent nature of people? Can we ever expect people to become nonviolent? Write an essay about these issues.
2. Write out the specific rules of the lottery according to the description in the story. Include all the details and the order in which the rules are administered. (You may work with a partner.)
3. Pretend you are a newspaper reporter covering the story of this town's lottery. Write an eyewitness account of what you observe.
4. Describe how one of Mrs. Hutchinson's children felt when his/her mother opened the piece of paper. Write the description in the first person.
5. Compare and contrast the use of atmosphere in "The Lottery" with another story in this book, such as "All Summer in a Day" by Ray Bradbury.
6. An *allegory* is defined as a story with characters and actions that symbolize ideas and morals. For example, in the fable "The Tortoise and the Hare," the tortoise symbolizes perseverance. Do you think "The Lottery" is an allegory? Write about what "The Lottery" could symbolize, using examples from the story.

Chapter 8
The One Day War JUDITH SOLOWAY

A | PRE-READING

1. Think Before You Read

Answer the following questions before you read the story:

1. What do you know about the Civil War in the United States?
2. What is a bicentennial celebration?
3. Have you ever seen a military cemetery? Describe what you remember.
4. Read the first paragraph only and try to guess what the story is about.
5. How do you feel when you see films about wars or read about them? Have you ever been in a war?

2. Literary Term: Satire

Do you sometimes say the opposite of what you mean? We often use sarcasm to show our disapproval of an action, idea, or person. When writers want to show disapproval, they may use **satire** to emphasize a human failure, weakness, or vice. Satire can be gentle and humorous or bitter and savage. The situations, characters, and language of satire help create the tone of the story.

3. Idioms and Expressions

Note the following idioms and expressions that appear in the story:

rolling along proceeding efficiently	**speak for** represent
fall into place work out well	**at a fraction of the cost** for much
know well in advance know at a much earlier time	less money

ABOUT THE AUTHOR

Judith Soloway (1950–) was born in Brooklyn, New York. While attending Hunter College High School in Manhattan, she wrote for the school newspaper and considered a career in journalism. Instead, after graduating from Queens College, she became a teacher; she has taught English in Maryland, Pennsylvania, and New York. Soloway is married, has four daughters, and currently teaches ESL at Broward Community College in Florida. She continues to write poetry and short stories in her spare time.

The inspiration for "The One Day War" came while Soloway was passing a large military cemetery during a motor trip. She was struck by the miles and miles of graves and their cold anonymity.

The One Day War

GOOD morning fellow Americans. Welcome to the One Day War. WCDW will be your eyes and ears for today bringing you live coverage of a momentous day in our history. As part of our bicentennial celebration of the Civil War, we are proud to participate in Professor Brainard's project, The One Day War.

I'm sure there isn't an American out there who hasn't heard of the project. It has been the most talked about subject in our country for many months. Now the great day, April 9, 2065, is here, and we are all part of it.

The weather is perfect and visibility is excellent. There isn't a cloud overhead; the sky is blue and clear. From our place here on the grandstand, we have a perfect vantage point. While we are waiting, we've arranged an exclusive interview with Professor Brainard, father of the One Day War.

"Professor, I know how busy you are supervising this enormous undertaking, and we appreciate your giving us an interview. To begin with, could you give us some background information about the project?"

"I am very pleased to speak with you. At this point, the project is rolling along according to schedule, and I am here to advise on any problems that may arise. You asked for some background. Well, as you may know, I'm considered an expert on the Civil War, and I was asked to plan a bicentennial celebration. One disturbing aspect of the Civil War, like any other war, was how expensive and inefficient it was. Using our modern day technology, we are able to reconstruct one battle that is the equivalent of all the battles fought during the entire war!

"The major expenses in any war involve the movement of troops and machinery, medical equipment and personnel, and burial expenses. Doing all this during wartime is difficult, expensive, and inefficient. Given our cultural and scientific development these past two hundred years, there was no reason we couldn't produce the same effect at a fraction of the cost. The most brilliant part of the plan was the most obvious – why not bury the soldiers right on the battlefield and eliminate a lot of cost and trouble. The battlefield becomes the cemetery! Once we settled on this idea, the other details fell into place.

"An assembly line procedure was adopted. The computer chose the soldiers. We hired digging crews, masons, gardeners, and florists. We saved a tremendous amount of money by not needing any war machinery except for one revolver per soldier. Naturally, there was no need for medical teams and supplies. The families of the soldiers knew well in advance, so they could plan accordingly and put their personal affairs in order."

"Did you encounter any difficulties with the plan?"

"A little, at first. Some members of Congress thought the plan was 'inhumane.' I explained to them that the net result was the same as waging the war for four years at a greater expense and inconvenience to the general population. Moreover, there would be no involvement with civilians whatsoever – no attacks, no burning of houses, no families killed by marauding soldiers. They agreed unanimously that my plan was safer, more efficient and more humane than the Civil War.

"We did encounter a strong objection from the Western Union lobby in Washington. They would be losing revenue from the telegrams usually sent to the families of the soldiers. We worked out an agreement allowing the company to manufacture the small American flags that will be given to each family."

"And now, Professor Brainard, after months of planning, your project is about to become a reality. Thank you, Professor. I know I speak for the entire nation when I salute you as a remarkable man and a true patriot."

It's 8:30, and we are almost ready for the project to get under way. Before us on this immense battlefield, stretched out for miles, are the two opposing armies. The soldiers stand at attention in neat rows – an army of blue facing an army of gray. They stand very still like marble statues. On our left, we can see the digging machines and their crews waiting silently. Behind them are the masons and gardeners.

On our right, we can see the florists.

Here in the grandstand are all the dignitaries: the President, Vice President, Speaker of the House, Senate Majority Leader, members of the Cabinet, the Supreme Court Justices and representatives of the Armed Forces.

We all rise for our National Anthem. The President approaches the podium. When he gives the signal, the band will play *Taps*, and on the last note of *Taps*, watch the soldiers.

With military precision, each man withdraws his pistol, places it to his temple, and in unison 204,000 shots ring out. The noise is deafening like a huge explosion. Gunsmoke fills the air. The sky is now gray as if a storm has suddenly blown in. The field is very quiet. The rows of gray and blue fallen bodies are now irregular. I guess it's hard to plan a perfect fall even with intensive training and devotion to one's country. The soldiers have done their part. Now it's time for the rest of the team to go to work.

The grandstand viewers file out of their seats and into the waiting limousines. The President shakes Professor Brainard's hand. As the last officials leave, the digging machines and their crews move onto the field. They work from left to right digging each trench, burying each body, and leveling the ground. The stone masons follow. They place a stone at each soldier's grave. Every stone has already been engraved with the soldier's name and dates of birth and death. The crews work efficiently, row after row. The landscapers follow the masons.

They place strips of sod over the newly dug earth. Now the florists unload their trucks and put fresh floral bouquets on each grave.

We are watching the final phase of the One Day War. The digging crews have left the field, the masons have gone, the florists are leaving, and the buses of widows and orphans are arriving. All the families of the soldiers will be here at the same time. They have all been transported here at government expense. They file out onto the field. The ushers and hostesses, dressed in tuxedos and long gowns, direct each family to its particular gravesite. Each family receives an identification tag and a small American flag. The military band is playing *When Johnny Comes Marching Home Again*. We all stand at attention as a gentle breeze blows over the field.

It is truly amazing what American ingenuity can accomplish. This morning what was an ordinary field has been transformed into a military cemetery. It has been a beautiful day! I've been honored to help bring this momentous project into your homes. Yes, it's been a perfect day. Good night, Americans. Sleep well.

C | AFTER READING

1. Comprehension

Answer these questions to determine how well you understood the story.

1. Where and when does this story take place? U.S 2065
2. Who is the narrator? To whom is he speaking? Report, speaking to the public
3. Who is Professor Brainard? Why is he called a patriot?
4. Which people are on the grandstand? the President, VP, Speaker, 3 House & Supreme Court
5. What does war machinery mean? more guns
6. What does an assembly line procedure mean? Why is it used?
7. Why do the grandstand viewers leave the scene of the battlefield?
8. Why are the families of the soldiers given American flags?

2. Vocabulary

Each of the numbered vocabulary words appears in Soloway's story. Look at the four definitions for each word and circle the correct one.

1. momentous
   a. soon
   b. motherly
   c. sudden
   d. important

2. vantage point
   a. pencil
   b. control
   c. viewing position
   d. power play

3. mason
   a. friend
   b. dancer
   c. enemy
   d. stonecutter

4. revolver
   a. door
   b. car
   c. gun
   d. sun

5. marauding
   a. controlled
   b. kind
   c. friendly
   d. rampaging

6. revenue
   a. income
   b. meeting
   c. memory
   d. dream

7. podium
   a. medicine
   b. platform
   c. vegetable
   d. hatred

8. sod
   a. earth with grass
   b. flower
   c. unhappy
   d. talked

9. visibility
   a. math function
   b. hat
   c. darkness
   d. clarity of the air

10. temple
    a. side of the forehead
    b. chin
    c. cheek
    d. neck

11. unison
    a. fictional animal
    b. only son
    c. happiness
    d. at the same time

The Unexpected Twist

12. usher
    a. winner
    b. sleeper
    c. escort
    d. doctor

13. ingenuity
    a. reality
    b. cleverness
    c. innocence
    d. integrity

3. Grammar: Active and Passive Voice

Sentences are written in either the active or passive voice. In the active voice, the subject is doing the action. For example, in "The One Day War" the narrator states:

"We **hired** digging crews, masons, gardeners, and florists."

In this sentence, the subject *we* did the hiring (performed the action). In the passive voice, the subject is acted upon. If we were to change the previous sentence to the passive voice, it would read like this:

The digging crews, masons, gardeners, and florists **were hired** by us.

Which sentence do you think is smoother? Obviously, the one in the active voice. It is generally better to write in the active voice because the active voice is more direct and stronger than the passive voice. If you use the passive voice excessively, it weakens your writing. However, there are times when the passive is preferred. For instance, the passive is generally used when the action is more important than the person doing the action. Look at the following sentences:

ACTIVE: The police **found** the lost child.
PASSIVE: The lost child **was found.** (The important fact is that the child was found. Who found the child is not as important.)
ACTIVE: Raul's mother **gave birth** to him in Chile.
PASSIVE: Raul **was born** in Chile.

The passive voice is formed by using the verb *to be* and a past participle. The object of the verb in an active sentence becomes the subject in a passive sentence; the subject from an active sentence becomes the agent preceded by the preposition *by.* When you change a verb from active to passive, make sure the new verb agrees with its subject. Note the following sentences:

```
           SUBJECT   VERB         OBJECT
ACTIVE:  Many people watch the television program.


PASSIVE:  The television program is watched by many people.
                 SUBJECT      PASSIVE VERB    AGENT
```

It often sounds awkward to use the preposition *by* and the agent. If this is the case, it may be better to leave them out of the sentence, as shown here:

AWKWARD: The skyscraper was built in 1924 by workers.
CORRECT: **The skyscraper was built in 1924.**

■ *Application*

For the next exercise, rewrite each active sentence as a passive sentence. For example,

ACTIVE: The coach **praised** the team.
PASSIVE: The team **was praised** by the coach.

1. The scientist supervised every aspect of the project.

   _____

2. They could produce the same effect more efficiently.

   _____

3. We worked out an agreement with the company.

   _____

4. We encountered a strong objection.

   _____

5. They approved the plan unanimously.

   _____

6. The soldiers heard the music.

   _____

7. The reporter interviewed Dr. Brainard.

_____

8. The ushers led the families to the gravesites.

_____

■ *Application*

For this exercise, rewrite each passive sentence in the active voice and then decide which sentence sounds better – the active or passive. Remember: When using the passive voice, you must use the past participle.

1. They were married in Las Vegas by a judge.

_____

2. The buildings were destroyed in the earthquake.

_____

3. My brother was fired from his job.

_____

4. The ruins of the ancient city were found in the desert.

_____

5. His car was hit by a motorcycle.

_____

6. He was told to apply for a fellowship.

_____

4. *Editing*

A television reporter was the first journalist on the scene of an explosion. The following story is what she reported. Edit the story by changing the active voice to the passive.

An explosion has destroyed the building. It killed many people. The explosion

injured many others. They are taking the injured to several hospitals in the area.

They have brought doctors and nurses here. The Red Cross has requested blood

donors to contact its offices. Police have blocked off the center of the city.

1. Sharing Ideas

Discuss the following questions with a partner, in a small group, or with the whole class:

1. At what point in the story do you realize what Brainard's project is really about?
2. According to Professor Brainard, what are some disturbing aspects of the Civil War?
3. Why is Brainard's plan efficient? Are there any faults in his plan? What are they?
4. How do you feel about the soldiers? Are they heroes?
5. How does the author feel about war?
6. The narrator states, "I guess it's hard to plan a perfect fall even with intensive training and devotion to one's country." Look for other examples of satire.

2. Writing

Read the writing ideas that follow. Your instructor may make specific assignments, or ask you to choose one of these.

1. Prepare to interview someone who survived a war. List some questions you would ask.
2. Pretend you are the president of the United States in 2065. Write a speech you would deliver to the nation on the day of Brainard's project.
3. Write a letter to the family of one of the soldiers who died.
4. Create a dialogue between the wife and child of a dead soldier.
5. Notice the contrast between the beautiful, clear weather and the purpose of the day. Does this contrast add to the irony of the story? What other words and images help create irony? Write about the irony in the story.
6. What are your own feelings about war? Are wars necessary? Write an essay about your views.

Summing Up

A | TAKE A CLOSER LOOK

1. Analyzing and Comparing

In each of the following sections, you are asked to think about and compare two of the stories in Part Two.

"The Lottery" and "The Ambitious Guest"

■ Compare the descriptions of the scenery in each story. How are they different?
■ Select several examples of irony from each story.
■ Who is more surprised by fate – Mrs. Hutchinson or the young traveler? Explain.
■ Which character are you more sympathetic with? Why?

"The Last Leaf" and "The Lottery"

■ Both of these stories deal with sacrifice. How are the sacrifices similar? How are they different?
■ Is Mrs. Hutchinson a heroine? Is the painter a hero?
■ Contrast the way each of these characters faces death.

"The Lottery" and "The One Day War"

■ Compare the way victims are chosen in both stories. Which method is more civilized? Defend your answer.
■ Compare the physical descriptions of the settings in both stories.

2. Freewriting

Fate is a theme in each of the stories in Part Two. For fifteen minutes, write about fate as it is treated in each of the stories. Could the characters escape their fates? If they could, how would the stories change? Have a character from one story give advice to a character in another story.

When you have finished writing, exchange papers with a classmate and discuss your reactions.

B WORDS FREQUENTLY CONFUSED

Words that have similar spellings, meanings, or pronunciations are often confused with one another. In the following exercise, you will use some of the words that appear in the stories in Part Two. For each section, choose the correct words and insert them in the sentences. Use your dictionary if you need help.

From "The Last Leaf"

> statue (noun), statute (noun), stature (noun)
>
> loose (adjective), lose (verb)
>
> except (preposition), accept (verb)
>
> light (verb), lit (verb)
>
> leave (verb), live (verb), life (noun)
>
> bored (verb), board (noun), boring (adjective)

1. She was very _____ by the _____ lecture.

2. We admired the _____ of Michelangelo's *David*.

3. The senators passed the _____ on the first vote.

4. The politician had lost his _____ in the community after the scandal.

5. He sawed the _____ into two pieces.

6. Put your keys in your pocket if you don't want to _____ them.

7. She likes to wear _____ clothes.

8. Did you _____ the fire in the fireplace?

9. Yes, I _____ the fire.

10. The teacher asked Leon to _____ the room.

11. Do you _____ with your family?

12. His grandfather lived a long _____.

13. I _____ your invitation and look forward to the party.

14. _____ for the bad weather, we had a wonderful vacation.

From "The Ambitious Guest"

imagine (verb), image (noun)

plain (adjective or noun), plane (noun)

affect (verb), effect (noun)

lonely (adjective), alone (adjective)

wail (noun or verb), whale (noun)

breathe (verb), breath (noun)

conscious (adjective), conscience (noun), conscientious (adjective)

1. The _____ is the largest living mammal.

2. We heard the _____ of the ambulance siren.

3. Can you _____ being an astronaut?

4. The little girl is the _____ of her mother.

5. The _____ stretched out before them for miles.

6. We flew to London on a private _____.

7. Liquor has a bad _____ on some people.

8. Drinking too much liquor may _____ your health.

9. She took a deep _____ before diving into the pool.

10. It is difficult to _____ at high altitudes.

11. She walked through the forest _____.

12. He felt _____ sitting by himself in the cafeteria.

13. She suddenly became _____ of someone following her on the dark street.

14. Her _____ is clear. She returned the wallet to its owner.

15. Teachers appreciate students who are _____ about doing assignments.

From "The Lottery"

precede (verb), proceed (verb)

rite (noun), right (adjective or noun), write (verb)

lead (noun or verb), led (verb)

draw (verb), drawer (noun)

1. Little children like to _____ with crayons.

2. The _____ in this antique desk is stuck.

3. Monday will always _____ Tuesday.

4. The judge said, "Shall we _____ with the hearing?"

5. "You can _____ a horse to water, but you cannot make it drink."

6. The conductor _____ the orchestra with great feeling.

7. The _____ in some paint can cause poisoning.

8. The word *ritual* is derived from the word _____.

9. The witness raised her _____ hand and swore to tell the truth.

10. It is a big accomplishment for a five-year-old child to _____ his or her name.

From "The One Day War"

rise (verb), raise (noun or verb)

human (noun), humane (adjective)

signal (noun or verb), sign (noun)

personal (adjective), personnel (noun)

noisy (adjective), nosey (adjective)

adopt (verb), adapt (verb), adept (adjective)

stripe (noun), striped (adjective), strip (noun), stripped (verb)

1. Antonio learned to _____ to his new school.

2. The young couple hoped to _____ a baby.

3. The sculptor was very _____ at working in stone.

4. What time do you _____ in the morning?

5. Did you _____ the shades to let in the sun?

6. I asked my boss for a(n) _____.

7. We hung the Welcome Home _____ over the door.

8. They could barely hear the S.O.S. _____ from the sinking ship.

9. The highway crew painted a yellow _____ on the road.

10. You should seal the package with a(n) _____ of tape.

11. She wore _____ pants and a red shirt.

12. The soldier was _____ of all his medals after he deserted his post.

13. The _____ children at the next table disturbed our dinner.

14. Our _____ neighbor likes to gossip about everyone on the street.

15. We belong to the _____ race, but we are not always _____.

16. We had a(n) _____ interest in the project.

17. When you interview for a job, you meet with someone in _____.

C SPELLING

Forming Noun Plurals and Past Tense Verbs

In Shirley Jackson's story, the *families* actually *enjoyed* the horrible custom of drawing names for the annual lottery. Notice that we change the *y* in family to an *i*, and then we add *-es* to pluralize the noun. With the verb *enjoy*, however, we form the past tense by keeping the *y* and adding *-ed*. Note the following rules for words ending in *y:*

1. If the *y* is preceded by a consonant, as in the noun *family*, we change the *y* to *i* and add *-es* to form the plural. The same is true for forming the past tense of verbs. *Study*, for example, becomes *studied* because the *y* is preceded by the consonant *d*. Here are some other examples:

Noun Singular/Plural	Verb Present/Past Tense
victory victories	**try** tried
ally allies	**reply** replied
fly flies	**lie** lied

2. If, however, the *y* is preceded by a vowel, we just add the suffix *-s* for a noun and *-ed* for a verb. Note these examples:

Noun Singular/Plural	Verb Present/Past Tense
day days	**employ** employed
valley valleys	**pray** prayed
toy toys	**play** played

For this exercise, form the plurals of the following nouns:

inquiry _____   history _____

baby _____   boy _____

community _____   alley _____

company _____   jury _____

bay _____   bunny _____

Now, form the past tense of these verbs:

comply _____   hurry _____

worry _____   destroy _____

supply _____   busy _____

annoy _____   apply _____

1. Roots, Prefixes, and Suffixes

Match the prefixes and roots in the left-hand column with the definitions on the right by writing the number of the correct definition in the space provided.

_____ micro	1. study	8. within	
_____ mal	2. love of	9. small	
_____ pre	3. not	10. before	
_____ log	4. earth	11. bad	
_____ phil	5. head	12. both	
_____ ambi	6. large	13. against	
_____ intra	7. lead		
_____ anti			
_____ geo			
_____ capi			

By studying the structure of the following words (their roots, prefixes, or suffixes), can you figure out their meanings? Write a definition or a synonym next to each word.

1. precede _____

2. transport _____

3. manuscript _____

4. biography _____

5. malnutrition _____

6. detach _____

7. antisocial _____

8. ambivalent _____

9. substandard _____

10. illiterate _____

2. Infinitives and Gerunds

Underline the correct infinitive or gerund in each of the following word combinations. For example,

enjoy (to go, <u>going</u>)

1. refuse (to come, coming)
2. want (to meet, meeting)
3. dislike (to take, taking)
4. decide (to buy, buying)
5. hope (to see, seeing)
6. try (to find, finding)
7. keep (to read, reading)
8. seems (to be, being)
9. delay (to write, writing)
10. avoid (to travel, traveling)

3. Adjectives

In the following sentences, there are errors in the use of adjectives. Underline the incorrect adjective and write the correct form in the space provided below each sentence.

1. This is the most prettiest scarf I have ever seen.

   _____

2. Of the two books, this one is the best.

   _____

3. I like that red small nice English bicycle.

   _____

4. We bought a lovely leather Italian brown handbag.

   _____

5. She has a colonial attractive brick old house.

   _____

6. You broke the vase. Please be carefuller in the future.

   _____

7. My headache got worser as the day wore on.

_____

8. Of all the children in the class, Henry is the most smart.

_____

9. The "ambitious" guest found an old charming wooden mountain cottage.

_____

10. The guest was a handsome young tall American man.

_____

4. Active and Passive Voice

In each of the following sentences, the verb is in either the active or passive voice. Underline the verb, and in the space provided to the right of each sentence, write *A* for active voice or *P* for passive voice.

1. The game was won by the Yankees's star pitcher. _____

2. The American Civil War was fought by the North and the South. _____

3. A lottery was held each year by the villagers. _____

4. Tess Hutchinson drew the paper with the black spot. _____

5. In the One Day War, 204,000 soldiers killed themselves with their own pistols. _____

6. The unknown guest sought refuge in a mountainside inn. _____

7. All the inhabitants were killed by a storm. _____

8. Mr. Behrman painted a leaf on a wall to save a young woman's life. _____

9. Many artists live in Greenwich Village. _____

10. The names of the families participating in the lottery were read by Mr. Summers. _____

Now, rewrite all of the sentences that are in the passive voice, putting them into the active voice.

Irony

IRONY, SOMETIMES defined as "a cruel twist of fate," is a technique used by many famous authors. Perhaps that is because in real life we're always running into ironic situations that make us realize how much our existence is governed by chance or luck. You have already encountered some ironic elements in Part Two. In "The Ambitious Guest," the stranger – who has such great expectations for his life – perishes with the family. The ultimate irony of the plot is that all the characters would have survived if they had stayed in the cottage.

■ Not all irony has to be tragic, however. You will be amused by the turn of events in "The Third Level," the first story in this part of the book.

Chapter 11

DÉSIRÉE'S BABY
– Kate Chopin

Chapter 9

The Third Level JACK FINNEY

A PRE-READING

1. Think Before You Read

Answer the following questions before you read the story:

1. If it were possible to travel back in time, what place and time in history would you choose?
2. Many people think that life was simpler a hundred years ago. Do you agree or disagree?
3. The following words refer to fashion styles in the 1890s. Try to find pictures of these styles in a dictionary or encyclopedia.

derby hat   high-buttoned shoes
leg-of-mutton sleeves   sideburns
handlebar mustache   sleeve protectors

2. Literary Term: Romanticism

The romantic movement in art, literature, and music began in the early nineteenth century in Europe. **Romanticism** reflects the writer's interest in nature and sentimental feelings about life. When we romanticize someone or something, we concentrate on all the good qualities and forget the negatives. Romanticism involves seeing life as we would like it to be, while looking at the world through rose-colored glasses.

3. Idioms and Expressions

Note the following idioms and expressions that appear in the story:

skin me cheat me, trick me out of money	**didn't pass a soul** didn't see anyone
ducked into bent one's head down to enter	**drew three hundred dollars out** took three hundred dollars out of a bank account
got lost couldn't find the way out	

B THE STORY

ABOUT THE AUTHOR

Jack Finney (1911–1995), a well-known novelist and short-story writer whose theme is usually traveling through time, was born in Milwaukee, Wisconsin. Finney lived in New York City for a while, working as an advertising copywriter and writing suspense stories for various magazines.

In 1954 he published his first novel, *Five against the House,* which details the plot of a group of college students to rob a casino in Reno, Nevada. The next year Finney published *The Body Snatchers,* which inspired the film *The Invasion of the Body Snatchers.* His most famous novel, *Time and Again,* was published in 1970; it is about an advertising artist who manages to break the time barrier and send himself to New York City in the 1880s.

You will find this same theme in "The Third Level," in which a commuter discovers a train that travels to the year 1894. You may also want to read Finney's sequel, *From Time to Time,* published in 1995, in which the main character travels back to the year 1912 in hopes of preventing the sinking of the *Titanic.*

The Third Level

THE PRESIDENTS of the New York Central and the New York, New Haven and Hartford railroads will swear on a stack of timetables that there are only two. But I say there are three, because I've *been* on the third level at Grand Central Station. Yes, I've taken the obvious step: I talked to a psychiatrist friend of mine, among others. I told him about the third level at Grand Central Station, and he said it was a waking-dream wish fulfillment. He said I was unhappy. That made my wife kind of mad, but he explained that he meant the modern world is full of insecurity, fear, war, worry and all the rest of it, and that I just want to escape. Well, who doesn't? Everybody I know wants to escape, but they don't wander down into any third level at Grand Central Station.

But that's the reason, he said, and my friends all agreed. Everything points to it, they claimed. My stamp collecting, for example; that's a "temporary refuge from reality." Well, maybe, but my grandfather didn't need any refuge from reality; things were pretty nice and peaceful in his day, from all I hear, and he started my collection. It's a nice collection, too, blocks of four of practically every U.S. issue, first-day covers, and so on. President Roosevelt collected stamps, too, you know.

Anyway, here's what happened at Grand Central. One night last summer I worked late at the office. I was in a hurry to get uptown to my apartment so I decided to take the subway from Grand Central because it's faster than the bus.

Now, I don't know why this should have happened to me. I'm just an ordinary guy named Charley, thirty-one years old, and I was wearing a tan gabardine suit and a straw hat with a fancy band; I passed a dozen men who looked just like me. And I wasn't trying to escape from anything; I just wanted to get home to Louisa, my wife.

I turned into Grand Central from Vanderbilt Avenue, and went down the steps to the first level, where you take trains like the Twentieth Century. Then I walked down another flight to the second level, where the suburban trains leave from, ducked into an arched doorway heading for the subway – and got lost. That's easy to do. I've been in and out of Grand Central hundreds of times, but I'm always bumping into new doorways and stairs and corridors. Once I got into a tunnel about a mile long and came out in the lobby of the Roosevelt Hotel. Another time I came up in an office building on Forty-sixth Street, three blocks away.

Sometimes I think Grand Central is growing like a tree, pushing out new corridors and staircases like roots. There's probably a long tunnel that nobody knows about feeling its way under the city right now, on its way to Times Square, and maybe another to

Central Park. And maybe – because for so many people through the years Grand Central *has* been an exit, a way of escape – maybe that's how the tunnel I got into . . . But I never told my psychiatrist friend about that idea.

The corridor I was in began angling left and slanting downward and I thought that was wrong, but I kept on walking. All I could hear was the empty sound of my own footsteps and I didn't pass a soul. Then I heard that sort of hollow roar ahead that means open space and people talking. The tunnel turned sharp left; I went down a short flight of stairs and came out on the third level at Grand Central Station. For just a moment I thought I was back on the second level, but I saw the room was smaller, there were fewer ticket windows and train gates, and the information booth in the center was wood and old-looking. And the man in the booth wore a green eyeshade and long black sleeve protectors. The lights were dim and sort of flickering. Then I saw why; they were open-flame gaslights.

There were brass spittoons on the floor, and across the station a glint of light caught my eye; a man was pulling a gold watch from his vest pocket. He snapped open the cover, glanced at his watch, and frowned. He wore a derby hat, a black four-button suit with tiny lapels, and he had a big, black, handlebar mustache. Then I looked around and saw that everyone in the station was dressed like eighteen-ninety-something; I never saw so many beards, sideburns and fancy mustaches in my life. A woman walked in through the train gate; she wore a dress with leg-of-mutton sleeves and skirts to the top of her high-buttoned shoes. Back of her, out on the tracks, I caught a glimpse of a locomotive, a very small Currier & Ives locomotive with a funnel-shaped stack. And then I knew.

To make sure, I walked over to a newsboy and glanced at the stack of papers at his feet. It was *The World*; and *The World* hasn't been published for years. The lead story said something about President Cleveland. I've found that front page since, in the Public Library files, and it was printed June 11, 1894.

I turned toward the ticket windows knowing that here – on the third level at Grand Central – I could buy tickets that would take Louisa and me anywhere in the United States we wanted to go. In the year 1894. And I wanted two tickets to Galesburg, Illinois.

Have you ever been there? It's a wonderful town still, with big old frame houses, huge lawns and tremendous trees whose branches meet overhead and roof the streets. And in 1894, summer evenings were twice as long, and people sat out on their lawns, the men smoking cigars and talking quietly, the women waving palm-leaf fans, with the fireflies all around, in a peaceful world. To be back there with the First World War still twenty years off, and World War II, over forty years in the future . . . I wanted two tickets for that.

The clerk figured the fare – he glanced at my fancy hatband, but he figured the fare – and I had enough for two coach tickets, one way. But when I counted out the money and looked up, the clerk was staring at me. He nodded at the bills. "That ain't money, mister," he said, "and if you're trying to skin me you won't get very far," and he glanced at the cash drawer beside him. Of course the money in his drawer was old-style bills, half again as big as the money we use nowadays, and different-looking. I turned away and got out fast. There's nothing nice about jail, even in 1894.

And that was that. I left the same way I came, I suppose. Next day, during lunch hour, I drew three hundred dollars out of the bank, nearly all we had, and bought old-style currency (that *really* worried my psychiatrist friend). You can buy old money at almost any coin dealer's, but you have to pay a premium. My three hundred dollars bought less than two hundred in old-style bills, but I didn't care; eggs were thirteen cents a dozen in 1894.

But I've never again found the corridor that leads to the third level at Grand Central Station, although I've tried often enough.

Louisa was pretty worried when I told her all this, and didn't want me to look for the third level any more, and after a while I stopped; I went back to my stamps. But now we're *both* looking, every weekend, because now we have proof that the third level is still there. My friend Sam Weiner disappeared! Nobody knew where, but I sort of suspected because Sam's a city boy, and I used to tell him about Galesburg – I went to school there –

and he always said he liked the sound of the place. And that's where he is, all right. In 1894.

Because one night, fussing with my stamp collection, I found – well, do you know what a first-day cover is? When a new stamp is issued, stamp collectors buy some and use them to mail envelopes to themselves on the very first day of sale; and the postmark proves the date. The envelope is called a first-day cover. They're never opened; you just put blank paper in the envelope.

That night, among my oldest first-day covers, I found one that shouldn't have been there. But there it was. It was there because someone had mailed it to my grandfather at his home in Galesburg; that's what the address on the envelope said. And it had been there since July 18, 1894 – the postmark showed that – yet I didn't remember it at all. The stamp was a six-cent, dull brown, with a picture of President Garfield. Naturally, when the envelope came to Granddad in the mail, it went right into his collection and stayed there – till I took it out and opened it.

The paper inside wasn't blank. It read:

941 Willard Street
Galesburg, Illinois
July 18, 1894

Charley:

I got to wishing that you were right. Then I got to believing you were right. And, Charley, it's true; I found the third level! I've been here two weeks, and right now, down the street at the

Dalys', someone is playing a piano, and they're all out on the front porch singing, "Seeing Nellie Home." And I'm invited over for lemonade. Come on back, Charley and Louisa. Keep looking till you find the third level! It's worth it, believe me!

The note is signed *Sam*.

At the stamp and coin store I go to, I found out that Sam bought eight hundred dollars' worth of old-style currency. That ought to set him up in a nice little hay, feed and grain business; he always said that's what he really wished he could do, and he certainly can't go back to his old business. Not in Galesburg, Illinois, in 1894. His old business? Why, Sam was my psychiatrist.

C | AFTER READING

1. Comprehension

Answer these questions to determine how well you understood the story.

1. In what city does most of the story take place? How do you know?
2. Who is the narrator?
3. Where is the third level?
4. What is Charley's hobby?
5. How does Charley know he has gone back in time? Give some specific details from the story.
6. What is the date on the newspaper *The World?*
7. What tickets does Charley want to buy? Why?
8. Who sent Charley a letter, and where was the letter from?

2. Vocabulary

The following sentences have been selected from "The Third Level." Substitute a *synonym* – a word with the same meaning – for each of the underlined words. Be careful to use synonyms that are appropriate for the way the words are used in these sentences. Line numbers are given in case you want to refer to the story. You may use your dictionary.

1. Yes, I've taken the <u>obvious</u> step. (lines 7–8) _____

2. Everything points to it, they <u>claimed</u>. My stamp collecting . . . that's a

   "temporary <u>refuge</u> from reality." (lines 23–26) _____

   _____

3. I was wearing a tan <u>gabardine</u> suit. (lines 46–47) _____

4. I'm always <u>bumping</u> into new doorways and stairs and <u>corridors.</u> (lines 62–64) _____ _____

5. The corridor I was in began <u>angling</u> left and <u>slanting</u> downward. (lines 83–84) _____ _____

6. I heard that sort of <u>hollow</u> roar. (lines 88–89) _____

7. I went down a short <u>flight</u> of stairs. (lines 91–92) _____

8. The lights were dim and sort of <u>flickering</u>. (lines 101–102) _____

9. I walked over to a newsboy and <u>glanced</u> at the stack of papers at his feet. (lines 126–128) _____

10. You can buy old money . . . but you have to pay a <u>premium</u>. (lines 180–182)

_____

Some of the words you have just defined can have alternate meanings. Look at these same words in the following sentences. Insert the appropriate synonyms, according to the way the words are used here.

1. It was <u>obvious</u> that Bob did not know the answer to the question.

_____

2. In 1849, when miners found gold in Alaska, they immediately staked a <u>claim</u>.

_____

3. When I fell down, I got a <u>bump</u> on my head. _____

4. Maria is always <u>angling</u> to get special favors. _____

5. A good reporter must never <u>slant</u> the news. _____

6. After his sickness, his face had a <u>hollow</u> look. _____

7. Our <u>flight</u> to North Carolina was a short one. _____

8. The bullet just <u>glanced</u> off the policeman's shoulder. It didn't hurt him.

_____

9. I must pay the <u>premium</u> on my insurance policy. _____

3. Grammar: Reflexive and Intensive Pronouns

In Jack Finney's story, the main character, Charley, discovers the third level by *himself*. What kind of pronoun is *himself*? It is called a **reflexive pronoun** because the word reflects back to the subject. For example, if you fell down and hurt your knee, you would say, "I hurt **myself**." Or, if you were trying to control a mischievous child, you might command, "Behave **yourself**."

Like other personal pronouns, the *self* words have both singular and plural forms. The singular pronouns are: *myself, yourself, himself, herself, oneself,* and *itself*. In the plural, we have: *ourselves, yourselves,* and *themselves*.

You may also use a *self* pronoun for emphasis. These pronouns are called **intensive pronouns,** and they are written exactly the same as the reflexive pronouns. If Charley's wife didn't believe his story about the third level, he would insist, "I **myself** saw it." Note that this *self* pronoun immediately follows the subject. Other examples are:

You **yourself** invited them.
He **himself** made the call.

We often use the *self* pronouns after the prepositions *by, to,* and *for*. For example,

She lives **by herself.**   (She lives alone.)
He always sits **by himself** in class.   (He sits away from others.)
Mary often talks **to herself** in class.   (She is not talking to others.)
Tom made dinner **for himself.**   (Tom prepared his own dinner.)

Note: With certain verbs you may **not** use a *self* pronoun. These verbs are: *feel, relax,* and *concentrate*. Here are some examples:

I feel tired today.   (*Not:* I feel myself tired.)
I can't concentrate with that loud music.   (*Not:* I can't concentrate myself.)
Tom should relax.   (*Not:* Tom should relax himself.)

Another important rule to remember: **Never** use the *self* pronouns as part of a compound subject. Look at these sentences:

INCORRECT: Charley and himself searched for the third level.
CORRECT: **Charley and he** searched for the third level.
INCORRECT: My friend and myself saw a great movie last night.
CORRECT: **My friend and I** saw a great movie last night.

Likewise, do **not** use a *self* pronoun as part of a compound object:

INCORRECT:	Charley never told Sam or themselves his secret.
CORRECT:	Charley never told **Sam or them** his secret.
INCORRECT:	Susan helped Frank and myself.
CORRECT:	Susan helped **Frank and me.**

Be careful not to confuse the *self* pronouns with the expression *each other*. Can you tell the difference in meaning between these two sentences?

Charley and Louise talk to themselves.

Charley and Louise talk to each other.

In the first sentence, both Charley and Louise have a problem; they speak aloud to themselves. In the second sentence, they communicate with each other; they carry on a conversation.

■ *Application*

In each of the following sentences, use a *self* pronoun or the expression *each other*.

1. Lonely people often talk to _____.

2. To have a successful marriage, it is necessary for a couple to communicate with _____.

3. Charley and Sam never told _____ how to reach the third level.

4. Charley promised _____ that he would find the third level again.

5. In "A Day's Wait," Schatz and his father did not discuss with _____ the child's fear.

6. Johnsy told _____ that she would die when the last leaf fell from the vine.

7. You must not expect the government to help you. You must help _____.

8. Vicky and her mother never talked to _____ about serious matters.

9. Mrs. Jones lived by _____.

10. When Mrs. Olafson followed Vicky to school, she told the principal, "I

_____ saw her steal from the store."

4. Editing

Underline and correct any errors you find in the following paragraph:

My friend, Nora and myself, have always been interested in stories about traveling through time. We found out for each other many authors who have used this theme in their work. Nora says that reading such stories helps her relax herself, and even when she is nervous, she can concentrate herself on the plot. For her birthday Nora bought some books by Jack Finney for herself. She also gave his novel to her sister and myself. This novel, *Time and Again,* is the kind of book my friend and myself can read aloud to ourselves when we get together.

D | THINKING ABOUT THE STORY

1. Sharing Ideas

Discuss the following questions with a partner, in a small group, or with the whole class:

1. What was life like in Galesburg, Illinois, in 1894?
2. Why do you think Charley has a desire to escape reality?
3. Why does Charley like to collect stamps?
4. Describe Charley's relationship with his wife Louisa.
5. Why does Charley tell Sam about the third level?
6. Why does Sam go to Galesburg?

2. Writing

Read the writing ideas that follow. Your instructor may make specific assignments, or ask you to choose one of these.

1. Imagine that Charley and his wife finally arrive in Galesburg, Illinois, in 1894. Write a dialogue between Charley and Sam when they meet.
2. Louisa decides that she doesn't like Galesburg and wants to return to New York. Continue the story.

3. Pretend that you have found the third level at Grand Central Station. To what place will you buy a ticket? Describe the place and your feelings when you arrive.
4. You are a person from the 1890s, and you have been transported to the future – the early twenty-first century. Describe what you see.
5. Select a famous person who lived in the 1890s, and write about him or her.
6. Use a history book to research some historical events that occurred in the 1890s. Write an essay about the events you studied.

Chapter 10
All Summer in a Day RAY BRADBURY

A | PRE-READING

1. Think Before You Read

Answer the following questions before you read the story:

1. Read the beginning of the story, which describes the atmosphere or setting. Make a list of the sound and sight images. What specific words do you like?
2. Have you ever visited a rain forest or seen a tropical rain forest in a zoo? Describe what you saw.
3. How does weather affect our personalities?
4. What kind of climate do you prefer to live in?

2. Literary Term: Atmosphere

An author creates a physical setting for a story as well as the characters that move the plot along. The setting or **atmosphere** may have a tremendous impact on the story. In fact, the entire story may depend on this atmosphere. For example, in "The Ambitious Guest," Hawthorne creates a forbidding atmosphere of a cold, stormy winter night in a remote mountain cottage. The atmosphere prepares the reader for the tragic ending.

3. Idioms and Expressions

Note the following idioms and expressions that appear in the story:

get away move away	**muffled cries** sounds that are covered or blocked; hard to hear
let out allowed to go free	
in a flash quickly	**gone wrong** changed unexpectedly
whitened away the color faded	**meet each other's glances** look at each other

B | THE STORY

ABOUT THE AUTHOR

Ray Bradbury (1920–), born in Waukegan, Illinois, has traveled to distant galaxies and to the future in many of his stories. He is referred to as a science fiction writer or fantasist. His characters are not always realistic, but they are human. His plots may be impossible, but we believe them.

As a child, Bradbury loved libraries and regarded books as an indispensable part of his life. The idea of book burning was loathsome to him and became a theme in many of his writings. In *Fahrenheit 451,* which was later made into a movie, books are burned in a futuristic totalitarian society. In real life, Bradbury had actual examples of repression and censorship, such as Nazi Germany, the blacklists of the McCarthy era, and the communist regimes. On a personal level, Bradbury's great-grandmother, ten times removed, had been accused and acquitted of being a witch during the Salem witch trials.

Bradbury began writing on a typewriter that he rented for ten cents a half hour. Perhaps this accounts for his brisk writing style. His writing is poetic and symbolic and leans toward the macabre. Though he began his career by writing for magazines, he has also written for television, theater, and Hollywood. He has even hosted a television show of his dramatized stories.

All Summer in a Day

"READY?"

"Ready."

"Now?"

"Soon."

5 "Do the scientists really know? Will it happen today, will it?"

"Look, look; see for yourself!"

The children pressed to each other like so many roses, so many weeds, intermixed, peering out for a look at 10 the hidden sun.

It rained.

It had been raining for seven years; thousands upon thousands of days compounded and filled from one end 15 to the other with rain, with the drum and gush of water, with the sweet crystal fall of showers and the concussion of storms so heavy they 20 were tidal waves come over the islands. A thousand forests had been crushed under the rain and grown up a thousand times to be crushed again. And this was the way life was forever 25 on the planet Venus, and this was the schoolroom of the children of the rocket men and women who had come to a raining world to set up civilization and live out their lives.

30 "It's stopping, it's stopping!"

"Yes, yes!"

Margot stood apart from them, from these children who could never remember a time when there wasn't 35 rain and rain and rain. They were all nine years old, and if there had been a day, seven years ago, when the sun came out for an hour and showed its face to the stunned world, they could 40 not recall. Sometimes, at night, she heard them stir, in remembrance, and she knew they were dreaming and remembering gold or a yellow crayon or a coin large enough to buy the world with. She knew they thought they 45 remembered a warmness, like a blushing in the face, in the body, in the arms and legs and trembling hands. But then they always awoke to the tatting drum, the endless shaking 50 down of clear bead necklaces upon the roof, the walk, the gardens, the forests, and their dreams were gone.

All day yesterday they had read in class about the sun. About how like a 55 lemon it was, and how hot. And they had written small stories or essays or poems about it:

I think the sun is a flower, 60
That blooms for just one hour.

That was Margot's poem, read in a quiet voice in the still classroom while the rain was falling outside. 65

"Aw, you didn't write that!" protested one of the boys.

"I did," said Margot. "I *did*."

"William!" said the teacher.

But that was yesterday. Now the rain 70 was slackening, and the children were crushed in the great thick windows.

"Where's teacher?"

"She'll be back."

"She'd better hurry, we'll miss it!" 75
They turned on themselves, like a

feverish wheel, all tumbling spokes.

Margot stood alone. She was a very frail girl who looked as if she had been lost in the rain for years and the rain had washed out the blue from her eyes and the red from her mouth and the yellow from her hair. She was an old photograph dusted from an album, whitened away, and if she spoke at all her voice would be a ghost. Now she stood, separate, staring at the rain and the loud wet world beyond the huge glass.

"What're *you* looking at?" said William.

Margot said nothing.

"Speak when you're spoken to." He gave her a shove. But she did not move; rather she let herself be moved only by him and nothing else.

They edged away from her, they would not look at her. She felt them go away. And this was because she would play no games with them in the echoing tunnels of the underground city. If they tagged her and ran, she stood blinking after them and did not follow. When the class sang songs about happiness and life and games her lips barely moved. Only when they sang about the sun and the summer did her lips move as she watched the drenched windows.

And then, of course, the biggest crime of all was that she had come here only five years ago from Earth, and she remembered the sun and the way the sun was and the sky was when she was four in Ohio. And they, they had been on Venus all their lives, and they had been only two years old when last the sun came out and had long since forgotten the color and heat of it and the way it really was. But Margot remembered.

"It's like a penny," she said once, eyes closed.

"No, it's not!" the children cried.

"It's like a fire," she said, "in the stove."

"You're lying, you don't remember!" cried the children.

But she remembered and stood quietly apart from all of them and watched the patterning windows. And once, a month ago, she had refused to shower in the school shower rooms, had clutched her hands to her ears and over her head, screaming the water mustn't touch her head. So after that, dimly, dimly, she sensed it, she was different and they knew her difference and kept away.

There was talk that her father and mother were taking her back to Earth next year; it seemed vital to her that they do so, though it would mean the loss of thousands of dollars to her family. And so, the children hated her for all these reasons of big and little consequence. They hated her pale snow face, her waiting silence, her thinness, and her possible future.

"Get away!" The boy gave her another push. "What're you waiting for?"

Then, for the first time, she turned and looked at him. And what she was waiting for was in her eyes.

"Well, don't wait around here!" cried the boy savagely. "You won't see nothing!"

Her lips moved.

"Nothing!" he cried. "It was all a joke, wasn't it?" He turned to the other children. "Nothing's happening today. *Is* it?"

They all blinked at him and then, understanding, laughed and shook their heads. "Nothing, nothing!"

"Oh, but," Margot whispered, her eyes helpless. "But this is the day, the scientists predict, they say, they *know,* the sun . . ."

"All a joke!" said the boy, and seized her roughly. "Hey, everyone, let's put her in a closet before teacher comes!"

"No," said Margot, falling back.

They surged about her, caught her up and bore her, protesting, and then pleading, and then crying, back into a tunnel, a room, a closet, where they slammed and locked the door. They stood looking at the door and saw it tremble from her beating and throwing herself against it. They heard her muffled cries. Then, smiling, they turned and went out and back down the tunnel, just as the teacher arrived.

"Ready, children?" She glanced at her watch.

"Yes!" said everyone.

"Are we all here?"

"Yes!"

The rain slackened still more.

They crowded to the huge door.

The rain stopped.

It was as if, in the midst of a film concerning an avalanche, a tornado, a hurricane, a volcanic eruption, something had, first, gone wrong with the sound apparatus, thus muffling and finally cutting off all noise, all of the blasts and repercussions and thunders, and then, second, ripped the film from the projector and inserted in its place a peaceful tropical slide which

did not move or tremor. The world ground to a standstill. The silence was so immense and unbelievable that you felt your ears had been stuffed or you had lost your hearing altogether. The children put their hands to their ears. They stood apart. The door slid back and the smell of the silent, waiting world came in to them.

The sun came out.

It was the color of flaming bronze and it was very large. And the sky around it was a blazing blue tile color. And the jungle burned with sunlight as the children, released from their spell, rushed out, yelling, into the springtime.

"Now, don't go too far," called the teacher after them. "You've only two hours, you know. You wouldn't want to get caught out!"

But they were running and turning their faces up to the sky and feeling the sun on their cheeks like a warm iron; they were taking off their jackets and letting the sun burn their arms.

"Oh, it's better than the sun lamps, isn't it?"

"Much, much better!"

They stopped running and stood in the great jungle that covered Venus, that grew and never stopped growing, tumultuously, even as you watched it. It was a nest of octopi, clustering up great arms of fleshlike weed, wavering, flowering in this brief spring. It was the color of rubber and ash, this jungle, from the many years without sun. It was the color of stones and white cheeses and ink, and it was the color of the moon.

The children lay out, laughing, on

the jungle mattress, and heard it sigh 245
and squeak under them, resilient and
alive. They ran among the trees, they
slipped and fell, they pushed each
other, they played hide-and-seek and
tag, but most of all they squinted at the 250
sun until tears ran down their faces,
they put their hands up to that
yellowness and that amazing blueness
and they breathed of the fresh, fresh air
and listened and listened to the silence 255
which suspended them in a blessed sea
of no sound and no motion. They
looked at everything and savored
everything. Then, wildly, like animals
escaped from their caves, they ran and 260
ran in shouting circles. They ran for an
hour and did not stop running.

And then –

In the midst of their running one of
the girls wailed. 265

Everyone stopped.

The girl, standing in the open, held
out her hand.

"Oh, look, look," she said, trembling.

They came slowly to look at her 270
opened palm.

In the center of it, cupped and huge,
was a single raindrop.

She began to cry, looking at it.

They glanced quietly at the sky. 275

"Oh. Oh."

A few cold drops fell on their noses
and their cheeks and their mouths. The
sun faded behind a stir of mist. A wind
blew cool around them. They turned 280
and started to walk back toward the
underground house, their hands at
their sides, their smiles vanishing away.

A boom of thunder startled them
and like leaves before a new hurricane, 285
they tumbled upon each other and ran.

Lightning struck ten miles away, five
miles away, a mile, a half mile. The sky
darkened into midnight in a flash.

They stood in the doorway of the 290
underground for a moment until it was
raining hard. Then they closed the
door and heard the gigantic sound of
the rain falling in tons and avalanches,
everywhere and forever. 295

"Will it be seven more years?"

"Yes. Seven."

Then one of them gave a little cry.

"Margot!"

"What?" 300

"She's still in the closet where we
locked her."

"Margot."

They stood as if someone had driven
them, like so many stakes, into the 305
floor. They looked at each other and
then looked away. They glanced out at
the world that was raining now and
raining and raining steadily. They
could not meet each other's glances. 310
Their faces were solemn and pale. They
looked at their hands and feet, their
faces down.

"Margot."

One of the girls said, "Well . . . ?" 315

No one moved.

"Go on," whispered the girl.

They walked slowly down the hall in
the sound of cold rain. They turned
through the doorway to the room in 320
the sound of the storm and thunder,
lightning on their faces, blue and
terrible. They walked over to the closet
door slowly and stood by it.

Behind the closet door was only 325
silence.

They unlocked the door, even more
slowly, and let Margot out.

1. Comprehension

Answer these questions to determine how well you understood the story.

1. Why didn't the children like Margot?
2. How does Margot describe the sun in her poem?
3. Why do the children lock Margot in the closet?
4. Why does one of the little girls cry when she feels something on her hand?
5. How do you think the children feel before they open the closet to free Margot?
6. How is the planet Venus described?

2. Vocabulary

Each of the numbered vocabulary words appears in the story. Match the words with their definitions. Write the letter of the correct definition on the line preceding each vocabulary word.

1. __f__ compounded	a. easing off, lessening
2. __C__ concussion	b. stifled, covered up
3. __a__ slackening	c. with great noise
4. __h__ surged	d. opened and closed an eye
5. __b__ muffled	e. pounding
6. __l__ solemn	f. added to
7. __d__ blinked	g. strong
8. __i__ feverish	h. pushed
9. __j__ savor	i. in a frenzy
10. __k__ tumbled	j. enjoy, taste
11. __g__ resilient	k. fell over
12. __c__ tumultuously	l. serious

3. Grammar: Pronoun Cases: Subjective and Objective

In "All Summer in a Day," Bradbury frequently uses the personal pronoun *they* when referring to Margot's classmates: "**They** were all nine years old." Then he switches to *them:* "She heard **them.**" Why does the author use *they* in one sentence and *them* in another? *They* is a subject pronoun and *them* is an object pronoun.

This grammatical construction is called **pronoun case.** Unlike nouns, personal pronouns have different cases. You must use *I,* for example, if the pronoun is the subject of the sentence and *me* if the word is the object. Remember: The subject of a sentence is the person or thing that is the *doer* of the action. For example,

Margot recalled her days on Earth.

Margot is the subject because she *recalls* her days. If we were to use a pronoun for the noun *Margot,* we would use *she.* **Other pronouns in the subjective (or nominative) case are:**

Singular	Plural
I	we
you	you
who, he, she, it	who, they

Here are some sentences that use subjective case pronouns:

Sam and **he** knew about the third level.
There were only Grace and **she** at the office.   (Note: The subject does not always
   come at the beginning of the sentence.)
My friend and **I** like to travel.
Who is it?

The pronoun *who* can also be a **relative pronoun,** which means that it relates to a noun or pronoun. In the following sentence, *who* is the subject of the verb *called* and "who" refers (relates) to "woman":

That woman **who** called me yesterday wants to know your name.

The problem with using the subjective or nominative case usually arises when we have double subjects; for example, **Margot and they** were waiting for the sun. If you cross out one of the subjects, such as *Margot and,* you will have no trouble using the correct pronoun, *they.* This sentence means that *Margot* was waiting for the sun, and *they* were waiting for the sun.

Look at this sentence: Both the **narrator and Sam** found the third level. The narrator and Sam are the subjects of this sentence because they are the *doers—* they found (verb). What did they find? They found *the third level. The third level* is the **object** of the sentence because it receives the action from the verb. **Pronouns in the objective case are:**

146
Irony

Singular	Plural
me	us
you	you
him, her, it	them
whom	whom

Here are some sentences that use objective case pronouns:

The teacher invited **us** for lunch.
She and Grace asked **him** for directions.
Mario and Carlos helped **my mother and me.**
Margot was the girl **whom** they locked in the closet.   (Note: *Whom* is the object of the verb *locked.*)

The objective case is also used for objects of prepositions. Prepositions, as you know, are words that indicate direction or relationship. Some commonly used prepositions are: *in, into, on, at, from, for, with, to, between,* and *among.* If you are going to use a pronoun at the end of a prepositional phrase, you must use the objective case:

Mary took her dog with **her.**   (object of the preposition *with*)
We bought a gift for Kim and **them.**   (object of the preposition *for*)
Let's keep the secret between **you and me.**   (object of the preposition *between*)

■ *Application*
As a review, underline the correct pronoun in each of these sentences.

1. Janet and (she, her) met Tom and (he, him) at the game.
2. My friend and (I, me) thought that Mario and (they, them) were in Spain.
3. That was Momoko (who, whom) you saw on the street yesterday.
4. At the party were Yuko and (they, them).
5. (He, him) and (I, me) found Sara and (she, her) in the library.
6. There is a good relationship between Maggie and (she, her) and between Alan and (he, him).
7. Among the three of (they, them) were Louise and (she, her).
8. We divided the profits between Alan and (he, him).
9. Bill and (we, us) invited Betty and (they, them), (who, whom) you met last summer.
10. The teacher and (he, him) produced the musical play written by the students and (they, them).

All Summer in a Day

4. Grammar: Possessive Case

Nouns In English, we usually show possession in nouns by using an apostrophe (') followed by an *s:*

mother's car
my country's flag
James's dog

For plurals ending in *s,* we generally show possession by putting the apostrophe after the *s.*

the mothers' cars
the countries' flags

When we refer to an inanimate object and want to show possession, we usually use the preposition *of.* We do this because inanimate objects cannot actively possess. Here are a few examples:

the color of the car
the author of the story
the time of day

Avoid using a series of possessives that sounds awkward:

AWKWARD:	The man's car's tire had a flat.
CORRECT:	**The tire of the man's car** had a flat.

■ *Application*

Rewrite each of the following sentences by substituting an *of* phrase for an *'s* form:

1. The woman's necklace's clasp was broken.

_____

2. She sewed the coat's pocket's hole.

_____

3. He licked the envelope's stamp's back.

_____

4. The flower's scent's effect was dramatic.

_____

5. We enjoyed the orchestra's music's sound.

_____

Pronouns The possessive pronouns (*my, your, his, her, its, our, your,* and *their*) are used as modifiers and precede a noun. Look at the following list. Note that the possessive *its* does *not* have an apostrophe. *It's* is the contraction for *it is.*

I **my**		*it* **its**
you **your**		*we* **our**
he **his**		*you* **your**
she **her**		*they* **their**

It is important not to confuse the possessive pronouns listed above with possessive pronouns that function as nouns (*mine, yours, his, hers, its, ours, yours,* and *theirs*). These sentences show correct usage:

It is **my** car.
The car is **mine.**

▪ *Application*

For this exercise, write the correct pronouns in the sentences that follow. More than one answer may be possible.

1. The little boy said, "Give me _____ toy. It's

   _____."

2. His sister answered, "No, it's not _____. Mommy bought it for

   me."

3. My friend Janet and I rode _____ bicycles to the beach. She

   parked _____ bicycle next to _____.

4. Our neighbors painted _____ house the same color as

   _____.

5. I found some money. Is it _____?

6. They lost _____ tickets to the ballet. An usher who found

   them said, "Are these _____?"

7. Shall we have dinner at _____ house or _____?

8. He offered _____ apology. The mistake was

   _____ .

9. Brad and Mary said, "_____ daughters love to play in the

   sandbox."

10. Brad and Mary said _____ daughters love to play in the

    sandbox.

11. Sharon likes to ride _____ bicycle through the park.

12. The football team celebrated _____ victory.

13. He told _____ mother he would call _____

    more often.

14. When are you going to do _____ homework?

15. I lent my car to my friend. He said he would treat it like _____

    own.

16. He said he would treat it as if it were _____ .

17. Howard and Sheila moved into a new apartment in _____

    building.

18. _____ apartment is on the same floor as _____ .

■ *Application*
Possessives in the story
Write the correct pronouns in these sentences, which are taken from Bradbury's
story.

1. The sun came out for an hour and showed _____ face.

2. If she spoke at all, _____ voice would be a ghost.

3. The rain had washed out the blue from _____ eyes.

4. They had been on Venus all _____ lives.

5. You felt _____ ears had been stuffed.

6. The children put _____ hands to _____ ears.

5. Editing

To review subjective, objective, and relative pronouns, try this practice exercise. Correct any errors you find in the following paragraph:

My brother Boris and me have a good relationship. It was him whom introduced me to the joys of travel. Every year we go to a new section of the United States. Between him and I we plan a great trip. We traveling together presents no problem. Boris and me get along very well, and he is a person whose tastes are like mines. Boris sends cards to his girlfriend and buys many gifts for ours mother and she. I like to see all the museums and talk to whoever we meet on the trip. When we return, all our friends enjoy us telling our parents and they the stories of our adventures.

D | THINKING ABOUT THE STORY

1. Sharing Ideas

Discuss the following questions with a partner, in a small group, or with the whole class:

1. Describe Margot. Use as many adjectives as possible.
2. Why doesn't Margot feel comfortable with the other children?
3. What could Margot have done when the children tried to put her in the closet? What would you have done?
4. How different is life on Venus after the sun comes out?
5. How do you think the children in the class feel about Margot after they open the closet?

2. Writing

Read the writing ideas that follow. Your instructor may make specific assignments, or ask you to choose one of these.

1. Bradbury creates an intense atmosphere of rain and wetness, which is reinforced throughout the story. Review the story and underline the words that help create this atmosphere. Make a list of opposite words that describe a world of heat and dryness. Then, write a story in which sunshine and heat create the setting. Think of yourself as the director of a movie based on your story. What

directions would you give the set designers and special effects people? What props would you use?

2. Describe the main character, Margot. What is she like physically and psychologically? Do you sympathize with her? Why?

3. Continue the story. Write about what happens to Margot and the other children.

4. Pretend you are Margot. Write a letter to your classmates after you've returned to Earth.

5. Compare the group behavior in this story with the way the villagers behaved in "The Lottery."

6. Why are some people cruel and discriminatory toward other people?

Chapter 11

Désirée's Baby KATE CHOPIN

A | PRE-READING

1. Think Before You Read

Answer the following questions before you read the story:

1. Look up Louisiana in your encyclopedia and find out when it became a state. Who were the first settlers in New Orleans? What is this city famous for?
2. What do you know about the early marriage laws in the southern states? Were they discriminatory?
3. Many nineteenth century authors used the word *Providence* to mean *God,* as you will note as you read "Désirée's Baby." Other terms you might want to look up are *bayous, corbeille, layette,* and *peignoir.*
4. How do you think slaves were treated on the average southern plantation? When was slavery declared illegal?

2. Literary Term: Tragedy

A **tragedy** occurs in a story or a play when the main character is defeated by the opposing force at the end of the story. The opposing force can be another person, nature, society, or the character's own personality. For example, in "The Ambitious Guest," the opposing force that causes the tragic deaths of the entire family and their unknown guest is nature – the avalanche. In "The Lottery," the opposing force is society, which adheres to a primitive custom of sacrificing a person every year to ensure a good crop. As you read "Désirée's Baby," decide who or what causes the tragedy.

3. Idioms and Expressions

Providence another name for God **contained himself** tried to be patient **like a pall** a gloomy effect	**closing about her** a feeling of being enveloped by something **stole away** left quietly

B | THE STORY

ABOUT THE AUTHOR

Kate Chopin (1851–1904) was born Katherine O'Flaherty in St. Louis, Missouri, to a prosperous Irish-born merchant father and a Creole mother. She learned both French and English, read widely, played the piano, wrote poetry, and lived an independent life. As she grew up, she was greatly admired for her wit and beauty. Among her suitors was Oscar Chopin, a Louisiana cotton trader, whom she married when she was nineteen. They settled first in New Orleans, and then on a plantation near Cloutiersville.

In their twelve years of married life, she bore six children. However, she refused to give up her independence; she dressed unconventionally, smoked cigarettes, and went wherever she pleased unescorted. When her husband died suddenly in 1882, Kate Chopin took over the management of his plantation and turned to writing. She published several short stories, most of them depicting the lives and emotions of southern women in Creole society. Chopin's masterpiece, *The Awakening,* a short novel published in 1899, tells the tragedy of a misunderstood woman in an unfulfilled marriage. You will find much the same theme in "Désirée's Baby."

Désirée's Baby

As the day was pleasant, Madame Valmondé drove over to L'Abri to see Désirée and the baby.

It made her laugh to think of Désirée with a baby. Why, it seemed but yesterday that Désirée was little more than a baby herself; when Monsieur in riding through the gateway of Valmondé had found her lying asleep in the shadow of the big stone pillar.

The little one awoke in his arms and began to cry for "Dada." That was as much as she could do or say. Some people thought she might have strayed there of her own accord, for she was of the toddling age. The prevailing belief was that she had been purposely left by a party of Texans, whose canvas-covered wagon, late in the day, had crossed the ferry that Coton Maïs kept, just below the plantation. In time Madame Valmondé abandoned every speculation but the one that Désirée had been sent to her by a beneficent Providence to be the child of her affection, seeing that she was without child of the flesh. For the girl grew to be beautiful and gentle, affectionate and sincere, – the idol of Valmondé.

It was no wonder, when she stood one day against the stone pillar in whose shadow she had lain asleep, eighteen years before, that Armand Aubigny riding by and seeing her there, had fallen in love with her. That was the way all the Aubignys fell in love, as if struck by a pistol shot. The wonder was that he had not loved her before; for he had known her since his father brought him home from Paris, a boy of eight, after his mother died there. The passion that awoke in him that day, when he saw her at the gate, swept along like an avalanche, or like a prairie fire, or like anything that drives headlong over all obstacles.

Monsieur Valmondé grew practical and wanted things well considered: that is, the girl's obscure origin. Armand looked into her eyes and did not care. He was reminded that she was nameless. What did it matter about a name when he could give her one of the oldest and proudest in Louisiana? He ordered the *corbeille* from Paris, and contained himself with what patience he could until it arrived; then they were married.

Madame Valmondé had not seen Désirée and the baby for four weeks. When she reached L'Abri she shuddered at the first sight of it, as she always did. It was a sad looking place, which for many years had not known the gentle presence of a mistress, old Monsieur Aubigny having married and buried his wife in France, and she having loved her own land too well ever to leave it. The roof came down steep and black like a cowl, reaching out beyond the wide galleries that encircled the yellow stuccoed house. Big, solemn oaks grew close to it, and their thick-leaved, far-reaching branches shadowed it like a pall. Young

Aubigny's rule was a strict one, too, and under it his negroes had forgotten how to be gay, as they had been during the old master's easy-going and indulgent lifetime.

The young mother was recovering slowly, and lay full length, in her soft white muslins and laces, upon a couch. The baby was beside her, upon her arm, where he had fallen asleep, at her breast. The yellow nurse woman sat beside a window fanning herself.

Madame Valmondé bent her portly figure over Désirée and kissed her, holding her an instant tenderly in her arms. Then she turned to the child.

"This is not the baby!" she exclaimed, in startled tones. French was the language spoken at Valmondé in those days.

"I knew you would be astonished," laughed Désirée, "at the way he has grown. The little *cochon de lait!*[1] Look at his legs, mamma, and his hands and fingernails, – real fingernails. Zandrine had to cut them this morning. Isn't it true, Zandrine?"

The woman bowed her turbaned head majestically, "Mais si, Madame."[2]

"And the way he cries," went on Désirée, "is deafening. Armand heard him the other day as far away as La Blanche's cabin."

Madame Valmondé had never removed her eyes from the child. She lifted it and walked with it over to the window that was lightest. She scanned the baby narrowly, then looked as searchingly at Zandrine, whose face was turned to gaze across the fields.

"Yes, the child has grown, has changed," said Madame Valmondé, slowly, as she replaced it beside its mother. "What does Armand say?"

Désirée's face became suffused with a glow that was happiness itself.

"Oh, Armand is the proudest father in the parish, I believe, chiefly because it is a boy, to bear his name; though he says not, – that he would have loved a girl as well. But I know it isn't true. I know he says that to please me. And mamma," she added, drawing Madame Valmondé's head down to her, and speaking in a whisper, "he hasn't punished one of them – not one of them – since baby is born. Even Négrillon, who pretended to have burnt his leg that he might rest from work – he only laughed, and said Négrillon was a great scamp. Oh, mamma, I'm so happy; it frightens me."

What Désirée said was true. Marriage, and later the birth of his son had softened Armand Aubigny's imperious and exacting nature greatly. This was what made the gentle Désirée

"This is not the baby!" she exclaimed, in startled tones.

---

[1] *cochon de lait:* piglet, little pig (a term of endearment).
[2] *Mais si, Madame:* Yes, Madam.

so happy, for she loved him desperately. When he frowned she trembled, but loved him. When he smiled, she asked no greater blessing of God. But Armand's dark, handsome face had not often been disfigured by frowns since the day he fell in love with her.

When the baby was about three months old, Désirée awoke one day to the conviction that there was something in the air menacing her peace. It was at first too subtle to grasp. It had only been a disquieting suggestion; an air of mystery among the blacks; unexpected visits from far-off neighbors who could hardly account for their coming. Then a strange, an awful change in her husband's manner, which she dared not ask him to explain. When he spoke to her, it was with averted eyes, from which the old love-light seemed to have gone out. He absented himself from home; and when there, avoided her presence and that of her child, without excuse. And the very spirit of Satan seemed suddenly to take hold of him in his dealings with the slaves. Désirée was miserable enough to die.

She sat in her room, one hot afternoon, in her *peignoir*, listlessly drawing through her fingers the strands of her long, silky brown hair that hung about her shoulders. The baby, half naked, lay asleep upon her own great mahogany bed, that was like a sumptuous throne, with its satin-lined half-canopy. One of La Blanche's little quadroon boys – half naked too – stood fanning the child slowly with a fan of peacock feathers. Désirée's eyes had been fixed absently and sadly upon the baby, while she was striving to penetrate the threatening mist that she felt closing about her. She looked from her child to the boy who stood beside him, and back again; over and over. "Ah!" It was a cry that she could not help; which she was not conscious of having uttered. The blood turned like ice in her veins, and a clammy moisture gathered upon her face.

She tried to speak to the little quadroon boy; but no sound would come, at first. When he heard his name uttered, he looked up, and his mistress was pointing to the door. He laid aside the great, soft fan, and obediently stole away, over the polished floor, on his bare tiptoes.

She stayed motionless, with gaze riveted upon her child, and her face the picture of fright.

Presently her husband entered the room, and without noticing her, went to a table and began to search among some papers which covered it.

"Armand," she called to him, in a voice which must have stabbed him, if he was human. But he did not notice.

When he spoke to her, it was with averted eyes, from which the old love-light seemed to have gone out.

"Armand," she said again. Then she rose and tottered towards him. "Armand," she panted once more, clutching his arm, "look at our child. What does it mean? tell me."

He coldly but gently loosened her fingers from about his arm and thrust the hand away from him. "Tell me what it means!" she cried despairingly.

"It means," he answered lightly, "that the child is not white; it means that you are not white."

A quick conception of all that this accusation meant for her nerved her with unwonted courage to deny it. "It is a lie; it is not true, I am white! Look at my hair, it is brown; and my eyes are gray, Armand, you know they are gray. And my skin is fair," seizing his wrist. "Look at my hand; whiter than yours, Armand," she laughed hysterically.

"As white as La Blanche's," he returned cruelly; and went away leaving her alone with their child.

When she could hold a pen in her hand, she sent a despairing letter to Madame Valmondé.

"My mother, they tell me I am not white. Armand has told me I am not white. For God's sake tell them it is not true. You must know it is not true. I shall die. I must die. I cannot be so unhappy, and live."

The answer that came was as brief:

"My own Désirée: Come home to Valmondé; back to your mother who loves you. Come with your child."

When the letter reached Désirée she went with it to her husband's study, and laid it open upon the desk before which he sat. She was like a stone image: silent, white, motionless after she placed it there.

In silence he ran his cold eyes over the written words. He said nothing. "Shall I go, Armand?" she asked in tones sharp with agonized suspense.

"Yes, go."

"Do you want me to go?"

"Yes, I want you to go."

He thought Almighty God had dealt cruelly and unjustly with him; and felt, somehow, that he was paying Him back in kind when he stabbed thus into his wife's soul. Moreover he no longer loved her, because of the unconscious injury she had brought upon his home and his name.

She turned away like one stunned by a blow, and walked slowly towards the door, hoping he would call her back.

"Good-bye, Armand," she moaned.

He did not answer her. That was his last blow at fate.

Désirée went in search of her child. Zandrine was pacing the sombre gallery with it. She took the little one from the nurse's arms with no word of explanation, and descending the steps, walked away, under the live-oak branches.

It was an October afternoon; the sun was just sinking. Out in the still fields the negroes were picking cotton.

Désirée had not changed the thin white garment nor the slippers which she wore. Her hair was uncovered and the sun's rays brought a golden gleam from its brown meshes. She did not take the broad, beaten road which led to the far-off plantation of Valmondé. She walked across a deserted field, where the stubble bruised her tender feet, so delicately shod, and tore her thin gown to shreds.

She disappeared among the reeds and willows that grew thick along the banks of the deep, sluggish bayou; and she did not come back again.

Some weeks later there was a curious scene enacted at L'Abri. In the centre of the smoothly swept back yard was a great bonfire. Armand Aubigny sat in the wide hallway that commanded a view of the spectacle; and it was he who dealt out to a half dozen negroes the material which kept this fire ablaze.

A graceful cradle of willow, with all its dainty furbishings, was laid upon the pyre, which had already been fed with the richness of a priceless *layette*. Then there were silk gowns, and velvet and satin ones added to these; laces, too, and embroideries; bonnets and gloves; for the *corbeille* had been of rare quality.

The last thing to go was a tiny bundle of letters; innocent little scribblings that Désirée had sent to him during the days of their espousal. There was the remnant of one back in the drawer from which he took them. But it was not Désirée's; it was part of an old letter from his mother to his father. He read it. She was thanking God for the blessing of her husband's love: –

"But, above all," she wrote, "night and day, I thank the good God for having so arranged our lives that our dear Armand will never know that his mother, who adores him, belongs to the race that is cursed with the brand of slavery."

C | AFTER READING

1. Comprehension

Answer these questions to determine how well you understood the story.

1. Although the story is set in America, why do all of the characters have French names?
2. What makes the reader think, at first, that Armand will be a good husband?
3. At what point in the story do you begin to suspect that there will be a problem?
4. Why does Armand assume that his wife is not a white woman?
5. What is the result of his cruelty to Désirée?
6. Explain the surprise at the end of the story.

2. Vocabulary

In each of the numbered examples, you will find a description of one of the words from "Désirée's Baby." Using the following list, write the word that best fits the description. Do not use the same word more than once. Some listed words are not to be used at all. Here is an example:

a current custom _____*prevailing*_____

scanned	beneficent 6	portly 1	somber 9
startled	spectacle 10	indulgent 5	unwonted 12
riveted 13	sumptuous 7	suffused 14	willow
pyre	listless 8	conception 11	menacing 3
corbeille	averted 4	imperious 2	

1. a heavyset figure _____

2. a haughty, proud man like Armand _____

3. a threatening gesture _____

4. eyes turned away _____

5. giving a child anything he or she wants _____

6. a kind and generous employer _____

7. a luxurious wedding reception _____

8. a tired feeling _____

9. a sad occasion _____

10. a remarkable sight _____

11. an idea or understanding _____

12. unusual behavior _____

13. a fascinated stare _____

14. spread colors over the sky _____

3. *Grammar: Participial Clauses*

"Désirée's Baby" contains many participial clauses. A participle is a word that usually ends in *ing* or *ed*. It looks like a verb but is used as an adjective, for example, the *running car*. A participial clause is an adjective clause, modifying (describing) a noun or pronoun in the sentence. For example, in the second paragraph of the story, Monsieur Valmondé "found her [Désirée] lying asleep in the shadow of the big stone pillar." What was the pronoun *her* doing? *Lying asleep*. This is a participial clause because it describes a pronoun. The verb *lying* can be both a verb and an adjective. In this case, it is used as an adjective.

Another participial clause occurs in the third paragraph: "seeing she was without child of the flesh." This participial clause describes the word *Providence*.

Present and past participles Often students are confused by the distinction between participles ending in *ing* (present) and those ending in *ed* (past). For example: Are you **interesting** or **interested** in sports? Is your teacher **boring** or **bored?** (We hope neither.) The following discussion may help clear up your confusion.

The present participle gives an **active meaning.** The noun or pronoun it modifies **does** something. For example: That movie was **exciting.** The movie *caused* excitement (active voice).

The past participle, on the other hand, gives a **passive meaning** to the noun or pronoun it modifies. For example: The audience was **excited by** the movie. The *audience* felt excitement (passive voice).

Here are some more examples:

Construction work is **exhausting.**   (present participle: The work *causes* exhaustion.)
The construction workers were **exhausted.**   (past participle: The *workers* felt exhaustion.)
The South Sea Islands are **fascinating.**   (present participle: The islands *cause* fascination.)
We were **fascinated by** the South Sea Islands.   (past participle: *We* felt fascination.)

Remember: The present participle causes the result. The past participle reacts to the cause.

◼ *Application*
Complete the sentences below by using either the present or past participle of the word in parentheses.

(annoy)   1. We were _____ by the constant noise of our

   neighbor.

   2. Our neighbors are always _____.

(confuse)	3. That math lesson is _____.
	4. I am _____ by the math lesson.
(disgust)	5. John's rude behavior is _____.
	6. We were _____ by John's rude behavior.
(frighten)	7. Désirée was _____ by her husband's cold manner.
	8. Armand's cold behavior was _____.
(horrify)	9. The earthquakes in Japan and Russia were _____.
	10. Readers were _____ by news reports of the earthquakes in Japan and Russia.
(thrill)	11. We were _____ by the enchanting ballet.
	12. That ballet performance was _____.
(please)	13. Her soft, melodic voice is _____ to the ear.
	14. The audience was _____ by her soft, melodic voice.
(irritate)	15. We were _____ every time we heard his monotonous list of complaints.
	16. His monotonous list of complaints is _____.
(amuse)	17. Maria's stories are always _____.
	18. Her classmates are always _____ by Maria's stories.
(amaze)	19. Your energy, even at the end of a long day, is _____.
	20. I'm _____ by your energy.

D | THINKING ABOUT THE STORY

1. Sharing Ideas

Discuss the following questions with a partner, in a small group, or with the whole class:

1. How is racism involved in the plot of the story?
2. What personality trait does Armand possess that creates the tragedy? Discuss by giving examples from the story.

3. Discuss the problem of slavery as it existed in the South before the Civil War. How did it eventually divide the Union?
4. Does racism or social class distinction exist in your native country? Explain.

2. *Writing*

Read the writing ideas that follow. Your instructor may make specific assignments, or ask you to choose one of these.

1. Pretend to be Armand and write a defense of your actions.
2. Tell the story from the viewpoint of one of Armand's slaves.
3. Let's suppose that Désirée's baby had survived and he meets his father twenty years later. Write a dialogue between the father and the son.
4. Write a description of a place you have seen that suggests a tragedy could have occurred there.
5. Reread the sixth paragraph of the story, which begins on line 60: "Madame Valmondé had not seen Désirée and the baby for four weeks. When she reached L'Abri she shuddered at the first sight of it, as she always did." Explain, by specific references to the text, how this paragraph foreshadows the tragedy in the story. What other paragraphs or sentences also hint at disaster? Write about this foreshadowing.

Summing Up

A | TAKE A CLOSER LOOK

1. Analyzing and Comparing

In each of the following sections, you are asked to think about and compare two of the stories in Part Three.

"All Summer in a Day" and "The Third Level"

▪ What is the irony in each story? Change the endings so that the irony would be eliminated. Are the stories as effective? Why?

▪ Contrast the differences in the types of irony used by each author. In which story is the irony tragic? In which story is the irony humorous? Which of the two is more powerful?

▪ Charley and Margot both want to escape from their environments. Compare the two characters. How are they alike? How are their situations different?

"All Summer in a Day" and "Désirée's Baby"

▪ Cruelty is a theme in both these stories. Describe the cruelty. Who inflicts the cruelty? Who are the victims?

▪ Contrast Désirée and Margot as they appear at the beginning of the stories. Which character changes? Why doesn't the other character change?

▪ How does prejudice bring about tragedy for each character?

"Désirée's Baby" and "The Third Level"

▪ A letter reveals the ironic endings. Which letter is tragic? Which is humorous?

▪ How do you think Armand reacted to his mother's letter? What do you think Charley did after receiving the letter from Sam?

▪ Which ending was more surprising? Which was more realistic?

2. Freewriting

Write the word *anger* in a circle. Think of things that make you angry and write them on lines that radiate from the circle. For fifteen minutes write about people or situations that make you angry and the ways you deal with your anger.

From "The Third Level"

In "The Third Level," Charley tries to *buy* (purchase) a ticket to Galesburg. Do you ever write this word for the preposition *by?* Another *bye* (as in *good-bye*) can sometimes be confusing, which is also true of the following words from the story. After you have learned their different meanings, write sentences using each word correctly.

knew (verb), new (adjective)

lead (noun and verb), led (verb)

mail (noun and verb), male (adjective and noun)

sail (noun and verb), sale (noun)

1. _____

2. _____

3. _____

4. _____

5. _____

6. _____

7. _____

8. _____

From "All Summer in a Day"

In this story, the children are nine years old. Frequently, we express the same idea another way: They are *nine-year-old* children. The meaning is the same, but the construction is different. In the first construction, the word *years* is used in the plural form because it is a noun. In the second construction, *nine-year-old* is hyphenated and the *s* is omitted. Because the expression precedes the noun it modifies, the entire expression, *nine-year-old,* is used as an adjective modifying *children.* Note these examples:

three-week vacation   a vacation of three weeks

two-day absence   an absence of two days

five-month-old baby   a baby five months old

Then, look up the following word distinctions from "All Summer in a Day":

sun (noun), son (noun)

remember (verb), memory (noun), remembrance (noun)

always (adverb), all ways (two words: adjective and noun)

pale (adjective), pail (noun)

From "Désirée's Baby"

In this story Désirée awoke one morning *conscious* that something was wrong. After his terrible act of cruelty, shouldn't Armand's *conscience* have bothered him? Do you know the difference in meaning between these two words? Study the following pairs of similar words and write sentences clearly illustrating their differences:

idol (noun), idle (adjective)

gentle (adjective), genteel (adjective)

mist (noun), missed (verb)

unwonted (adjective), unwanted (adjective)

1. _____

2. _____

3. _____

4. _____

5. _____

6. _____

7. _____

8. _____

C | SPELLING

In "The Third Level," Charley *received* a letter from his psychiatrist, Sam. Note the spelling of the word *received*. Do you have trouble getting the *ie* and *ei* words straight? If so, memorize this rhyme: Put *i* before *e* (*niece*) except after *c* (*receive*), or when sounded like *a* as in *neighbor* or *weigh*.

Keeping this pattern in mind, look at the following lists. Practice spelling each of these words by using them in sentences. Or, write a paragraph in which you use at least five *ie* and five *ei* words.

ie		*ei*	
belief (believe)	friend	ceiling	perceive
brief	grief	conceit	receipt
chief	piece	deceit	reign (an *a* sound)
field	relief (relieve)	freight (an *a* sound)	vein (an *a* sound)

D REVIEW TEST

In each of the following sentences, circle the correct choice:

1. (Its, It's) too bad that it rained yesterday. We had to cancel the game.
2. They object to (your, you) playing the radio so loudly.
3. Our house needs repair. (It's, Its) roof is leaking.
4. To (who, whom) am I speaking?
5. Margot was the girl (who, whom) remembered the sun.
6. John and Mary had a quarrel. They are no longer speaking to (themselves, each other).
7. My mother and (I, myself) have a good relationship.
8. Between you and (I, me), I don't believe Harry and (he, him).
9. Désirée and (he, him) had a good marriage until the baby was born.
10. That program is so (bored, boring). I want to look at something (interested, interesting).
11. The drilling outside my window is very (annoyed, annoying).
12. I, too, am very (irritated, irritating) by it.
13. Our last speaker told (fascinated, fascinating) tales about his adventures.
14. We admire (them, their) behaving in such an honorable way.
15. (Dickens, Dickens's) novels are famous in every country.
16. (Margot, Margot's) dream of once more seeing the sun was shattered.
17. My name is Susan. What's (your, yours)?
18. My friend and (I, me) like (their, theirs) home very much.
19. The teacher told Frank and (I, me) a good story.
20. We bought a gift for (our, ours) teacher.
21. The reader is shocked by (Armand, Armand's) behavior. (He, His) treating Désirée with contempt led to tragedy.
22. Jack is very generous to my mother and (I, me).
23. Let's divide the profits among José, Carmen, and (she, her).
24. Phil and (he, him) were chosen to head the committee instead of Ted and (she, her).
25. (Your, You're) going to the game, aren't you?

FROM BIRTH until death we have to deal with the first people who come into our lives – our parents and siblings. Even if your home life is essentially happy, there are many problems in close relationships. Perhaps you believe that your mother favors your brother or sister, or you don't quite understand your father. Resentments and misunderstandings repressed in childhood can often surface in adult years. Or, conversely, what you once perceived as cruelty can be viewed later as kindness, as you will see in one of the stories from this part.

■ All three selections in this part deal with the most complex relationships of life – living day by day with other human beings in a group we call *family*.

Chapter 14

MY FATHER SITS IN THE DARK

– *Jerome Weidman*

Chapter 12

A Visit to Grandmother WILLIAM MELVIN KELLEY

A PRE-READING

1. Think Before You Read

Answer the following questions before you read the story:

1. It is especially challenging to raise children in a large family. How do parents show their love for each child? How do they avoid playing favorites?
2. In what special ways did your parents show their love for you when you were a child?
3. Did your parents show favoritism to a brother or sister? How did you feel?
4. What are the qualities of a good parent?

2. Literary Term: Conflict

Conflict between characters, ideologies, or countries creates interest in the plot of a story. As readers, we become absorbed in the story and want to see what happens at the end. The conflict can be an internal psychological struggle within one of the characters, or it can be a major eruption between people or nations. Conflict allows the writer to explore and use human emotions such as love, hate, sorrow, joy, and fear.

3. Idioms and Expressions

Note the following idioms and expressions that appear in the story:

go along join	**laid up** in bed, debilitated
heading to going in a certain direction	**offhand way** casually
	I reckon I guess

B | THE STORY

ABOUT THE AUTHOR

William Melvin Kelley (1937–) was born in the Bronx, New York, and attended the Fieldston School, a private school in Riverdale. He went on to Harvard University, where he studied under Archibald MacLeish. He describes his desire to write as "a vague undergraduate yearning." After Harvard, however, he was convinced that writing would be his career.

At the age of twenty-five, his first novel, *A Different Drummer,* was published. Reviewers praised the book, and it received the Richard and Hinda Rosenthal Award of the National Institute of Arts and Letters. Additional novels include *A Drop of Patience* (1965), *dem* (1967), and *Dunsford Travels Everywhere* (1970).

Dancers on the Shore, published in 1964, is a collection of short stories, one of which is "A Visit to Grandmother." In the preface to *Dancers on the Shore,* Kelley says, "A writer should ask questions. He should depict people, not symbols or ideas disguised as people."

A Visit to Grandmother

CHIG KNEW SOMETHING was wrong the instant his father kissed her. He had always known his father to be the warmest of men, a man so kind that when people ventured timidly into his office, it took only a few words from him to make them relax, and even laugh. Doctor Charles Dunford cared about people.

But when he had bent to kiss the old lady's black face, something new and almost ugly had come into his eyes: fear, uncertainty, sadness, and perhaps even hatred.

Ten days before in New York, Chig's father had decided suddenly he wanted to go to Nashville to attend his college class reunion, twenty years out. Both Chig's brother and sister, Peter and Connie, were packing for camp and besides were too young for such an affair. But Chig was seventeen, had nothing to do that summer, and his father asked if he would like to go along. His father had given him additional reasons: "All my running buddies got their diplomas and were snapped up by them crafty young gals, and had kids within a year – now all those kids, some of them gals, are your age."

The reunion had lasted a week. As they packed for home, his father, in a far too offhand way, had suggested they visit Chig's grandmother. "We this close. We might as well drop in on her and my brothers."

So, instead of going north, they had gone farther south, had just entered her house. And Chig had a suspicion now that the reunion had been only an excuse to drive south, that his father had been heading to this house all the time.

His father had never talked much about his family, with the exception of his brother, GL, who seemed part con man, part practical joker and part Don Juan; he had spoken of GL with the kind of indulgence he would have shown a cute, but ill-behaved and potentially dangerous, five-year-old.

Chig's father had left home when he was fifteen. When asked why, he would answer: "I wanted to go to school. They didn't have a Negro high school at home, so I went up to Knoxville and lived with a cousin and went to school."

They had been met at the door by Aunt Rose, GL's wife, and ushered into the living room. The old lady had looked up from her seat by the window. Aunt Rose stood between the visitors.

The old lady eyed his father. "Rose, who that? Rose?" She squinted. She looked like a doll, made of black straw, the wrinkles in her face running in one direction like the head of a broom. Her hair was white and coarse and grew out straight from her head. Her eyes were brown – the whites, too, seemed light brown – and were hidden behind thick glasses, which remained somehow on a tiny nose. "That Hiram?" That was another of his father's brothers. "No, it ain't Hiram; too big for Hiram." She turned then to Chig. "Now that man, he look like Eleanor, Charles's wife, but Charles wouldn't never send my grandson to see me. I never even hear from Charles." She stopped again.

"It Charles, Mama. That who it is."

Aunt Rose, between them, led them closer. "It Charles come all the way from New York to see you, and brung little Charles with him."

The old lady stared up at them. "Charles? Rose, that really Charles?" She turned away, and reached for a handkerchief in the pocket of her clean, ironed, flowered housecoat, and wiped her eyes. "God have mercy. Charles." She spread her arms up to him, and he bent down and kissed her cheek. That was when Chig saw his face, grimacing. She hugged him; Chig watched the muscles in her arms as they tightened around his father's neck. She half rose out of her chair. "How are you, son?"

Chig could not hear his father's answer.

She let him go, and fell back into her chair, grabbing the arms. Her hands were as dark as the wood, and seemed to become part of it. "Now, who that standing there? Who that man?"

"That's one of your grandsons, Mama." His father's voice cracked. "Charles Dunford, Junior. You saw him once, when he was a baby, in Chicago. He's grown now."

"I can see that, boy!" She looked at Chig squarely. "Come here, son, and kiss me once." He did. "What they call you? Charles too?"

"No, ma'am, they call me Chig."

She smiled. She had all her teeth, but they were too perfect to be her own. "That's good. Can't have two boys answering to Charles in the same house. Won't nobody at all come. So you that little boy. You don't remember me, do you. I used to take you to church in Chicago, and you'd get up and hop in time to the music. You studying to be a preacher?"

"No, ma'am. I don't think so. I might be a lawyer."

"You'll be an honest one, won't you?"

"I'll try."

"Trying ain't enough! You be honest, you hear? Promise me. You be honest like your daddy."

"All right. I promise."

"Good. Rose, where's GL at? Where's that thief? He gone again?"

"I don't know, Mama." Aunt Rose looked embarrassed. "He say he was going by his liquor store. He'll be back."

"Well, then where's Hiram? You call up those boys, and get them over here – now! You got enough to eat? Let me go see." She started to get up. Chig reached out his hand. She shook him off. "What they tell you about me, Chig? They tell you I'm all laid up? Don't believe it. They don't know nothing about old ladies. When I want help, I'll let you know. Only time I'll need help getting anywheres is when I dies and they lift me into the ground."

She was standing now, her back and shoulders straight. She came only to Chig's chest. She squinted up at him. "You eat much? Your daddy ate like two men."

"Yes, ma'am."

"That's good. That means you ain't nervous. Your mama, she ain't nervous. I remember that. In Chicago, she'd sit down by a window all afternoon and never say nothing, just knit." She smiled. "Let me see what we got to eat."

"I'll do that, Mama." Aunt Rose spoke softly. "You haven't seen Charles in a long time. You sit and talk."

The old lady squinted at her. "You can do the cooking if you promise it ain't because you think I can't."

Aunt Rose chuckled. "I know you can do it, Mama."

"All right. I'll just sit and talk a spell." She sat again and arranged her skirt around her short legs.

Chig did most of the talking, told all about himself before she asked. His father only spoke when he was spoken to, and then, only one word at a time, as if by coming back home, he had become a small boy again, sitting in the parlor while his mother spoke with her guests.

When Uncle Hiram and Mae, his wife, came they sat down to eat. Chig did not have to ask about Uncle GL's absence; Aunt Rose volunteered an explanation: "Can't never tell where the man is at. One Thursday morning he left here and next thing we knew, he was calling from Chicago, saying he went up to see Joe Louis fight. He'll be here though; he ain't as young and footloose as he used to be." Chig's father had mentioned driving down that GL was about five years older than he was, nearly fifty.

Uncle Hiram was somewhat smaller than Chig's father; his short-cropped kinky hair was half gray, half black. One spot, just off his forehead, was totally white. Later, Chig found out it had been that way since he was twenty. Mae (Chig could not bring himself to call her Aunt) was a good deal younger than Hiram, pretty enough so that Chig would have looked at her twice on the street. She was a honey-colored woman, with long eye lashes. She was wearing a white sheath.

At dinner, Chig and his father sat on one side, opposite Uncle Hiram and Mae; his grandmother and Aunt Rose sat at the ends. The food was good; there was a lot and Chig ate a lot. All through the meal, they talked about the family as it had been thirty years before, and particularly about the young GL. Mae and Chig asked questions; the old lady answered; Aunt Rose directed the discussion, steering the old lady onto the best stories; Chig's father laughed from time to time; Uncle Hiram ate.

"Why don't you tell them about the horse, Mama?" Aunt Rose, over Chig's weak protest, was spooning mashed potatoes onto his plate. "There now, Chig."

"I'm trying to think." The old lady was holding her fork halfway to her mouth, looking at them over her glasses. "Oh, you talking about that crazy horse GL brung home that time."

"That's right, Mama." Aunt Rose nodded and slid another slice of white meat on Chig's plate.

Mae started to giggle. "Oh, I've heard this. This is funny, Chig."

The old lady put down her fork and began: Well, GL went out of the house one day with an old, no-good chair I wanted him to take over to the church for a bazaar, and he met up with this man who'd just brung in some horses from out West. Now, I reckon you can expect one swindler to be in every town, but you don't rightly think there'll be two, and God forbid they should ever meet – but they did, GL and his chair, this man and his horses. Well, I wished I'd-a been there; there must-a been some mighty high-powered talking going on. That man with his horses, he told GL them horses was half Arab, half Indian, and GL told that man the chair was an antique he'd stole from some rich white folks. So they swapped. Well, I was a-looking out the window and seen GL dragging this animal to the house. It looked pretty gentle and its eyes was most closed and its feet was shuffling.

"GL, where'd you get that thing?" I says.

"I swapped him for that old chair, Mama," he says. "And made myself a bargain. This is even better than Papa's horse."

Well, I'm a-looking at this horse and noticing how he be looking more and more wide awake every minute, sort of warming up like a teakettle until, I swears to you, that horse is blowing steam out its nose.

"Come on, Mama," GL says, "come on and I'll take you for a ride." Now George, my husband, God rest his tired soul, he'd brung home this white folks' buggy which had a busted wheel

and fixed it and was to take it back that day and GL says: "Come on, Mama, we'll use this fine buggy and take us a ride."

"GL," I says, "no, we ain't. Them white folks'll burn us alive if we use their buggy. You just take that horse right on back." You see, I was sure that boy'd come by that animal ungainly.

"Mama, I can't take him back," GL says.

"Why not?" I says.

"Because I don't rightly know where that man is at," GL says.

"Oh," I says. "Well, then I reckon we stuck with it." And I turned around to go back into the house because it was getting late, near dinnertime, and I was cooking for ten.

"Mama," GL says to my back. "Mama, ain't you coming for a ride with me?"

"Go on, boy. You ain't getting me inside kicking range of that animal." I was eyeing that beast and it was boiling hotter all the time. I reckon maybe that man had drugged it. "That horse is wild, GL," I says.

"No, he ain't. He ain't. That man say he is buggy- and saddle-broke and as sweet as the inside of an apple."

My oldest girl, Essie, had-a come out on the porch and she says: "Go on, Mama. I'll cook. You ain't been out the house in weeks."

"Sure, come on, Mama," GL says. "There ain't nothing to be fidgety about. This horse is gentle as a rose petal." And just then that animal snorts so hard it sets up a little dust storm around its feet.

"Yes, Mama," Essie says, "you can

see he gentle." Well, I looked at Essie and then at that horse because I didn't think we could be looking at the same animal. I should-a figured how Essie's eyes ain't never been so good.

"Come on, Mama," GL says.

"All right," I says. So I stood on the porch and watched GL hitching that horse up to the white folks' buggy. For a while there, the animal was pretty quiet, pawing a little, but not much. And I was feeling a little better about riding with GL behind that crazy-looking horse. I could see how GL was happy I was going with him. He was scurrying around that animal, buckling buckles and strapping straps, all the time smiling, and that made me feel good.

Then he was finished, and I must say, that horse looked mighty fine hitched to that buggy and I knew anybody what climbed up there would look pretty good too. GL came around and stood at the bottom of the steps, and took off his hat and bowed and said: "Madam," and reached out his hand to me and I was feeling real elegant like a fine lady. He helped me up to the seat and then got up beside me and we moved out down our alley. And I remember how colored folks come out on their porches and shook their heads, saying: "Lord now, will you look at Eva Dunford, the fine lady! Don't she look good sitting up there!" And I pretended not to hear and sat up straight and proud.

We rode on through the center of town, up Market Street, and all the way out where Hiram is living now, which in them days was all woods, there not being even a farm in sight and that's when that horse must-a first realized he weren't at all broke or tame or maybe thought he was back out West again, and started to gallop.

"GL," I says, "now you ain't joking with your mama, is you? Because if you is, I'll strap you purple if I live through this."

Well, GL was pulling on the reins with all his meager strength, and yelling, "Whoa, you. Say now, whoa!" He turned to me just long enough to say, "I ain't fooling with you, Mama. Honest!"

I reckon that animal weren't too satisfied with the road, because it made a sharp right turn just then, down into a gulley, and struck out across a hilly meadow. "Mama," GL yells. "Mama, do something!"

I didn't know what to do, but I figured I had to do something so I stood up, hopped down onto the horse's back and pulled it to a stop. Don't ask me how I did that; I reckon it was that I was a mother and my baby asked me to do something, is all.

"Well, we walked that animal all the way home; sometimes I had to club it over the nose with my fist to make it come, but we made it, GL and me. You remember how tired we was, Charles?"

"I wasn't here at the time." Chig turned to his father and found his face completely blank, without even a trace of a smile or a laugh.

"Well, of course you was, son. That happened in . . . in . . . it was a hot summer that year and –"

"I left here in June of that year. You wrote me about it."

The old lady stared past Chig at him. They all turned to him; Uncle Hiram looked up from his plate.

"Then you don't remember how we all laughed?"

"No, I don't, Mama. And I probably wouldn't have laughed. I don't think it was funny." They were staring into each other's eyes.

"Why not, Charles?"

"Because in the first place, the horse was gained by fraud. And in the second place, both of you might have been seriously injured or even killed." He broke off their stare and spoke to himself more than to any of them: "And if I'd done it, you would've beaten me good for it."

"Pardon?" The old lady had not heard him; only Chig had heard.

Chig's father sat up straight as if preparing to debate. "I said that if I had done it, if I had done just exactly what GL did, you would have beaten me good for it, Mama." He was looking at her again.

"Why you say that, son?" She was leaning toward him.

"Don't you know? Tell the truth. It can't hurt me now." His voice cracked, but only once. "If GL and I did something wrong, you'd beat me first and then be too tired to beat him. At dinner, he'd always get seconds and I wouldn't. You'd do things with him, like ride in that buggy, but if I wanted you to do something with me, you were always too busy." He paused and considered whether to say what he finally did say: "I cried when I left here. Nobody loved me, Mama. I cried all the way up to Knoxville. That was the last time I ever cried in my life."

"Oh, Charles." She started to get up, to come around the table to him.

He stopped her. "It's too late."

"But you don't understand."

"What don't I understand? I understood then; I understand now."

Tears now traveled down the lines in her face, but when she spoke, her voice was clear. "I thought you knew. I had ten children. I had to give all of them what they needed most." She nodded. "I paid more mind to GL. I had to. GL could-a ended up swinging if I hadn't. But you was smarter. You was more growed up than GL when you was five and he was ten, and I tried to show you that by letting you do what you wanted to do."

"That's not true, Mama. You know it. GL was light-skinned and had good hair and looked almost white and you loved him for that."

"Charles, no. No, son. I didn't love any one of you more than any other."

"That can't be true." His father was standing now, his fists clenched tight. "Admit it, Mama . . . please!" Chig looked at him, shocked; the man was actually crying.

"It may not-a been right what I done, but I ain't no liar." Chig knew she did not really understand what had happened, what he wanted of her. "I'm not lying to you, Charles."

Chig's father had gone pale. He spoke very softly. "You're about thirty years too late, Mama." He bolted from the table. Silverware and dishes rang and jumped. Chig heard him hurrying up to their room.

They sat in silence for a while and

then heard a key in the front door. A man with a new, lacquered straw hat came in. He was wearing brown-and-white two-tone shoes with very pointed toes and a white summer suit. "Say now! Man! I heard my brother was in town. Where he at? Where that rascal?"

He stood in the doorway, smiling broadly, an engaging, open, friendly smile, the innocent smile of a five-year-old.

C | AFTER READING

1. Comprehension

Answer these questions to determine how well you understood the story.

1. What emotions does Chig see in his father's eyes as Charles kisses his mother?
2. How old is Chig?
3. How old was Charles when he left home?
4. Describe Charles's brother GL.
5. How old was Chig when he had last seen his grandmother?
6. What one word would you use to describe the grandmother?
7. Find a sentence in which the grandmother compliments her son Charles.

2. Vocabulary

The following vocabulary words appear in Kelley's story. Write the appropriate word(s) in each sentence. Use each word only once.

crafty	venture	indulgence	swapped
grimaced	fidgety	practical joker	swinging
housecoat	footloose	shuffled	

1. We _____ at the sound of her fingernails on the blackboard.

2. The old woman was dressed in a floral _____.

3. She _____ around the kitchen in her slippers and prepared breakfast.

4. The _____ thief moved among the people at the parade.

5. Ben and Jerry _____ stories about their business _____.

6. He treated his inheritance in a casual way and decided to live a(n)

   _____ , carefree life.

7. The little girl was adored by her father, who offered her every

   _____ money could buy.

8. Margaret's nervous, _____ behavior made everyone tense.

9. The _____ was an annoyance to his friends because he

   constantly tried to trick them.

10. The child enjoyed _____ on the old tire.

3. Grammar: Subject-Verb Agreement

If a subject is singular, the verb must be singular. If the subject is plural, the verb must be plural. Easy? Not always. In some sentences, it is difficult to figure out what the subject of each verb is. Look at this sentence:

The arrival of the tourists seems imminent.

Here, the subject is *arrival,* not tourists. Therefore, the verb must agree with the **singular** subject, *arrival.* Now look at this sentence:

The tourists seem tired.

Here, the subject is *tourists* (a plural). Therefore, the verb must agree and be **plural.**

■ *Application*
In each of the following sentences, underline the subject with one line and the verb with two lines:

1. All the children want toys for Christmas.

2. Each of the pianists is very talented.

3. The color of the roses was so unusual.

4. Mathematics is a challenging subject.

5. Sometimes the news is very depressing.

   In sentences 4 and 5, the subjects sound plural but are treated as singular nouns. Additional words that are considered singular appear on the following page. Use each of them in a sentence. Be sure your subject and verb agree.

aerobics	politics	United States
economics	physics	United Nations

1. _____

2. _____

3. _____

4. _____

5. _____

6. _____

If singular subjects are joined by *either . . . or, neither . . . nor,* the word *or,* or the word *nor,* we use singular verbs. Note the following examples:

Neither Michelle nor Lisa **has been** to China.
Either the man or the woman **asks** for directions.

If one subject is singular and one is plural, the verb should agree with the subject that is closest. For example,

Neither my sister nor my **brothers want** to travel this year.

■ *Application*
Correct the verbs in the following sentences:

1. Neither the coach nor the football players expects _____ to win

the game.

2. Either the subway or the busses isn't _____ working today.

3. Neither she nor her friends hopes _____ to win the lottery.

4. I don't know if David or Mark have seen _____ the movie.

5. Neither the bank nor the library are closed _____ today.

6. If my friends or my brother come _____ , I'll call you.

Many English sentences begin with *there is* or *there are.* The word *there* fills in for the actual subject, which occurs later in the sentence.

In each sentence that follows, underline the actual subject of the sentence and make sure it agrees with the verb you insert (*is* or *are*).

1. There _____ many banks in my city.

2. There _____ a group of children standing near the playground.

3. There _____ some examples of metaphors in the story.

4. There _____ milk in the refrigerator.

5. There _____ neither a letter nor a card in the mailbox.

6. There _____ either a concert or a dance recital every week at

   school.

7. There _____ questions nobody can answer.

8. There _____ good news about his job interview.

Other words or phrases that take singular verbs include *each, every, everyone, everybody, anyone, anybody, one of,* and *each of.* Note these examples:

Everybody **is** responsible for her own actions.
Each of the spectators **hopes** the team will win.

■ *Application*
Write the correct verb(s) in each of the following sentences:

1. One of my sisters _____ (work, works) at a television station.

2. Every member of the orchestra _____ (practice, practices) three

   hours a day.

3. Each of the children _____ (want, wants) a toy for Christmas.

4. One of my favorite foods _____ (is, are) chocolate.

5. Anyone who _____ (know, knows) her _____

   (like, likes) her.

6. Everyone she asked _____ (feel, feels) enthusiastic about the

   trip.

4. Grammar: Collective Nouns

English has many collective nouns that are treated as singular nouns even though they refer to a collection of individuals. Some examples are listed here. Use each of these collective nouns in a sentence.

army	chorus	family	jury
audience	class	government	orchestra
band	crowd	group	team

1. _____

2. _____

3. _____

4. _____

5. _____

6. _____

7. _____

8. _____

9. _____

10. _____

11. _____

12. _____

1. Sharing Ideas

Discuss the following questions with a partner, in a small group, or with the whole class:

1. Why does Charles want to visit his family after his long absence?
2. Why does Charles bring Chig with him?
3. How does Charles feel about his mother?
4. What did he want from her as a child?
5. What is the significance of the story about the runaway horse? What purpose does this story serve in the plot?
6. What do we know about GL? Describe him.
7. Does Chig like his grandmother? Explain your answer.

2. Writing

Read the writing ideas that follow. Your instructor may make specific assignments, or ask you to choose one of these.

1. What do you think Chig is feeling as he observes the confrontation between his father and grandmother at the dinner table? Write about Chig's feelings.
2. Create a conversation between Chig and Charles later that evening or the next day.
3. Write an essay in which Chig describes his grandmother to one of his friends when he gets back home.
4. GL is not a fully developed character in this story, and yet he serves an important role. Discuss his significance to the plot.
5. Compare and contrast the relationship between Charles and Chig and Charles and his mother.
6. Describe the conflict in this story and discuss whether or not you think it is resolved by the end of the story.

Chapter 13

Too Soon a Woman DOROTHY M. JOHNSON

A | PRE-READING

1. Think Before You Read

Answer the following questions before you read the story:

1. What do you know about pioneer life in America's West?
2. What qualities of character would have been helpful to pioneers beginning a new life in the West?
3. Look up the meaning of the following terms that apply to the early settlers: *prairie, homesteader, teamster,* and *covered wagon.*
4. What dangers do you think pioneers faced?
5. Why would it be unwise to eat a mushroom you found in the woods?

2. Literary Term: Characterization

Every story depends on **characters** to develop the plot. The actions, personalities, and subconscious motivations of these characters make us, the readers, interested in them. The author reveals characters through physical descriptions, dialogues, thoughts, feelings, and the observations of other characters. As you read "Too Soon a Woman," see what you learn about the main character from the observations of the narrator.

3. Idioms and Expressions

Note the following idioms and expressions that appear in the story:

two-bit of small worth	**hide nor hair** a trace of something
grub food	**all-fired (all fired up)** enthusiastic
rigged up put together	**plumb** completely

B THE STORY

ABOUT THE AUTHOR

Dorothy M. Johnson (1905–1984) lived all of her life in the West. She was born in McGregor, Iowa, and later moved to Montana, where she attended the state university. After graduating from college, she worked as an editor at several magazines until 1952, when she was appointed as professor of journalism at Montana State University. During and after her time as editor, she wrote many short stories, which she incorporated into a book entitled *The Hanging Tree*. The principal story in this collection was made into a movie in 1959. At that time, Johnson had also written a novel, *Buffalo Woman,* for which she received an award from the Western Writers of America. In 1969 she wrote a biography of Sitting Bull, the famous Indian. The book so pleased the Blackfoot tribe that they made her an honorary member.

Johnson's work has been praised for its realism and strong characters, like the protagonist (the main character) in "Too Soon a Woman."

Too Soon a Woman

WE LEFT the home place behind, mile by slow mile, heading for the mountains, across the prairie where the wind blew forever.

At first there were four of us with the one-horse wagon and its skimpy load. Pa and I walked, because I was a big boy of eleven. My two little sisters romped and trotted until they got tired and had to be boosted up into the wagon bed.

That was no covered Conestoga, like Pa's folks came West in, but just an old farm wagon, drawn by one weary horse, creaking and rumbling westward to the mountains, toward the little woods town where Pa thought he had an old uncle who owned a little two-bit sawmill.

Two weeks we had been moving when we picked up Mary, who had run away from somewhere that she wouldn't tell. Pa didn't want her along, but she stood up to him with no fear in her voice.

"I'd rather go with a family and look after kids," she said, "but I ain't going back. If you won't take me, I'll travel with any wagon that will."

Pa scowled at her, and her wide blue eyes stared back.

"How old are you?" he demanded.

"Eighteen," she said. "There's teamsters come this way sometimes. I'd rather go with you folks. But I won't go back."

"We're prid'near[1] out of grub," my father told her. "We're clean out of money. I got all I can handle without taking anybody else." He turned away as if he hated the sight of her. "You'll have to walk," he said.

So she went along with us and looked after the little girls, but Pa wouldn't talk to her.

On the prairie, the wind blew. But in the mountains, there was rain. When we stopped at little timber claims along the way, the homesteaders said it had rained all summer. Crops among the blackened stumps were rotted and spoiled. There was no cheer anywhere, and little hospitality. The people we talked to were past worrying. They were scared and desperate.

So was Pa. He traveled twice as far each day as the wagon, ranging through the woods with his rifle, but he never saw game. He had been depending on venison. But we never got any except as a grudging gift from the homesteaders.

He brought in a porcupine once, and that was fat meat and good. Mary roasted it in chunks over the fire, half crying with the smoke. Pa and I rigged up the tarp sheet for shelter to keep the rain from putting the fire clean out.

The porcupine was long gone, except for some of the tried-out fat that

[1] *prid'near:* pretty near (almost).

Mary had saved, when we came to an old, empty cabin. Pa said we'd have to stop. The horse was wore out, couldn't pull anymore up those grades on the deep-rutted roads in the mountains.

At the cabin, at least there was shelter. We had a few potatoes left and some corn meal. There was a creek that probably had fish in it, if a person could catch them. Pa tried it for half a day before he gave up. To this day I don't care for fishing. I remember my father's sunken eyes in his gaunt, grim face.

He took Mary and me outside the cabin to talk. Rain dripped on us from branches overhead.

"I think I know where we are," he said. "I calculate to get to old John's and back in about four days. There'll be grub in the town, and they'll let me have some whether old John's still there or not."

He looked at me. "You do like she tells you," he warned. It was the first time he had admitted Mary was on earth since we picked her up two weeks before.

"You're my pardner," he said to me, "but it might be she's got more brains. You mind what she says."

He burst out with bitterness. "There ain't anything good left in the world, or people to care if you live or die. But I'll get grub in the town and come back with it."

He took a deep breath and added, "If you get too all-fired hungry, butcher the horse. It'll be better than starvin'."

He kissed the little girls good-bye and plodded off through the woods with one blanket and the rifle.

The cabin was moldy and had no floor. We kept a fire going under a hole in the roof, so it was full of blinding smoke, but we had to keep the fire so as to dry out the wood.

The third night we lost the horse. A bear scared him. We heard the racket, and Mary and I ran out, but we couldn't see anything in the pitch-dark.

In gray daylight I went looking for him, and I must have walked fifteen miles. It seemed like I had to have that horse at the cabin when Pa came or he'd whip me. I got plumb lost two or three times and thought maybe I was going to die there alone and nobody would ever know it, but I found the way back to the clearing.

That was the fourth day, and Pa didn't come. That was the day we ate up the last of the grub.

The fifth day, Mary went looking for the horse. My sisters whimpered, huddled in a quilt by the fire, because they were scared and hungry.

I never did get dried out, always having to bring in more damp wood and going out to yell to see if Mary would hear me and not get lost. But I couldn't cry like the little girls did, because I was a big boy, eleven years old.

It was near dark when there was an answer to my yelling, and Mary came into the clearing.

Mary didn't have the horse – we never saw hide nor hair of that old horse again – but she was carrying something big and white that looked like a pumpkin with no color to it.

She didn't say anything, just looked around and saw Pa wasn't there yet, at the end of the fifth day.

Too Soon a Woman

"What's that thing?" my sister Elizabeth demanded.

"Mushroom," Mary answered. "I bet it hefts ten pounds."

160 "What are you going to do with it now?" I sneered. "Play football here?"

"Eat it – maybe," she said, putting it in a corner. Her wet hair hung over her shoulders. She huddled by the fire.

165 My sister Sarah began to whimper again. "I'm hungry!" she kept saying.

"Mushrooms ain't good eating," I said. "They can kill you."

170 "Maybe," Mary answered. "Maybe they can. I don't set up to know all about everything, like some people."

"What's that mark on your shoulder?" I asked her. "You tore your dress on the brush."

175 "What do you think it is?" she said, her head bowed in the smoke.

"Looks like scars," I guessed.

180 "'Tis scars. They whipped me. Now mind your own business. I want to think."

Elizabeth whimpered, "Why don't Pa come back?"

185 "He's coming," Mary promised. "Can't come in the dark. Your pa'll take care of you soon's he can."

She got up and rummaged around in the grub box.

190 "Nothing there but empty dishes," I growled. "If there was anything, we'd know it."

Mary stood up. She was holding the can with the porcupine grease. "I'm 195 going to have something to eat," she said coolly. "You kids can't have any yet. And I don't want any squalling, mind."

It was a cruel thing, what she did then. She sliced that big, solid 200 mushroom and heated grease in a pan.

The smell of it brought the little girls out of their quilt, but she told them to go back in so fierce a voice that they obeyed. They cried to break your heart. 205

I didn't cry. I watched, hating her.

I endured the smell of the mushroom frying as long as I could. Then I said, "Give me some."

"Tomorrow," Mary answered. 210 "Tomorrow, maybe. But not tonight." She turned to me with a sharp command: "Don't bother me! Just leave me be."

She knelt there by the fire and 215 finished frying the slice of mushroom.

If I'd had Pa's rifle, I'd have been willing to kill her right then and there.

She didn't eat right away. She looked at the brown, fried slice for a while and 220 said, "By tomorrow morning, I guess you can tell whether you want any."

The little girls stared at her as she ate. Sarah was chewing an old leather glove.

When Mary crawled into the quilts 225 with them, they moved away as far as they could get.

I was so scared that my stomach heaved, empty as it was.

Mary didn't stay in the quilts long. 230 She took a drink out of the water bucket and sat down by the fire and looked through the smoke at me.

She said in a low voice, "I don't know how it will be if it's poison. Just 235 do the best you can with the girls. Because your pa will come back, you know. . . . You better go to bed. I'm going to sit up."

And so would you sit up. If it might 240

be your last night on earth and the pain of death might seize you at any moment, you would sit up by the smoky fire, wide-awake, remembering whatever you had to remember, savoring life.

We sat in silence after the girls had gone to sleep. Once I asked, "How long does it take?"

"I never heard," she answered. "Don't think about it."

I slept after a while, with my chin on my chest. Maybe Peter dozed that way at Gethsemane as the Lord knelt praying.

Mary's moving around brought me wide-awake. The black of night was fading.

"I guess it's all right," Mary said. "I'd be able to tell by now, wouldn't I?"

I answered gruffly, "I don't know."

Mary stood in the doorway for a while, looking out at the dripping world as if she found it beautiful. Then she fried slices of the mushroom while the little girls danced with anxiety.

We feasted, we three, my sisters and I, until Mary ruled, "That'll hold you," and would not cook any more. She didn't touch any of the mushroom herself.

That was a strange day in the moldy cabin. Mary laughed and was gay; she told stories, and we played "Who's Got the Thimble?" with a pine cone.

In the afternoon we heard a shout, and my sisters screamed and I ran ahead of them across the clearing.

The rain had stopped. My father came plunging out of the woods leading a pack horse – and well I remember the treasures of food in that pack.

He glanced at us anxiously as he tore at the ropes that bound the pack.

"Where's the other one?" he demanded.

Mary came out of the cabin then, walking sedately. As she came toward us, the sun began to shine.

My stepmother was a wonderful woman.

C | AFTER READING

1. Comprehension

Answer these questions to determine how well you understood the story.

1. Why didn't the father in the story want to let Mary come along with his family?
2. Where was the family going? How do we know that they were poor?
3. Why wouldn't she let the children eat the mushroom at first? When did she finally cook it for them?
4. Give three examples of Mary's courage.
5. Explain the meaning of the last sentence in the story.
6. How does the title of this story explain Mary's situation?

2. Vocabulary

The numbered vocabulary words are from "Too Soon a Woman." Look at the four definitions for each word and circle the correct one.

1. romp
   a. play actively
   b. sit quietly
   c. jump
   d. shout

2. boosted
   a. bragged
   b. lowered
   c. raised up
   d. tied together

3. scowl
   a. look with displeasure
   b. scold
   c. smile
   d. protect

4. gaunt
   a. fall
   b. gruesome
   c. thin
   d. unhappy

5. grim
   a. frightened
   b. dirty
   c. harsh
   d. suffering

6. plod
   a. run quickly
   b. walk heavily
   c. explore
   d. plan

7. moldy
   a. small animal
   b. damp
   c. shapely
   d. stale

8. whimper
   a. cry softly
   b. plead
   c. scream
   d. face bravely

9. grudgingly
   a. generously
   b. giving reluctantly
   c. selfishly
   d. in a hospitable manner

10. savor
    a. keep for future use
    b. substitute
    c. cook with skill
    d. taste with pleasure

11. sedately
    a. producing sleepiness
    b. noisily
    c. in a dignified manner
    d. rushing forward

12. skimpy
    a. large
    b. move with leaps
    c. deficient in size
    d. cheap

3. Grammar: Mood

Verbs, like people, have moods. In English, there are three moods, which are determined by the verb. These moods are **indicative, imperative,** and **subjunctive.**

Indicative The **indicative** mood makes a statement or asks a question. In English, we use the indicative mood most frequently. These sentences are in the indicative mood:

We like ballet. Do you like ballet?
They seem happy. Do they seem happy?
She gave him a present. Did she give him a present?

■ *Application*
Write five statements using the indicative mood. Then rewrite each sentence as a question.

1. _____
2. _____
3. _____
4. _____
5. _____

Imperative Sentences in the **imperative** mood give orders or directions. The subject of an imperative sentence is *you* (understood). Imperative sentences are commonly found on signs, recipes, manuals, and so forth. We also use the imperative in speaking, as shown in the following examples:

Don't walk on the grass.
Add one cup of sugar.
Turn on the power.
Welcome to our class.

Write five imperative sentences.

1. _____

2. _____

3. _____

4. _____

5. _____

Subjunctive   The subjunctive mood is often the hardest for students to master. **Subjunctive** sentences have dependent (*that*) clauses, which follow such verbs as *wish, suggest, request, recommend, urge,* or *insist.* The word *that* may be omitted. Note these sentences:

His teacher **suggested** (that) he study harder.
We **requested** (that) a refund be sent to us.

   Be is the most irregular verb in the English language. It has eight forms: *am, is, are, was, were, be, been,* and *being.* In the subjunctive mood, *be* is used in the present for singular and plural:

I suggest that he **be** considered for the job.
We request that you **be** at the graduation.

Were is used in the past tense for singular and plural:

If I **were** you, I wouldn't take that job.
If we **were** there, we could have helped them.

■ *Application*
Write six sentences using *wish, suggest, request, recommend, urge,* and *insist* in the independent clause.

1. _____

2. _____

3. _____

4. _____

5. _____

6. _____

4. Grammar: Conditional Sentences

The subjunctive mood is more commonly found in conditional sentences. Conditional sentences are categorized as future conditional, present conditional, or past conditional.

Future conditional We use the **future conditional** when we refer to something that may happen in the future if a certain condition exists. *If* introduces the conditional clause and the verb is in the simple present or present progressive tense. The result clause (what will happen if the condition exists) is in the future tense, and the future tense verb is often accompanied by a modal. Look at these sentences:

If I **buy** a ticket, I **may win** the lottery.
If she **leaves** now, she **will be** on time for her job.
If he **is running** for Congress, he **will need** volunteers.

If the conditional clause comes at the beginning of the sentence, it must be separated from the result clause with a comma. However, the order of the clauses may be reversed. Then, no comma is used to separate the clauses, as shown here:

I may win the lottery if I buy a ticket.
She will be on time for her job if she leaves now.

▨ Application
Finish the following sentences by writing a result clause:

1. If I finish my homework,

   I will _____

2. If she tells the police about the money she found,

   they _____

3. If we take a shortcut to the airport,

   _____

4. If you lend me your car,

   _____

5. If you are polite to people,

   _____

Rewrite the preceding sentences by putting the result clause before the conditional (*if*) clause. Do not put a comma between the clauses!

1. _____

2. _____

3. _____

4. _____

5. _____

In the future conditional, it is possible that things can happen. We use the present tense of the verb even though we are indicating a future action.

> INCORRECT: If I will study, I will succeed in school.
> CORRECT: **If I study, I will succeed** in school.

Present conditional   We use the **present conditional** when we refer to how situations might be different from the way they are now. Sometimes, this conditional is called the **contrary to fact,** or **unreal, conditional.** Note these examples:

If I were a bird, I could fly.   (I am not a bird. I can't fly.)
If they had money, they would travel.   (They don't have money. They won't travel.)

The conditional clause uses the past tense, and the result clause uses *would* + the base form of the verb.

When the verb *be* occurs in a present conditional clause, we use *were* for both singular and plural subjects. For example,

If **I were** a bird, I would fly.
If **we were** birds, we would fly.

■ *Application*
In the following exercise, combine each pair of sentences into one present conditional sentence. For example,

She doesn't know how to dance. She can't enter the contest.

If she knew how to dance, she could enter the contest.

1. We don't speak Chinese. We can't converse with our Chinese neighbor.

_____

2. They don't know where the treasure is buried. They don't have a map.

_____

3. I am not the president. I can't declare a war on drugs.

_____

4. It's not raining. I'm not carrying an umbrella.

_____

5. I am not you. I won't call your mother.

_____

Past conditional Present and future conditionals are possible situations: If you do something in the present, something may happen in the future. Past conditionals, however, are impossible situations. We use the **past conditional** when we are guessing about how things might have been different in the past. We are altering the past by going back in time. The if-clause uses the verb in the past perfect tense (*had* + the past participle). The main clause uses *would have, could have,* or *should have* + the past participle. Look at the following examples:

"If I'd had Pa's rifle, I'd have been willing to kill her right then and there."
   (from the story)
If he had gone with his friends, he could have seen the football game.

■ *Application*
In the following exercise, combine each pair of sentences into one past conditional sentence. For example,

We weren't home. We didn't watch the program.

If we had been home, we would have watched the program.

1. I wasn't at the lecture. I didn't hear the professor speak about geopolitics.

_____

2. He didn't pay attention to the rules. He didn't stay in the company.

_____

3. Our team didn't practice every day. We didn't win the championship game.

_____

Too Soon a Woman

4. Bill and Eva didn't enjoy the concert. They didn't stay until the end.

_____

5. Brad didn't go to Paris. He didn't see the Eiffel Tower.

_____

Using conditionals in other ways We also use conditionals to add politeness to requests and wishes. For example,

Would you like to order dinner now?
I would like a cup of coffee.
Could you help me carry this carton?

■ *Application*
Write five sentences using polite conditionals.

1. _____

2. _____

3. _____

4. _____

5. _____

■ *Application*
The following exercise involves future conditionals. You may work with a partner or in a group. List some popular superstitions using future conditional sentences. Here is an example:

If you break a mirror, you will have bad luck for seven years.

1. _____

2. _____

3. _____

4. _____

5. _____

6. _____

7. _____

8. _____

Using the present conditional, list some of the things you would, could, or should do.

If I won the lottery,

       I would _____

       I could _____

      I should _____

If I were invisible,

       I would _____

       I could _____

      I should _____

■ *Application*

Using the past conditional, list some of the things you would have, should have, or could have done.

If I had known my future,

     I would have _____

     I could have _____

    I should have _____

D | THINKING ABOUT THE STORY

1. *Sharing Ideas*

Discuss the following questions with a partner, in a small group, or with the whole class:

1. Why do you think Mary ran away? Why wouldn't she tell what happened to her?
2. Why does the author tell the story from the viewpoint of an eleven-year-old boy?
3. How do we know that the narrator is recalling the story many years after it happened?
4. How does the title describe Mary?
5. Give examples from the story that show a change in the boy's attitude toward Mary.
6. Explain the effect produced by these sentences: "Mary came out of the cabin then, walking sedately. As she came toward us, the sun began to shine."

2. Writing

Read the writing ideas that follow. Your instructor may make specific assignments, or ask you to choose one of these.

1. The story is told by an unnamed narrator, an eleven-year-old boy. Write it from Mary's viewpoint or from Pa's.
2. Write Mary's thoughts as she sat up all night waiting to find out if the mushroom was poisonous.
3. Make up a dialogue creating a scene that is suggested but does not actually occur in the story, for example, Pa falling in love with Mary, their wedding day, or Mary's relationship with her stepson.
4. Comment on this statement: "One must sometimes be cruel in order to be kind." Write about how this refers to "Too Soon a Woman," to any other story you may have read, or to an incident in your own life.
5. Read another story about pioneer life and compare it in character and theme to "Too Soon a Woman." Some suggestions are the stories of Willa Cather or Bret Harte, or other stories by Dorothy Johnson in her collection, *The Hanging Tree*.

Chapter 14

My Father Sits in the Dark JEROME WEIDMAN

A PRE-READING

1. Think Before You Read

Answer the following questions before you read the story:

1. Do you ever wonder what people are thinking when you see them sitting alone on a bus, a plane, or in a restaurant?
2. Do you have any memories that you would like to keep to yourself?
3. How do you feel about sitting alone in the dark? Would you rather have a light on?
4. Can you picture your father when he was young? What kind of boy do you think he was?
5. Do you know anything about Eugene Debs or Theodore Roosevelt (referred to as T.R. in the story)? If not, look them up in an encyclopedia.

2. Literary Term: Interior Monologue

An author often uses the thoughts and impressions of one character to tell the story. This **interior monologue** gives an intimate and revealing picture of the characters' reactions to other characters or events. In the story you are about to read, we learn about the father through the ongoing thoughts of his son. This device, popularized by the Irish writer James Joyce, is also called **stream of consciousness.**

3. Idioms and Expressions

Note the following idioms and expressions that appear in the story:

knock wood a superstitious practice in which believers knock on a piece of wood to ward off an unpleasant experience	**a funny feeling** a strange or odd feeling
	get to the bottom of this find out the cause
the small hours of the night after midnight	**take it easy** relax

---

B | THE STORY

ABOUT THE AUTHOR

Except for a few years when he lived in Connecticut, Jerome Weidman (1913–1998) spent his long life in New York City, where he was born on the Lower East Side.

He became a writer during America's Great Depression through a curious incident. As a young man of twenty-one, Weidman worked in an accounting firm doing odd jobs. One day he delivered coffee to one of the female clerks, who was telling a story to her co-workers about an incident that had happened to her on New Year's Eve. Weidman realized she was telling the story so badly that no one was listening. The incident, however, struck Weidman as worthy of being formed into a good story if related properly. This he did within an hour, and so began his writing career.

Weidman published more than a dozen novels, over two hundred short stories, and wrote the text for several Broadway plays, including *Fiorello*, the life of a famous mayor of New York, Fiorello La Guardia. Most of Weidman's short stories, though, deal with ordinary people, such as the father in "My Father Sits in the Dark."

MY FATHER HAS a peculiar habit. He is fond of sitting in the dark, alone. Sometimes I come home very late. The house is dark. I let myself in quietly because I do not want to disturb my mother. She is a light sleeper. I tiptoe into my room and undress in the dark. I go to the kitchen for a drink of water. My bare feet make no noise. I step into the room and almost trip over my father. He is sitting in a kitchen chair, in his pajamas, smoking his pipe.

"Hello, Pop," I say.

"Hello, son."

"Why don't you go to bed, Pa?"

"I will," he says.

But he remains there. Long after I am asleep I feel sure that he is still sitting there, smoking.

Many times I am reading in my room. I hear my mother get the house ready for the night. I hear my kid brother go to bed. I hear my sister come in. I hear her do things with jars and combs until she, too, is quiet. I know she has gone to sleep. In a little while I hear my mother say good night to my father. I continue to read. Soon I become thirsty. (I drink a lot of water.) I go to the kitchen for a drink. Again I almost stumble across my father. Many times it startles me. I forget about him. And there he is – smoking, sitting, thinking.

"Why don't you go to bed, Pop?"

"I will, son."

But he doesn't. He just sits there and smokes and thinks. It worries me. I can't understand it. What can he be thinking about? Once I asked him.

"What are you thinking about, Pa?"

"Nothing," he said.

Once I left him there and went to bed. I awoke several hours later. I was thirsty. I went to the kitchen. There he was. His pipe was out. But he sat there, staring into a corner of the kitchen. After a moment I became accustomed to the darkness. I took my drink. He still sat and stared. His eyes did not blink. I thought he was not even aware of me. I was afraid.

"Why don't you go to bed, Pop?"

"I will, son," he said. "Don't wait up for me."

"But," I said, "you've been sitting here for hours. What's wrong? What are you thinking about?"

"Nothing, son," he said. "Nothing. It's just restful. That's all."

The way he said it was convincing. He did not seem worried. His voice was even and pleasant. It always is. But I could not understand it. How could it be restful to sit alone in an uncomfortable chair far into the night, in darkness?

What can it be?

I review all the possibilities. It can't be money. I know that. We haven't much, but when he is worried about money he makes no secret of it. It can't be his health. He is not reticent about that either. It can't be the health of anyone in the family. We are a bit short on money, but we are long on health. (Knock wood, my mother would say.) What can it be? I am afraid I do not know. But that does not stop me from worrying.

Maybe he is thinking of his brothers in the old country. Or of his mother and two step-mothers. Or of his father. But they are all dead. And he would not brood about them like that. I say brood, but it is not really true. He does not brood. He does not even seem to be thinking. He looks too peaceful, too, well not contented, just too peaceful, to be brooding. Perhaps it is as he says. Perhaps it is restful. But it does not seem possible. It worries me.

If I only knew what he thinks about. If I only knew that he thinks at all. I might not be able to help him. He might not even need help. It may be as he says. It may be restful. But at least I would not worry about it.

Why does he just sit there, in the dark? Is his mind failing? No, it can't be. He is only fifty-three. And he is just as keen-witted as ever. In fact, he is the same in every respect. He still likes beet soup. He still reads the second section of the *Times* first. He still wears wing collars. He still believes that Debs could have saved the country and that T.R. was a tool of the moneyed interests. He is the same in every way. He does not even look older than he did five years ago. Everybody remarks about that. Well-preserved, they say. But he sits in the dark, alone, smoking, staring straight ahead of him, unblinking, into the small hours of the night.

If it is as he says, if it is restful, I will let it go at that. But suppose it is not.

Suppose it is something I cannot fathom. Perhaps he needs help. Why doesn't he speak? Why doesn't he frown or laugh or cry? Why doesn't he do something? Why does he just sit there?

Finally I become angry. Maybe it is just my unsatisfied curiosity. Maybe I *am* a bit worried. Anyway, I become angry.

"Is something wrong, Pop?"

"Nothing, son. Nothing at all."

But this time I am determined not to be put off. I am angry.

"Then why do you sit here all alone, thinking, till late?"

"It's restful, son. I like it."

I am getting nowhere. Tomorrow he will be sitting there again. I will be puzzled. I will be worried. I will not stop now. I am angry.

"Well, what do you *think* about, Pa? Why do you just sit here? What's worrying you? What do you think about?"

"Nothing's worrying me, son. I'm all right. It's just restful. That's all. Go to bed, son."

My anger has left me. But the feeling of worry is still there. I must get an answer. It seems so silly. Why doesn't he tell me? I have a funny feeling that unless I get an answer I will go crazy. I am insistent.

"But what do you *think* about, Pa? What is it?"

"Nothing, son. Just things in general. Nothing special. Just things."

I can get no answer.

It is very late. The street is quiet and the house is dark. I climb the steps softly, skipping the ones that creak. I let myself in with my key and tiptoe into my room. I remove my clothes and remember that I am thirsty. In my bare feet I walk to the kitchen. Before I reach it I know he is there.

I can see the deeper darkness of his hunched shape. He is sitting in the same chair, his elbows on his knees, his cold pipe in his teeth, his unblinking eyes staring straight ahead. He does not seem to know I am there. He did not hear me come in. I stand quietly in the doorway and watch him.

Everything is quiet, but the night is full of little sounds. As I stand there motionless I begin to notice them. The ticking of the alarm clock on the icebox. The low hum of an automobile passing many blocks away. The swish of papers moved along the street by the breeze. A whispering rise and fall of sound, like low breathing. It is strangely pleasant.

The dryness in my throat reminds me. I step briskly into the kitchen.

"Hello, Pop," I say.

"Hello, son," he says. His voice is low and dreamlike. He does not change his position or shift his gaze.

I cannot find the faucet. The dim shadow of light that comes through the window from the street lamp only makes the room seem darker. I reach for the short chain in the center of the room. I snap on the light.

He straightens up with a jerk, as though he has been struck. "What's the matter, Pop?" I ask.

"Nothing," he says. "I don't like the light."

"What's the matter with the light?" I say. "What's wrong?"

"Nothing," he says. "I don't like the light."

I snap the light off. I drink my water slowly. I must take it easy, I say to myself. I must get to the bottom of this.

"Why don't you go to bed? Why do you sit here so late in the dark?"

"It's nice," he says. "I can't get used to lights. We didn't have lights when I was a boy in Europe."

My heart skips a beat and I catch my breath happily. I begin to think I understand. I remember the stories of his boyhood in Austria. I see the wide-beamed *kretchma*, with my grandfather behind the bar. It is late, the customers are gone, and he is dozing. I see the bed of glowing coals, the last of the roaring fire. The room is already dark, and growing darker. I see a small boy, crouched on a pile of twigs at one side of the huge fireplace, his starry gaze fixed on the dull remains of the dead flames. The boy is my father.

I remember the pleasure of those few moments while I stood quietly in the doorway watching him.

"You mean there's nothing wrong? You just sit in the dark because you like it, Pop?" I find it hard to keep my voice from rising in a happy shout.

"Sure," he says. "I can't think with the light on."

I set my glass down and turn to go back to my room. "Good night, Pop," I say.

"Good night," he says.

Then I remember. I turn back. "What do you think about, Pop?" I ask.

His voice seems to come from far away. It is quiet and even again. "Nothing," he says softly. "Nothing special."

My Father Sits in the Dark

C AFTER READING

1. Comprehension

Answer these questions to determine how well you understood the story.

1. According to the son, what "peculiar habit" does his father have?
2. Why is the son worried about his father?
3. Why doesn't the father turn on a light?
4. Describe the father.
5. At what point in the story does the son begin to understand his father's habit?

2. Vocabulary

The numbered vocabulary words have been selected from "My Father Sits in the Dark." Match the words in the first column with the definitions in the second column by writing the letter of the best meaning to the left of each word. To prevent guessing, there are more meanings than there are words.

   After you finish the matching exercise, select one word from the list and write a paragraph using that word to describe a person or a situation.

_____ g 1. tiptoe   a. in good condition despite age
_____ c 2. startle   b. bent over
_____ f 3. convincing   c. surprise suddenly
_____ e 4. reticent   d. a hissing sound
_____ k 5. brood   e. slow in understanding
_____ m 6. keen-witted   f. persuasive
_____ a 7. well-preserved   g. walk softly
_____ l 8. fathom   h. hurry
_____ b 9. hunched   i. aloof, shy
_____ d 10. swish   j. carefree
                                 k. think of sad things
                                 l. try to understand
                                 m. bright, alert

3. Grammar: Verb Tense Changes

Authors sometimes switch tenses to indicate the difference in time. A story can, for example, begin in the past tense as the characters recall what happened and then switch to the present because that is what is happening now. In this story, Weidman begins in the present tense. Why do you think he has chosen not to write it in the past? Rewrite the first paragraph in the simple past tense. Compare it with the original version. Which one is more effective? Why?

Occasionally, the author switches to the present continuous tense, such as in line 21, when he says, "I **am reading** in my room," or when he asks his father, "What **are you thinking** about?" What is the difference between the **simple present** and the **present continuous tense?** Compare these two sentences:

Maybe he **thinks** of his brothers in the old country.   (simple present)
Maybe he **is thinking** of his brothers in the old country.   (present continuous)

In the story, the author frequently uses the verb *hear* in the present tense. Why doesn't he say, I am hearing my mother get the house ready for the night? That is because *hear* is one of the verbs that cannot be used in the continuous tense. Other verbs that cannot be used in the continuous tense include the following:

believe	know	prefer	seem
belong	like (dislike)	realize	understand
forget	love	remember	want
hate	need	see	

■ *Application*

From the story "My Father Sits in the Dark," choose five verbs that can be used in both the simple present and the present continuous tense. Explain the differences in meaning that result from changing tenses. Here is an example:

Sometimes I come home very late.   (simple present, meaning: It is the narrator's habit to come home late on occasion.)
Sometimes when I am coming home late, I see my father sitting in the dark. (present continuous, meaning: The narrator sees his father at the moment of coming home.)

1. _____

2. _____

3. _____

4. _____

5. _____

4. Editing

Correct the following paragraph for errors in use of tense:

Often when people are young, they are believing that they completely understand their parents. They are forgetting that one cannot know the thoughts and emotions of another person, even in the same family. Sometimes a parent can be seeming to be unhappy when he is really just being serious. Just because a person is quiet, it doesn't mean he is needing help or even advice. When we are loving our family, we are disliking to see any one of them not choosing to confide in us. We are not realizing that people need space, even those closest to us.

D | THINKING ABOUT THE STORY

1. Sharing Ideas

Discuss the following questions with a partner, in a small group, or with the whole class:

1. In this story, the son reveals himself as much as the father. In your opinion, what kind of person is the son?
2. We never meet the son's mother, sister, or brother, but they are mentioned in the story. What sort of relationship do you think they had with the father?
3. Contrast or compare the father in the story with your own father or a close male relative.
4. What words or sentences in the story tell the reader that the son is needlessly worrying about his father?
5. Did you ever have a moment in your life when you suddenly understood something about your parents? Describe that moment.

2. Writing

Read the writing ideas that follow. Your instructor may make specific assignments, or ask you to choose one of these.

1. Expand the scene in which the son begins to imagine his father as a small boy in Austria.
2. Write a different scene, in which the father has sad thoughts of his boyhood in an Austrian inn.
3. Interview an older person (perhaps one of your parents) and ask, What are the best (or saddest) memories of your childhood? Write down the results of your interview.
4. Assume that twenty years have passed and the narrator of the story is attending his father's funeral. Write about the son's memories of and feelings toward his father.
5. Contrast the father's memories of his boyhood with Charles's recollection of his home life in "A Visit to Grandmother." Write about the differences.

Summing Up

TAKE A CLOSER LOOK

1. *Analyzing and Comparing*

In the next sections, you are asked to think about and compare two of the stories in Part Four. In the final section, compare all three stories.

"A Visit to Grandmother" and "Too Soon a Woman"

- How are the families in each of the stories similar? How are they different?
- Compare the grandmother from "A Visit to Grandmother" with Mary from "Too Soon a Woman."
- How do they relate to children? How do they show their love and concern?

"My Father Sits in the Dark" and "A Visit to Grandmother"

Compare the relationship between the father and son in the Weidman story with the relationship between Charles and his mother.

- How well do the father and son know each other? What is the son afraid of? How do they communicate with each other?
- How well do the mother and son understand each other? How do they communicate? Does their reunion help or hurt their relationship?

All Three Stories

- What is the conflict in each story?
- Are the lines of communication improved at the end of each story? How?
- Describe how the main characters in each story learn more about themselves and their relatives.

2. *Freewriting*

Communication among family members is a theme in each of the stories in Part Four. Write the word *family* on a piece of paper. Now write any words you associate with the word *family*. Write for fifteen minutes about your own family.

From "A Visit to Grandmother"

In this story, Charles cannot *excuse* his mother's *excuses* of GL's outrageous behavior. Notice the use of the same word as both a verb and a noun. The following pairs of words also occur in "A Visit to Grandmother." Write sentences correctly using each of them. Since you have learned the rules of subject and verb agreement in this chapter, test your knowledge by underlining the subject of each sentence with one line and the verb with two lines.

> weak (adjective), week (noun)
>
> bazaar (noun), bizarre (adjective)
>
> beat (verb), beet (noun)

1. _____

2. _____

3. _____

4. _____

5. _____

6. _____

From "Too Soon a Woman"

The boy in the story is *scared* that Mary will die from eating the mushroom. Mary's arm is *scarred* from the whipping she received. What is the difference in meaning between the two words? There is also another word, *sacred,* that you would use when referring to religion, church, or holy things. Here are some other groups of words that might confuse you. Write sentences correctly using each of them.

> four (adjective), fourth (adjective), forth (adverb)
>
> break (noun and verb), brake (noun and verb)
>
> pain (noun and verb), pane (noun)

1. _____

2. _____

3. _____

4. _____

5. _____

6. _____

7. _____

From "My Father Sits in the Dark"

The narrator's father was *accustomed* to sitting in the dark. What was his *custom?* Write sentences using the following pairs of words from "My Father Sits in the Dark":

almost (adverb), most (adjective and adverb)

preserve (verb), persevere (verb)

special (adjective), especially (adverb)

1. _____

2. _____

3. _____

4. _____

5. _____

6. _____

C | SPELLING

Forming the Present Participle

From the spelling patterns for Part One, you learned not to drop the final vowel of a verb to form the past tense. For example, *care* became *cared* in the past; *hope* became *hoped.* However, when adding the suffix *-ing,* we must do the opposite: We must drop the final vowel before adding *-ing. Care* becomes *caring,* and *hope* becomes *hoping.* Here are some other examples:

Present	Past	Present Participle
date	dated	dating
injure	injured	injuring
dine	dined	dining

For the past tense of most verbs ending in *y*, we change the *y* to *i* (unless the *y* is preceded by a vowel) and add *-ed*. *Study*, for instance, becomes *studied*. When adding *-ing* to the root word (when forming the present participle), we keep the *y*. *Study* becomes *studying*. More examples follow:

Present	Past	Present Participle
reply	replied	replying
worry	worried	worrying
try	tried	trying

As a review, complete the following chart by writing each verb in its past tense and present participle form:

Present	Past	Present Participle
say	_____	_____
envy	_____	_____
cry	_____	_____
suppose	_____	_____
judge	_____	_____
dry	_____	_____
raise	_____	_____
arrive	_____	_____
produce	_____	_____
graduate	_____	_____

Some of the following sentences are correct; others contain an error (or errors) in the use of verb tense, subject-verb agreement, or conditionals. If the sentence is correct, write the letter *C* in the space below each sentence. If the sentence is incorrect, underline the error or errors and rewrite the sentence correctly. For example,

> INCORRECT: Not one of us <u>want</u> to go to the game.
> CORRECT: *Not one of us wants to go to the game.*

1. Charles, Chig's father, rarely visit his own mother.

_____

2. Here come Jack and Jill.

_____

3. There go Jack with Jill.

_____

4. If I was you, I wouldn't sign that contract.

_____

5. If we had the money, we would buy a more expensive car.

_____

6. The narrator's father was sitting in the dark every night when his
   son comes home.

_____

7. No one know why he sit there alone.

_____

8. Neither you nor I are to blame.

_____

9. Every one of us are responsible.

_____

10. Each of us does good work.

_____

11. There are a pen and a pencil on the desk.

_____

12. The treasure is jewels.

_____

13. Chig, as well as his father, were surprised to see GL.

_____

14. Charles's mother thinks she understand her son.

_____

15. If it don't rain, we'll go to the park.

_____

16. The dog has tore a hole in my sock.

_____

17. If the mushroom were poisonous, Mary would have died.

_____

18. Mary suggested to the boy that he obeys her.

_____

19. The son and his father understands each other.

_____

20. If Pa hadn't allowed Mary to join the family, the children will have starved.

_____

Meeting Challenges

IN THE LATTER part of the twentieth century, human beings challenged the universe. We landed on the moon, penetrated the mysteries of space, developed computer technology to a science, climbed mountains, and made remarkable archaeological discoveries. All challenges, however, do not have to be physical or phenomenal. Every day we take up small challenges; we fight daily battles of our own.

■ There are innumerable situations that have tested you since the days of your childhood: your first day at school, meeting new friends, and adjusting to unfamiliar environments. Currently, you might be competing for a job or trying to break a bad habit. Whatever you are facing now, you should be able to relate to the challenges of the characters in this final part of the book.

■ *Chapter 17*

THE WARRIORS
– Anna Lee Walters

■ *Chapter 18*

TALKING TO THE DEAD
– Sylvia Watanabe

Chapter 15
A Rice Sandwich SANDRA CISNEROS

A | PRE-READING

1. Think Before You Read

Answer the following questions before you read the story:

1. Think back to when you were a young child. Was there something you wanted very much? How did you convince your parents to give it to you?
2. Did you ever cry in school because you were embarrassed or afraid? How did you cope with your emotions?
3. How did other people react to your tears?
4. What are your memories of your early school days? Did you like or dislike school?

2. Literary Term: Tone

Tone shows the mood of the story. It reflects the author's attitude, which may be serious, humorous, romantic, or even tragic. In "A Rice Sandwich," Cisneros treats the main character with affection and humor and thereby establishes the tone of the story.

3. Idioms and Expressions

Note the following idioms and expressions that appear in the story:

get to eat be allowed to eat	**I bet** I have a strong feeling
got it in my head had an idea	**next thing you know** soon, the result will be
get to go have an opportunity to go	

B   THE STORY

ABOUT THE AUTHOR

The daughter of a Mexican father and a Mexican-American mother, Sandra Cisneros was born in Chicago in 1954. After graduating from college, she worked as a teacher to high school dropouts, and she also wrote poetry and short stories. Her poems and fiction won her two fellowships in creative writing, and she later taught creative writing at several Midwest colleges.

Cisneros is the author of four books of poetry and two books of short stories, *The House on Mango Street* and *Woman Hollering Creek*. She often dedicates her books to her mother, whom she calls "la smart cookie." As you read the story, think about whether the mother of the main character might be based on the author's parent.

A Rice Sandwich

THE SPECIAL KIDS, the ones who wear keys around their necks, get to eat in the canteen. The canteen! Even the name sounds important. And these kids at lunch time go there because their mothers aren't home or home is too far away to get to.

My home isn't far but it's not close either, and somehow I got it in my head one day to ask my mother to make me a sandwich and write a note to the principal so I could eat in the canteen too.

Oh no, she says pointing the butter knife at me as if I'm starting trouble, no sir. Next thing you know everybody will be wanting a bag lunch – I'll be up all night cutting bread into little triangles, this one with mayonnaise, this one with mustard, no pickles on mine, but mustard on one side please. You kids just like to invent more work for me.

But Nenny says she doesn't want to eat at school – ever – because she likes to go home with her best friend Gloria who lives across the schoolyard. Gloria's mama has a big color T.V. and all they do is watch cartoons. Kiki and Carlos, on the other hand, are patrol boys. They don't want to eat at school either. They like to stand out in the cold especially if it's raining. They think suffering is good for you ever since they saw that movie "300 Spartans."

I'm no Spartan and hold up an anemic wrist to prove it. I can't even blow up a balloon without getting dizzy. And besides, I know how to make my own lunch. If I ate at school there'd be less dishes to wash. You would see me less and less and like me better. Everyday at noon my chair would be empty. Where is my favorite daughter you would cry, and when I came home finally at 3 p.m. you would appreciate me.

Okay, okay, my mother says after three days of this. And the following morning I get to go to school with my mother's letter and a rice sandwich because we don't have lunch meat.

Mondays or Fridays, it doesn't matter, mornings always go by slow and this day especially. But lunch time came finally and I got to get in line with the stay-at-school kids. Everything is fine until the nun who knows all the canteen kids by heart looks at me and says: you, who sent you here? And since I am shy, I don't say anything, just hold out my hand with the letter. This is no good, she says, till Sister Superior gives the okay. Go upstairs and see her. And so I went.

I had to wait for two kids in front of me to get hollered at, one because he did something in class, the other because he didn't. My turn came and I stood in front of the big desk with holy pictures under the glass while the Sister Superior read my letter. It went like this:

Dear Sister Superior, Please let Esperanza eat in the lunch room because she lives too far away and she gets tired. As you can see she is very skinny. I hope to God she does not faint. Thanking you, Mrs. E. Cordero.

80   You don't live far, she says. You live across the boulevard. That's only four blocks. Not even. Three maybe. Three long blocks away from here. I bet I can see your house from my window.
85   Which one? Come here. Which one is your house?

And then she made me stand up on a box of books and point. That one? she said pointing to a row of ugly 3- flats, the ones even the raggedy men are ashamed to go into. Yes, I nodded even though I knew that wasn't my house and started to cry. I always cry when nuns yell at me, even if they're not yelling.

Then she was sorry and said I could stay – just for today, not tomorrow or the day after – you go home. And I said yes and could I please have a Kleenex – I had to blow my nose.

In the canteen, which was nothing special, lots of boys and girls watched while I cried and ate my sandwich, the bread already greasy and the rice cold.

C AFTER READING

1. Comprehension

Answer these questions to determine how well you understood the story.

1. Who is the narrator of the story?
2. Why does Esperanza want to eat in the canteen?
3. Why doesn't the mother want to make a sandwich for Esperanza?
4. Who are Kiki and Carlos?
5. What happens when Esperanza tries to blow up a balloon?
6. How does Esperanza convince her mother to write a note to the principal?
7. Why doesn't the nun allow her to have lunch in the canteen every day? Do you think Esperanza is disappointed by this decision? Explain.

2. Vocabulary

The vocabulary words on the following page appear in Cisneros's story. For each definition, write the correct vocabulary word on the line. Notice that you have been given the part of speech with each definition. Try to do this exercise without using your dictionary.

Spartan	canteen	anemic	nodded
skinny	dizzy	hollered	
raggedy	faint	boulevard	
nun	greasy	suffer	

1. _____ wide street (noun)

2. _____ swoon, pass out (verb)

3. _____ to endure, be in pain (verb)

4. _____ very thin (adjective)

5. _____ yelled (verb)

6. _____ worn out, tattered (adjective)

7. _____ weak, lacking enough red blood cells (adjective)

8. _____ cafeteria (noun)

9. _____ self-disciplined, not afraid of pain or danger

10. _____ moved the head downward to signal approval (verb)

11. _____ unsteady (adjective)

12. _____ a woman who is a member of a religious order (noun)

13. _____ oily (adjective)

3. Grammar: Simple Sentences

In Part Four, you learned about subject-verb agreement, and you focused on simple sentences. A **simple** sentence must have at least one subject and one verb and must express a complete thought. As we become more proficient in a language, we speak and write in more complex sentences.

4. Grammar: Compound Sentences

A **compound** sentence has at least two main clauses. Each clause has its own subject and verb and can stand on its own (an independent clause). This is a compound sentence:

My home isn't far, but it's not close either.

In this sentence, the two independent (main) clauses are joined by the conjunction *but*. Other conjunctions are *and, or, nor, so (therefore), for (because),* and *yet (but).* When a conjunction joins two independent clauses, it should be preceded by a comma.

■ *Application*

In the following exercise, use a conjunction to combine the simple sentences into compound sentences. Underline the subject of each clause once and the verb twice.

1. We like to go to the movies. We like to see Broadway shows.

2. He waited a long time for the train. He was late for work.

3. She looked in the mailbox for his letter. He had not written to her.

4. Please let Esperanza eat in the lunch room. She lives too far away.

5. I was a good runner. I ran as hard as I could.

6. We hope it doesn't snow. We won't be able to get home.

7. We liked the movie. The book was better.

8. They planned a surprise party for Anna. They sent out invitations.

5. Grammar: Complex Sentences

A **complex** sentence consists of one independent clause with one or more dependent clauses. Look at the following sentence:

When the siren wailed, I jumped.

In this sentence, "When the siren wailed" is the dependent clause, and "I jumped" is the independent clause.

Certain words act as markers or flags that signal the beginning of a dependent clause. Some of these words are: *who, whom, whose, which,* and *that.* These pronouns are called **relative pronouns.** They introduce clauses that modify (describe) nouns.

Who and *whom* refer to people: *who* is the subjective case, *whom* is the objective case. *Whose* is a possessive pronoun that is used for people, animals, and things. *Which* and *that* are interchangeable. In informal speech, *that* is sometimes used for *who.* Note the following examples:

The girl **who** borrowed the library book never returned it.
Mr. Gold, **whom** I have always admired, is a dynamic speaker.
The neighbors complained about the dog **whose** barking kept them awake.

Other words and phrases also serve as markers or flags and introduce dependent clauses. These include: *after, as, as long as, although, because, before, even if, even though, if, since, unless, until, when, whenever, whether,* and *while.* If a clause marker comes before the main or independent clause, it must be followed by a comma (as in the sentence you just read). Clause markers do not need a comma when they follow the main clause (as shown in this sentence).

■ *Application*

In the sentences that follow, underline the subject in each clause with one line and the verb with two lines. Then, circle the clause marker that introduces the dependent clause. For example,

(When) the <u>astronauts</u> <u>landed</u>, the <u>people</u> <u>cheered</u> and <u>clapped</u>.

1. Because I am shy, I don't say anything.

2. Nenny doesn't want to eat at school because she likes to go home with Gloria.

3. I stood in front of the big desk while the Sister Superior read my letter.

4. You would appreciate me when I came home finally at 3 p.m.

5. Lots of boys and girls watched while I ate my sandwich.

Now, change the order of the clauses in the preceding sentences. Remember to punctuate properly.

1. _____

2. _____

3. _____

4. _____

5. _____

6. *Grammar: Compound-Complex Sentences*

The **compound-complex** sentence has at least two independent clauses and at least one dependent clause. For example,

This is a story that you've heard many times, but I know you will like it.

■ *Application*

In the sentences that follow, underline the subjects in each clause with one line and the verb with two lines. Remember: There will be at least three clauses in each sentence.

1. You said you were my friend, but you weren't honest when you deceived me.

2. I tried to eat, but the food, which I usually enjoyed, was no longer appealing.

3. The hurricane caused such devastation that people couldn't recognize their neighborhoods, and the police had to patrol the area.

4. The school was smaller than I remembered, and the wooden desks were old and worn.

5. The house was dark, and we heard strange sounds that frightened us and made us run away.

It is important to know the following rule: A sentence is a clause, but not every clause is a sentence. If a clause starts with a clause marker or flag, it's waving at you and warning you: I'm not a sentence; I'm a sentence fragment. When you read dependent clauses aloud, and listen to the way they sound, you can often tell that they are sentence fragments.

■ *Application*

This exercise starts with a list of simple sentences. In each sentence, underline the simple subject with one line and the main verb plus any auxiliary verbs with two lines. Then, expand each sentence by adding dependent or independent clauses. Here are some examples:

Beth likes flowers.

Beth likes flowers, and she enjoys spending time in her garden.

Everyone watched the parade.

While everyone watched the parade, we prepared lunch.

1. Even the name sounds important.

_____

2. The baby shook the rattle.

_____

3. Today is sunny and warm.

_____

4. The painting is valuable.

_____

5. The patient will be all right.

_____

6. He must know the value of a good education.

_____

7. I heard a noise behind me.

_____

8. She became a famous writer.

_____

9. They don't want to eat at school either.

_____

10. I had to blow my nose.

_____

D | THINKING ABOUT THE STORY

1. Sharing Ideas

Discuss the following questions with a partner, in a small group, or with the whole class:

1. Describe Esperanza. Use as many adjectives as you can.
2. In what ways are you like Esperanza when you try to get things you want?
3. How does the mother show she is sensitive to Esperanza's desires?
4. Discuss the reaction of the nuns to Mrs. Cordero's letter.
5. Why does Esperanza cry?

2. Writing

Read the writing ideas that follow. Your instructor may make specific assignments, or ask you to choose one of these.

1. Write an essay describing the relationship between Esperanza and her mother.
2. What do you think the nuns should have said to Esperanza? Write a dialogue that is different from the one in the story.
3. Are teachers as sensitive to children as they should be? Write about a teacher you remember who was very thoughtful and kind to you.
4. What are the qualities of a good teacher? Imagine that you are a teacher and write about how you would treat your students.
5. What does Esperanza learn? Write a sentence that describes the moral of the story and then elaborate on your idea.
6. Compare Esperanza to Margot from "All Summer in a Day."

Chapter 16

The Circus   WILLIAM SAROYAN

A PRE-READING

1. Think Before You Read

Answer the following questions before you read the story:

1. What do you think of when you hear the word *circus?*
2. Why do you think people join a circus?
3. When spring comes, do you notice a difference in the way people behave? What is the difference?
4. If you could be anywhere else right now, where would you want to be?
5. As you read this story, try to remember what you were like when you were in fifth grade (ten or eleven years old).

2. Literary Term: Dialogue

An author will often use **dialogue** (conversation) to develop the plot of a story. This story has a lot of dialogue, much of which is written in a regional dialect. The characters become even more real when we hear them speak to each other.

3. Idioms and Expressions

Note the following idioms and expressions that appear in the story:

run hog-wild be wild	**figured** thought
give us a hand help	**came tearing into** ran quickly into a place
going to the dogs becoming bad	
whacks hits, slaps	**by rights** correctly, as one should
pulling for all we were worth using all our energy	**on account of** because
powerful strapping strong whipping	**cussing** cursing

B | THE STORY

ABOUT THE AUTHOR

William Saroyan (1908–1981) was descended from an Armenian family that settled in Fresno, California. As a teenager, he decided to be a writer. He sold his first story to a Boston newspaper, and it was later included in the anthology *Best Short Stories of 1934*. "The Daring Young Man on the Flying Trapeze" was the story that made Saroyan famous. In 1940, Saroyan won the Pulitzer Prize for his play, *The Time of Your Life*.

Saroyan's characters are based on his relatives and members of the community from his childhood. The strong influence of the family is felt in the stories, and there are often conflicts between ethnic family values and the desire to assimilate into American culture.

My Name Is Aram, the novel from which the story "The Circus" is taken, is one of Saroyan's most popular works. It is a coming-of-age book set in the 1940s in California, but it is universal in its insights about a young boy's development.

The Circus

ANY TIME a circus used to come to town, that was all me and my old pal Joey Renna needed to make us run hog-wild, as the saying is. All we needed to do was see the signs on the fences and in the empty store windows to start going to the dogs and neglecting our educations. All we needed to know was that a circus was on its way to town for me and Joey to start wanting to know what good a little education ever did anybody anyway.

After the circus *reached* town we were just no good at all. We spent all our time down at the trains, watching them unload the animals, walking out Ventura Avenue with the wagons with lions and tigers in them and hanging around the grounds, trying to win the favor of the animal men, the workers, the acrobats, and the clowns.

The circus was everything everything else we knew wasn't. It was adventure, travel, danger, skill, grace, romance, comedy, peanuts, popcorn, chewing-gum and soda-water. We used to carry water to the elephants and stand around afterwards and try to seem associated with the whole magnificent affair, the putting up of the big tent, the getting everything in order, and the worldly-wise waiting for the people to come and spend their money.

One day Joey came tearing into the classroom of the fifth grade at Emerson School ten minutes late, and without so much as removing his hat or trying to explain his being late, shouted, Hey, Aram, what the hell are you doing here? The circus is in town.

And sure enough I'd forgotten. I jumped up and ran out of the room with poor old Miss Flibety screaming after me, Aram Garoghlanian, you stay in this room. Do you hear me, Aram Garoghlanian?

I heard her all right and I knew what my not staying would mean. It would mean another powerful strapping from old man Dawson. But I couldn't help it. I was just crazy about a circus.

I been looking all over for you, Joey said in the street. What happened?

I forgot, I said. I knew it was coming all right, but I forgot it was today. How far along are they?

I was at the trains at five, Joey said. I been out at the grounds since seven. I had breakfast at the circus table. Boy, it was good.

Honest, Joey? I said. How were they?

They're all swell, Joey said. Couple more years, they told me, and I'll be ready to go away with them.

As what? I said. Lion-tamer, or something like that?

I guess maybe not as a lion-tamer, Joey said. I figure more like a workman till I learn about being a clown or something, I guess. I don't figure I could work with lions right away.

We were out on Ventura Avenue, headed for the circus grounds, out near the County Fairgrounds, just north of the County Hospital.

Boy, what a breakfast, Joey said. Hot-cakes, ham and eggs, sausages, coffee. Boy.

Why didn't you tell me? I said.

I thought you knew, Joey said. I thought you'd be down at the trains same as last year. I would have told you if I knew you'd forgotten. What made you forget?

I don't know, I said. Nothing, I guess.

I was wrong there, but I didn't know it at the time. I hadn't really forgotten. What I'd done was *remembered*. I'd gone to work and remembered the strapping Dawson gave me last year for staying out of school the day the circus was in town. That was the thing that had kind of kept me sleeping after four-thirty in the morning when by rights I should have been up and dressing and on my way to the trains. It was the memory of that strapping old man Dawson had given me, but I didn't know it at the time. We used to take them strappings kind of for granted, me and Joey, on account of we wanted to be fair and square with the Board of Education and if it was against the rules to stay out of school when you weren't sick, and if you were supposed to get strapped for doing it, well, there we were, we'd done it, so let the Board of Education balance things the best way they knew how. They did that with a strapping. They used to threaten to send me and Joey to Reform School but they never did it.

Circus? old man Dawson used to say. I see. *Circus*. Well, bend down, boy.

So, first Joey, then me, would bend down and old man Dawson would get some powerful shoulder exercise while we tried not to howl. We wouldn't howl for five or six licks, but after that we'd howl like Indians coming. They used to be able to hear us all over the school and old man Dawson, after our visits got to be kind of regular, urged us politely to try to make a little less noise, inasmuch as it was a school and people were trying to study.

It ain't fair to the others, old man Dawson said. They're trying to learn something for themselves.

We can't help it, Joey said. It hurts.

That I know, old man Dawson said, but it seems to me there's such a thing as modulation. I believe a lad can overdo his howling if he ain't thoughtful of others. Just try to modulate that awful howl a little. I think you can do it.

Then he gave Joey a strapping of twenty and Joey tried his best not to howl so loud. After the strapping his face was very red and old man Dawson was very tired.

How was that? Joey said.

That was better, old man Dawson said. By far the most courteous you've managed yet.

I did my best, Joey said.

I'm grateful to you, old man Dawson said.

He was tired and out of breath. I moved up to the chair in front of him that he furnished during these matters to help us suffer the stinging pain. I got in the right position and he said, Wait a minute, Aram. Give a man a chance to get his breath. I'm not twenty-three years old. I'm *sixty*-three. Let me rest a minute.

All right, I said, but I sure would like to get this over with.

Don't howl too loud, he said. Folks passing by in the street are liable to think this is a veritable chamber of tortures. Does it really hurt that much?

You can ask Joey, I said.

How about it, Joey? old man Dawson said. Aren't you lads exaggerating just a little? Perhaps to impress someone in your room? Some girl, perhaps?

We don't howl to impress anybody, Mr. Dawson, Joey said. We wouldn't howl if we could help it. Howling makes us feel ashamed, doesn't it, Aram?

It's awfully embarrassing to go back to our seats in our room after howling that way, I said. We'd rather not howl if we could help it.

Well, old man Dawson said, I'll not be unreasonable. I'll only ask you to try to modulate it a little.

I'll do my best, Mr. Dawson, I said. Got your breath back?

Give me just a moment longer, Aram, Mr. Dawson said.

When he got his breath back he gave me my twenty and I howled a little louder than Joey and then we went back to class. It was awfully embarrassing. Everybody was looking at us.

Well, Joey said, what did you expect? The rest of you would fall down and die if you got twenty. You wouldn't *howl a little,* you'd die.

Now the circus was back in town . . .

That'll be enough out of you, Miss Flibety said.

Well, it's true, Joey said. They're all scared. A circus comes to town and what do they do? They come to school. They don't go out to the circus.

That'll be enough, Miss Flibety said.

Who do they think they are, giving us dirty looks? Joey said.

Miss Flibety lifted her hand, hushing Joey.

Now the circus was back in town, another year had gone by, it was April again, and we were on our way out to the grounds. Only this time it was worse than ever because they'd seen us at school and knew we were going out to the circus.

Do you think they'll send Stafford after us? I said.

Stafford was the truant officer.

We can always run, Joey said. If he comes, I'll go one way, you go another. He can't chase *both* of us. At least one of us will get away.

All right, I said. Suppose one of us gets caught?

Well, let's see, Joey said. Should the one who isn't caught give himself up or should he wreck Stafford's Ford?

I vote for wreck, I said.

So do I, Joey said, so wreck it is.

When we got out to the grounds a couple of the little tents were up, and the big one was going up. We stood around and watched. It was great the way they did it. Just a handful of guys who looked like tramps doing work you'd think no less than a hundred men could do. Doing it with style, too.

All of a sudden a man everybody called Red hollered at me and Joey.

Here, you Arabs,[1] he said, give us a hand.

Me and Joey ran over to him.

Yes, sir, I said.

He was a small man with very broad shoulders and very big hands. You didn't feel that he was small, because he seemed so powerful and because he had so much thick red hair on his head. You thought he was practically a giant.

He handed me and Joey a rope. The rope was attached to some canvas that was lying on the ground.

This is going to be easy, Red said. As the boys lift the pole and get it in place you keep pulling the rope, so the canvas will go up with the pole.

Yes, sir, Joey said.

Everybody was busy when we saw Stafford.

We can't run now, I said.

Let him come, Joey said. We told Red we'd give him a hand and we're going to do it.

I'll tell you what, I said. We'll tell him we'll go with him after we get the canvas up; then we'll run.

All right, Joey said.

Stafford was a big fellow in a business suit who had a beef-red face and looked as if he ought to be a lawyer or something. He came over and said, All right you hooligans, come along with me.

We promised to give Red a hand, Joey said. We'll come just as soon as we get this canvas up.

We were pulling for all we were worth, slipping and falling. The men were all working hard. Red was hollering orders, and then the whole thing was over and we had done our part.

We didn't even get a chance to find out what Red was going to say to us, or if he was going to invite us to sit at the table for lunch, or what.

Joey busted loose and ran one way and I ran the other and Stafford came after *me*. I heard the circus men laughing and Red hollering, Run, boy, run. He can't catch *you*. He's soft. Give him a good run. He needs the exercise.

I could hear Stafford, too. He was very sore and he was cussing.

I got away, though, and stayed low until I saw him drive off in his Ford. Then I went back to the big tent and found Joey.

We'll get it this time, Joey said.

I guess it'll be Reform School this time, I said.

No, Joey said. I guess it'll be thirty. We're going to do some awful howling if it is. Thirty's a lot of whacks even if he *is* sixty-three years old. He ain't exactly a weakling.

Thirty? I said. Ouch. That's liable to make me cry.

Maybe, Joey said. Me too, maybe. Seems like ten can make you cry, then you hold off till it's eleven, then twelve, and you think you'll start crying on the next one, but you don't. We haven't so far, anyway. Maybe we will when it's thirty.

[1] *Arabs:* slang term for circus workers.

Oh, well, I said, that's tomorrow.

Red gave us some more work to do around the grounds and let us sit next to him at lunch. It was swell. We talked to some acrobats who were Spanish, and to a family of Italians who worked with horses. We saw both shows, the afternoon one and the evening one, and then we helped with the work, taking the circus to pieces again; then we went down to the trains, and then home. I got home real late. In the morning I was sleepy when I had to get up for school.

They were waiting for us. Miss Flibety didn't even let us sit down for the roll call. She just told us to go to the office. Old man Dawson was waiting for us, too. Stafford was there, too, and very sore.

I figured, Well, here's where we go to Reform School.

Here they are, Mr. Dawson said to Stafford. Take them away, if you like.

It was easy to tell they'd been talking for some time and hadn't been getting along any too well. Old man Dawson seemed irritated and Stafford seemed sore at him.

In *this* school, old man Dawson said, I do any punishing that's got to be done. Nobody else. I can't stop you from taking them to Reform School, though.

Stafford didn't say anything. He just left the office.

Well, lads, old man Dawson said. How was it?

We had lunch with them, Joey said.

Let's see now, old man Dawson said. What offense is this, the sixteenth or the seventeenth?

It ain't that many, Joey said. Must be eleven or twelve.

Well, old man Dawson said, I'm sure of one thing. This is the time I'm supposed to make it thirty.

I think the next one is the one you're supposed to make thirty, Joey said.

No, Mr. Dawson said, we've lost track somewhere, but I'm sure this is the time it goes up to thirty. Who's going to be first?

Me, I said.

All right, Aram, Mr. Dawson said. Take a good hold on the chair, brace yourself, and try to modulate your howl.

Yes, sir, I said. I'll do my best, but thirty's an awful lot.

Well, a funny thing happened. He gave me thirty all right and I howled all right, but it *was* a modulated howl. It was the most modulated howl I ever howled; because it was the *easiest* strapping I ever got. I counted them and there were thirty all right, but they didn't hurt, so I didn't cry, as I was afraid I might.

It was the same with Joey. We stood together waiting to be dismissed.

I'm awfully grateful to you boys, old man Dawson said, for modulating your howls so nicely this time. I don't want people to think I'm killing you.

We wanted to thank him for giving us such easy strappings, but we couldn't say it. I think he knew the way we felt, though, because he smiled in a way that gave us an idea he knew.

Then we went back to class.

It was swell because we knew everything would be all right till the County Fair opened in September.

AFTER READING

1. Comprehension

Answer these questions to determine how well you understood the story.

1. Who is the narrator?
2. How does the narrator describe the circus? What are his exact words?
3. What is the name of the school Joey and Aram attend? What grade are they in?
4. In what month does the story take place?
5. Who is Mr. Stafford? Mr. Dawson?
6. Is this story humorous or sad?
7. How does Saroyan create the mood of the story? Cite examples from the story.

2. Vocabulary

The following vocabulary words appear in Saroyan's story. Write the appropriate word(s) in each sentence.

sore	reform school	modulation	tramps
irritated	liable	hooligans	truant officer
veritable	wrecked	howl	
canvas	exaggerating	hollered	

1. A(n) _____ reports students who are not in school.

2. Truant students who got into trouble used to be called _____.

3. If a teenager repeatedly commits crimes, he or she may be sent to

   _____.

4. When we lower the sound of music or speaking, we use _____.

5. His father was very _____ and _____ when Tom

   _____ the car.

6. _____ is a strong fabric used to make tents and sails for boats.

7. The fisherman was _____ when he described the size of the fish

   he had caught.

8. During the Depression, many homeless people were referred to as

   _____ .

9. He was _____ to hear our secret, so we whispered to each

   other.

10. We could hear the wind _____ through the trees as the storm

    increased in intensity.

11. The city seems like a(n) _____ desert in the early morning hours.

12. Aram's mother _____ at him when she found out he had left

    school.

3. Grammar: Transitional Words

In "The Circus," Saroyan uses short, simple sentences because he is telling the story from the viewpoint of a young boy. However, if he had used transitional words, the effect would have been different. Look at the following sentences:

Joey and Aram wanted to go to the circus.
They left school.

These sentences could be connected with a transitional like *therefore*, as shown in these examples:

Joey and Aram wanted to go to the circus; therefore, they left school.
Joey and Aram wanted to go to the circus. Therefore, they left school.

Transitionals connect words and sentences to create a smoother style of writing. You should be familiar with the following transitional words:

also	furthermore	nevertheless	still
although	however	nonetheless	then
consequently	instead	otherwise	therefore
finally	meanwhile	similarly	

Use the transitionals in the preceding list to join the pairs of sentences that follow.

1. We trekked through the jungle for four days. We arrived at the village.

   _____

2. She had studied the piano for many years. She never got over her fear of playing for an audience.

   _____

3. We thought we had enough money for our vacation. We ran out of cash after the first week.

   _____

4. They didn't invite me. I can't go to the party with you.

   _____

5. He learned French many years ago. He remembers many words.

   _____

6. I walked through the city. My friend preferred to take a bus.

   _____

7. The jury doubted his innocence. He was convicted.

   _____

8. Before the performance began, the orchestra was practicing. The chorus was rehearsing its songs.

   _____

9. Joey and Aram were afraid of Mr. Dawson. They were afraid of Mr. Stafford.

   _____

10. We couldn't get tickets. We waited in line for two hours.

    _____

4. Grammar: Transitional Phrases

Transitional phrases are also frequently used to connect words and sentences.

■ Application

Look at the following list of transitional phrases. Compare their meanings with the preceding transitional words and write the equivalent single transitional word next to each phrase. Then, rewrite the preceding ten sentences using transitional phrases instead of transitional words.

after all _____	in fact _____
as a result _____	in other words _____
at any rate _____	on the contrary _____
for example _____	on the other hand _____
in addition _____	

1. _____

2. _____

3. _____

4. _____

5. _____

6. _____

7. _____

8. _____

9. _____

10. _____

5. Editing

Rewrite the following story using transitional words and phrases. You may work alone or with a partner. Fill in your own missing word at the end of the paragraph.

Then, write another paragraph, continuing the story and the use of transitionals.

A little girl walked to her friend's house. She became tired. She was hungry. She was lost. She wasn't afraid. She had gone to her friend's house many times before. She found a compass in her pocket. She looked at the compass. It didn't help her find the path to her friend's house. It didn't help her at all. She became angry. She became sad. She looked in her pocket again. This time she found something to help her. She found a(n) _____.

D | THINKING ABOUT THE STORY

1. Sharing Ideas

Discuss the following questions with a partner, in a small group, or with the whole class:

1. Why do Aram and Joey like the circus?
2. Why did Aram forget to wake up early and go to the circus with Joey?
3. How do people from the circus treat the two boys?
4. How does the principal, Mr. Dawson, deal with the boys' truancy?
5. Do you like the boys? How does the author make the boys appealing or annoying?

2. Writing

Read the writing ideas that follow. Your instructor may make specific assignments, or ask you to choose one of these.

1. If you were the principal, how would you treat Joey and Aram? Create a dialogue between the principal (you) and the boys.
2. Did you ever want to run away from home? Pretend you are twelve years old and you join a circus. Write about what your life would be like.
3. Do the strappings stop the boys from running off to see the circus every year? Write about another way the principal might have dealt with their truancy.
4. How does Saroyan create a humorous mood? Write an essay about the humor in the story, citing the sections that make you smile as you read them.
5. In some school systems, when students break the rules, they receive physical punishments. Write about whether you agree or disagree with this type of policy.
6. The story is written as a first-person narrative. Retell the story from another character's viewpoint.

Chapter 17

The Warriors ANNA LEE WALTERS

A   PRE-READING

1. Think Before You Read

Answer the following questions before you read the story:

1. What does the word *warrior* suggest? Can it apply to anything else besides warfare?
2. Do you know anything about the history of the Pawnee Indians? If not, look in an encyclopedia or history book.
3. What problems do you think Native Americans encounter in today's society?
4. Do you have a favorite uncle or any other male relative who has made an impression on you? In what way has he influenced you?

2. Literary Term: Local Color

Local color is the use of specific details describing the dialect, dress, customs, and scenery associated with a particular region. An example of local color would be the stories of Bret Harte, who described life in America's Wild West during the period of the Gold Rush in the mid-1800s. His characters speak in "cowboy" dialect, ride horses, and often frequent saloons. Mark Twain is another American author who used local color to create the atmosphere of life along the Mississippi River. You will learn much about the Pawnee way of life when you read "The Warriors."

3. *Idioms and Expressions*

Note the following idioms and expressions that appear in the story:

hobo a homeless person who travels from place to place	**had a bite to it** sharp
brave all storms face up to all problems with courage	**exploded like a fire cracker** lost his temper
stand their ground resist, never give up	**followed at his heels** followed him around all day
at the top of their lungs in a loud voice	**a vacant look** an expression that indicates a person is not functioning normally

B | THE STORY

ABOUT THE AUTHOR

Anna Lee Walters (1946–) is a Native-American poet, essayist, novelist, and short-story writer, as well as a publisher. She was born in Oklahoma but later moved to a Navajo reservation in Arizona, where she has devoted her life to Native-American cultural affairs.

She studied at the College of Santa Fe in New Mexico and married a Navajo artist, Harry Walters. She began her literary career as a technical writer and editor at the Navajo Community College Press, where she is presently director.

All of her articles and fictional pieces deal with Native-American life. She published a novel, *The Ghost Singer,* in 1988 and has published several collections of short stories over the last twenty years. Walters works tirelessly promoting Native-American literature and has edited an anthology entitled *Neon Powwow: New Native American Voices of the Southwest.* For her own short stories, Walters draws from her Pawnee ancestry to create interesting tales, as you will see when you read "The Warriors."

The Warriors

IN OUR YOUTH, we saw hobos come and go, sliding by our faded white house like wary cats who did not want us too close. Sister and I waved at the strange procession of passing men and women hobos. Just between ourselves, Sister and I talked of that hobo parade. We guessed at and imagined the places and towns we thought the hobos might have come from or had been. Mostly they were white or black people. But there were Indian hobos, too. It never occurred to Sister and me that this would be Uncle Ralph's end.

Sister and I were little, and Uncle Ralph came to visit us. He lifted us over his head and shook us around him like gourd rattles. He was Momma's younger brother, and he could have disciplined us if he so desired. That was part of our custom. But he never did. Instead, he taught us Pawnee words. "*Pari* is Pawnee and *pita* is man," he said. Between the words, he tapped out drumbeats with his fingers on the table top, ghost dance and round dance songs that he suddenly remembered and sang. His melodic voice lilted over us and hung around the corners of the house for days. His stories of life and death were fierce and gentle. Warriors dangled in delicate balance.

He told us his version of the story of Pahukatawa, a Skidi Pawnee warrior. He was killed by the Sioux, but the animals, feeling compassion for him, brought Pahukatawa to life again.

"The Evening Star and the Morning Star bore children and some people say that these offspring are who we are," he often said. At times he pointed to those stars and greeted them by their Pawnee names. He liked to pray for Sister and me, for everyone and every tiny thing in the world, but we never heard him ask for anything for himself from *Atius,* the Father.

"For beauty is why we live," Uncle Ralph said when he talked of precious things only the Pawnees know. "We die for it, too." He called himself an ancient Pawnee warrior when he was quite young. He told us that warriors must brave all storms and odds and stand their ground. He knew intimate details of every battle the Pawnees ever fought since Pawnee time began, and Sister and I knew even then that Uncle Ralph had a great battlefield of his own.

As a child I thought that Uncle Ralph had been born into the wrong time. The Pawnees had been ravaged so often by then. The tribe of several thousand when it was at its peak over a century before were then a few hundred people who had been closely confined for more than a hundred years. The warrior life was gone. Uncle Ralph was trapped in a transparent bubble of a new time. The bubble bound him tight as it blew around us.

Uncle Ralph talked obsessively of warriors, painted proud warriors who shrieked poignant battle cries at the top of their lungs and died with honor.

Sister and I were little then, lost from him in the world of children who saw everything with children's eyes. And though we saw with wide eyes the painted warriors that he fantasized and heard their fierce and haunting battle cries, we did not hear his. Now that we are old and Uncle Ralph has been gone for a long time, Sister and I know that when he died, he was tired and alone. But he was a warrior.

The hobos were always around in our youth. Sister and I were curious about them, and this curiosity claimed much of our time. They crept by the house at all hours of the day and night, dressed in rags and odd clothing. They wandered to us from the railroad tracks where they had leaped from slow-moving boxcars onto the flatland. They hid in high clumps of weeds and brush that ran along the fence near the tracks. The hobos usually traveled alone, but Sister and I saw them come together, like poor families, to share a can of beans or a tin of sardines that they ate with sticks or twigs. Uncle Ralph also watched them from a distance.

One early morning, Sister and I crossed the tracks on our way to school and collided with a tall, haggard white man. He wore a very old-fashioned pin-striped black jacket covered with lint and soot. There was fright in his eyes when they met ours. He scurried around us, quickening his pace. The pole over his shoulder where his possessions hung in a bundle at the end bounced as he nearly ran from us.

"Looks just like a scared jackrabbit," Sister said, watching him dart away.

That evening we told Momma about the scared man. She warned us about the dangers of hobos as our father threw us a stern look. Uncle Ralph was visiting but he didn't say anything. He stayed the night and Sister asked him, "Hey, Uncle Ralph, why do you suppose they's hobos?"

Uncle Ralph was a large man. He took Sister and put her on one knee. "You see, Sister," he said, "hobos are a different kind. They see things in a different way. Them hobos are kind of like us. We're not like other people in some ways and yet we are. It has to do with what you see and feel when you look at this old world."

His answer satisfied Sister for a while. He taught us some more Pawnee words that night.

Not long after Uncle Ralph's explanation, Sister and I surprised a black man with white whiskers and fuzzy hair. He was climbing through the barbed-wire fence that marked our property line. He wore faded blue overalls with pockets stuffed full of handkerchiefs. He wiped sweat from his face. When it dried, he looked up and saw us. I remembered what Uncle Ralph had said and wondered what the black man saw when he looked at us standing there.

"We might scare him," Sister said softly to me, remembering the white man who had scampered way.

Sister whispered, "Hi," to the black man. Her voice was barely audible.

"Boy, it's sure hot," he said. His voice was big and he smiled.

"Where are you going?" Sister asked.

"Me? Nowheres, I guess," he muttered.

"Then what you doing here?" Sister went on. She was bold for a seven-year-old kid. I was older but I was also quieter. "This here place is ours," she said.

He looked around and saw our house with its flowering mimosa trees and rich green mowed lawn stretching out before him. Other houses sat around ours.

"I reckon I'm lost," he said.

Sister pointed to the weeds and brush further up the road. "That's where you want to go. That's where they all go, the hobos."

I tried to quiet Sister but she didn't hush. "The hobos stay up there," she said. "You a hobo?"

He ignored her question and asked his own. "Say, what is you all? You not black, you not white. What is you all?"

Sister looked at me. She put one hand on her chest and the other hand on me. "We Indians!" Sister said.

He stared at us and smiled again. "Is that a fact?" he said.

"Know what kind of Indians we are?" Sister asked him.

He shook his fuzzy head. "Indians is Indians, I guess," he said.

Sister wrinkled her forehead and retorted, "Not us! We not like others. We see things different. We're Pawnees. We're warriors!"

I pushed my elbow into Sister's side. She quieted.

The man was looking down the road and he shuffled his feet. "I'd best go," he said.

Sister pointed to the brush and weeds one more time. "That way," she said.

He climbed back through the fence and brush as Sister yelled, "Bye now!" He waved a damp handkerchief.

Sister and I didn't tell Momma and Dad about the black man. But much later Sister told Uncle Ralph every word that had been exchanged with the black man. Uncle Ralph listened and smiled.

Months later when the warm weather had cooled and Uncle Ralph came to stay with us for a couple of weeks, Sister and I went to the hobo place. We had planned it for a long time. That afternoon when we pushed away the weeds, not a hobo was in sight.

The ground was packed down tight in the clearing among the high weeds. We walked around the encircling brush and found folded cardboards stacked together. Burned cans in assorted sizes were stashed under the cardboards, and there were remains of old fires. Rags were tied to the brush, snapping in the hard wind.

Sister said, "Maybe they're all in the boxcars now. It's starting to get cold."

She was right. The November wind had a bite to it and the cold stung our hands and froze our breaths as we spoke.

"You want to go over to them boxcars?" she asked. We looked at the Railroad Crossing sign where the boxcars stood.

I was prepared to answer when a voice roared from somewhere behind us.

"Now, you young ones, you git on home! Go on! Git!"

A man crawled out of the weeds and

looked angrily at us. His eyes were red and his face was unshaven. He wore a red plaid shirt with striped gray and black pants too large for him. His face was swollen and bruised. An old woolen pink scarf hid some of the bruise marks around his neck, and his topcoat was splattered with mud.

Sister looked at him. She stood close to me and told him defiantly, "You can't tell us what to do! You don't know us!"

He didn't answer Sister but tried to stand. He couldn't. Sister ran to him and took his arm and pulled on it. "You need help?" she questioned.

He frowned at her but let us help him. He was tall. He seemed to be embarrassed by our help.

"You Indian, ain't you?" I dared to ask him.

He didn't answer me but looked at his feet as if they could talk so he wouldn't have to. His feet were in big brown overshoes.

"Who's your people?" Sister asked. He looked to be about Uncle Ralph's age when he finally lifted his face and met mine. He didn't respond for a minute. Then he sighed. "I ain't got no people," he told us as he tenderly stroked his swollen jaw.

"Sure you got people. Our folks says a man's always got people," I said softly. The wind blew our clothes and covered the words.

But he heard. He exploded like a firecracker. "Well I don't! I ain't got no people! I ain't got nobody!"

"What you doing out here anyway?" Sister asked. "You hurt? You want to come over to our house?"

"Naw," he said. "Now you little ones, go on home. Don't be walking round out here. Didn't nobody tell you little girls ain't supposed to be going round by themselves? You might git hurt."

"We just wanted to talk to hobos," Sister said.

"Naw, you don't. Just go on home. Your folks is probably looking for you and worrying 'bout you."

I took Sister's arm and told her we were going home. Then we said bye to the man. But Sister couldn't resist a few last words, "You Indian, ain't you?"

He nodded his head like it was a painful thing to do. "Yeah, I'm Indian."

"You ought to go on home yourself," Sister said. "Your folks probably looking for you and worrying 'bout you."

His voice rose again as Sister and I walked away from him. "I told you kids, I don't have no people!" There was exasperation in his voice.

Sister would not be outdone. She turned and yelled, "Oh yeah? You Indian ain't you? Ain't you?" she screamed. "We your people!"

His topcoat and pink scarf flapped in the wind as we turned away from him.

We went home to Momma and Dad and Uncle Ralph then. Uncle Ralph met us at the front door. "Where you all been?" he asked looking toward the railroad tracks. Momma and Dad were talking in the kitchen.

"Just playing, Uncle," Sister and I said simultaneously.

Uncle Ralph grabbed both Sister

and me by our hands and yanked us out the door. *"Awkuh!"* he said, using the Pawnee expression to show his dissatisfaction.

Outside, we sat on the cement porch. Uncle Ralph was quiet for a long time, and neither Sister nor I knew what to expect.

"I want to tell you all a story," he finally said. "Once, there were these two rats who ran around everywhere and got into everything all the time. Everything they were told not to do, well they went right out and did. They'd get into one mess and then another. It seems that they never could learn."

At that point Uncle Ralph cleared his throat. He looked at me and said, "Sister, do you understand this story? Is it too hard for you? You're older."

I nodded my head up and down and said, "I understand."

Then Uncle Ralph looked at Sister. He said to her, "Sister, do I need to go on with this story?"

Sister shook her head from side to side. "Naw, Uncle Ralph," she said.

"So you both know how this story ends?" he said gruffly. Sister and I bobbed our heads up and down again.

We followed at his heels the rest of the day. When he tightened the loose hide on top of his drum, we watched him and held it in place as he laced the wet hide down. He got his drumsticks down from the top shelf of the closet and began to pound the drum slowly.

"Where you going, Uncle Ralph?" I asked. Sister and I knew that when he took his drum out, he was always gone shortly after.

"I have to be a drummer at some doings tomorrow," he said.

"You a good singer, Uncle Ralph," Sister said. "You know all them old songs."

"The young people nowadays, it seems they don't care 'bout nothing that's old. They just want to go to the Moon." He was drumming low as he spoke.

"We care, Uncle Ralph," Sister said.

"Why?" Uncle Ralph asked in a hard, challenging tone that he seldom used on us.

Sister thought for a moment and then said, "I guess because you care so much, Uncle Ralph."

His eyes softened as he said, "I'll sing you an *Eruska* song, a song for the warriors."

The song he sang was a war dance song. At first Sister and I listened attentively, but then Sister began to dance the men's dance. She had never danced before and tried to imitate what she had seen. Her chubby body whirled and jumped the way she'd seen the men dance. Her head tilted from side to side the way the men moved theirs. I laughed aloud at her clumsy effort, and Uncle Ralph laughed heartily, too.

Uncle Ralph went in and out of our lives after that. We heard that he sang at one place and then another, and people came to Momma to find him. They said that he was only one of a few who knew the old ways and the songs.

When he came to visit us, he always brought something to eat. The Pawnee custom was that the man, the warrior, should bring food, preferably meat.

Then, whatever food was brought to the host was prepared and served to the man, the warrior, along with the host's family. Many times Momma and I, or Sister and I, came home to an empty house to find a sack of food on the table. Momma or I cooked it for the next meal, and Uncle Ralph showed up to eat.

As Sister and I grew older, our fascination with the hobos decreased. Other things took our time, and Uncle Ralph did not appear as frequently as he did before.

Once while I was home alone, I picked up Momma's old photo album. Inside was a gray photo of Uncle Ralph in an army uniform. Behind him were tents on a flat terrain. Other photos showed other poses but only in one picture did he smile. All the photos were written over in black ink in Momma's handwriting. "Ralphie in Korea," the writing said.

Other photos in the album showed our Pawnee relatives. Dad was from another tribe. Momma's momma was in the album, a tiny gray-haired woman who no longer lived. And Momma's momma's dad was in the album; he wore old Pawnee leggings and the long feathers of a dark bird sat upon his head. I closed the album when Momma, Dad, and Sister came home.

Momma went into the kitchen to cook. She called me and Sister to help. As she put on a bibbed apron, she said, "We just came from town, and we saw someone from home there." She meant someone from her tribal community.

"This man told me that Ralphie's been drinking hard," she said sadly. "He used to do that quite a bit a long time ago, but we thought it had stopped. He seemed to be all right for a few years." We cooked and then ate in silence.

Washing the dishes, I asked Momma, "How come Uncle Ralph never did marry?"

Momma looked up at me but was not surprised by my question. She answered, "I don't know, Sister. It would have been better if he had. There was one woman who I thought he really loved. I think he still does. I think it had something to do with Mom. She wanted him to wait."

"Wait for what?" I asked.

"I don't know," Momma said, and sank into a chair.

After that we heard unsettling rumors of Uncle Ralph drinking here and there.

He finally came to the house once when only I happened to be home. He was haggard and tired. His appearance was much like that of the white man that Sister and I met on the railroad tracks years before.

I opened the door when he tapped on it. Uncle Ralph looked years older than his age. He brought food in his arms. "*Nowa,* Sister," he said in greeting. "Where's the other one?" He meant my sister.

"She's gone now, Uncle Ralph. School in Kansas," I answered. "Where you been, Uncle Ralph? We been worrying about you."

He ignored my question and said, "I bring food. The warrior brings home food. To his family, to his people." His face was lined and had not been cleaned for days. He smelled of cheap wine.

I asked again, "Where you been, Uncle Ralph?"

He forced himself to smile. "Pumpkin Flower," he said, using the Pawnee name, "I've been out with my warriors all this time."

He put one arm around me as we went to the kitchen table with the food. "That's what your Pawnee name is. Now don't forget it."

"Did somebody bring you here, Uncle Ralph, or are you on foot?" I asked him.

"I'm on foot," he answered. "Where's your Momma?"

I told him that she and Dad would be back soon. I started to prepare the food he brought.

Then I heard Uncle Ralph say, "Life is sure hard sometimes. Sometimes it seems I just can't go on."

"What's wrong, Uncle Ralph?" I asked.

Uncle Ralph let out a bitter little laugh. "What's wrong?" he repeated. "What's wrong? All my life, I've tried to live what I've been taught, but Pumpkin Flower, some things are all wrong!"

He took a folded pack of Camel cigarettes from his coat pocket. His hand shook as he pulled one from the pack and lit the end. "Too much drink," he said sadly. "That stuff is bad for us."

"What are you trying to do, Uncle Ralph?" I asked him.

"Live," he said.

He puffed on the shaking cigarette a while and said, "The old people said to live beautifully with prayers and song. Some died for beauty, too."

"How do we do that, Uncle Ralph, live for beauty?" I asked.

"It's simple, Pumpkin Flower," he said. "Believe!"

"Believe what?" I asked.

He looked at me hard. *"Awkuh!"* he said. "That's one of the things that is wrong. Everyone questions. Everyone doubts. No one believes in the old ways anymore. They want to believe when it's convenient, when it doesn't cost them anything and they get something in return. There are no more believers. There are no more warriors. They are all gone. Those who are left only want to go to the Moon."

A car drove up outside. It was Momma and Dad. Uncle Ralph heard it too. He slumped in the chair, resigned to whatever Momma would say to him.

Momma came in first. Dad then greeted Uncle Ralph and disappeared into the back of the house. Custom and etiquette required that Dad, who was not a member of Momma's tribe, allow Momma to handle her brother's problems.

She hugged Uncle Ralph. Her eyes filled with tears when she saw how thin he was and how his hands shook.

"Ralphie," she said, "you look awful, but I am glad to see you."

She then spoke to him of everyday things, how the car failed to start and the latest gossip. He was silent, tolerant of the passing of time in this way. His eyes sent me a pleading look while his hands shook and he tried to hold them still.

245
The Warriors

When supper was ready, Uncle Ralph went to wash himself for the meal. When he returned to the table, he was calm. His hands didn't shake so much.

At first he ate without many words, but in the course of the meal he left the table twice. Each time he came back, he was more talkative than before, answering Momma's questions in Pawnee. He left the table a third time and Dad rose.

Dad said to Momma, "He's drinking again. Can't you tell?" Dad left the table and went outside.

Momma frowned. A determined look grew on her face.

When Uncle Ralph sat down to the table once more, Momma told him, "Ralphie, you're my brother but I want you to leave now. Come back when you're sober."

He held a tarnished spoon in mid-air and put it down slowly. He hadn't finished eating, but he didn't seem to mind leaving. He stood, looked at me with his red eyes, and went to the door. Momma followed him. In a low voice she said, "Ralphie, you've got to stop drinking and wandering – or don't come to see us again."

He pulled himself to his full height then. His frame filled the doorway. He leaned over Momma and yelled, "Who are you? Are you God that you will say what will be or will not be?"

Momma met his angry eyes. She stood firm and did not back down.

His eyes finally dropped from her face to the linoleum floor. A cough came from deep in his throat.

"I'll leave here," he said. "But I'll get all my warriors and come back! I have thousands of warriors and they'll ride with me. We'll get our bows and arrows. Then we'll come back!" He staggered out the door.

In the years that followed, Uncle Ralph saw us only when he was sober. He visited less and less. When he did show up, he did a tapping ritual on our front door. We welcomed the rare visits. Occasionally he stayed at our house for a few days at a time when he was not drinking. He slept on the floor.

He did odd jobs for minimum pay but never complained about the work or money. He'd acquired a vacant look in his eyes. It was the same look that Sister and I had seen in the hobos when we were children. He wore a similar careless array of clothing and carried no property with him at all.

The last time he came to the house, he called me by my English name and asked if I remembered anything of all that he'd taught me. His hair had turned pure white. He looked older than anyone I knew. I marveled at his appearance and said, "I remember everything." That night I pointed out his stars for him and told him how Pahukatawa lived and died and lived again through another's dreams. I'd grown, and Uncle Ralph could not hold me on his knee anymore. His arm circled my waist while we sat on the grass.

He was moved by my recitation and clutched my hand tightly. He said, "It's more than this. It's more than just repeating words. You know that, don't you?"

I nodded my head. "Yes, I know.

The recitation is the easiest part but it's more than this, Uncle Ralph."

He was quiet, but after a few minutes his hand touched my shoulder. He said, "I couldn't make it work. I tried to fit the pieces."

"I know," I said.

"Now before I go," he said, "do you know who you are?"

The question took me by surprise. I thought very hard. I cleared my throat and told him, "I know that I am fourteen. I know that it's too young."

"Do you know that you are a Pawnee?" he asked in a choked whisper.

"Yes, Uncle," I said.

"Good," he said with a long sigh that was swallowed by the night.

Then he stood and said, "Well, Sister, I have to go. Have to move on."

"Where are you going?" I asked. "Where all the warriors go?" I teased.

He managed a smile and a soft laugh. "Yeah, wherever the warriors are, I'll find them."

I said to him, "Before you go, I want to ask you . . . Uncle Ralph, can women be warriors too?"

He laughed again and hugged me merrily. "Don't tell me you want to be one of the warriors too?"

"No, Uncle," I said. "Just one of yours." I hated to let him go because I knew I would not see him again.

He pulled away. His last words were, "Don't forget what I've told you all these years. It's the only chance not to become what everyone else is. Do you understand?"

I nodded and he left.

I never saw him again.

The years passed quickly. I moved away from Momma and Dad and married. Sister left before I did.

Years later in another town, hundreds of miles away, I awoke in a terrible gloom, a sense that something was gone from the world the Pawnees knew. The despair filled days, though the reason for the sense of loss went unexplained. Finally, the telephone rang. Momma was on the line. She said, "Sister came home for a few days not too long ago. While she was here and alone, someone tapped on the door, like Ralphie always does. Sister yelled, 'Is that you, Uncle Ralphie? Come on in.' But no one entered."

Then I understood that Uncle Ralph was dead. Momma probably knew too. She wept softly into the phone.

Later Momma received an official call confirming Uncle Ralph's death. He had died from exposure in a hobo shanty, near the railroad tracks outside a tiny Oklahoma town. He'd been dead for several days and nobody knew but Momma, Sister, and me.

Momma reported to me that the funeral was well attended by the Pawnee people. Uncle Ralph and I had said our farewells years earlier. Momma told me that someone there had spoken well of Uncle Ralph before they put him in the ground. It was said that "Ralphie came from a fine family, an old line of warriors."

1. Comprehension

Answer these questions to determine how well you understood the story.

1. Why did the children enjoy Uncle Ralph's visits?
2. What were some of the things he taught them?
3. Why were the narrator and her sister fascinated with hobos? What connection do the hobos have to the rest of the story?
4. What was Uncle Ralph's problem?
5. How did the narrator, her sister, and her mother know that Uncle Ralph was dead even before they received an official call reporting his death?

2. Vocabulary

The following vocabulary words appear in Walters's story. From their context in these sentences, you may be able to figure out their meanings. Write the appropriate word in each sentence. If you need help, you may use your dictionary.

wary	obsessively	haggard	etiquette
gourd	poignant	exasperation	array
melodic	fantasized	rumors	offspring
ravage	collided	unsettling	

1. The weary mother had her hands full taking care of six noisy

   _____.

2. When the soldier returned from battle and saw his child for the first time, it

   was a(n) _____ scene.

3. Books of _____ indicate that gifts should be acknowledged

   with a letter of appreciation.

4. During the American Civil War, General Sherman, a Yankee commander,

   ordered his troops to _____ the countryside and burn Atlanta.

5. Uncle Ralph _____ about bringing thousands of warriors to

   avenge the insults he felt he had received.

6. Uncle Ralph spoke _____ of the warriors and his Pawnee heritage.

7. The children were enchanted with the _____ of toys they saw in the shop window.

8. In the summer, people should be _____ of ticks, especially in wooded areas.

9. The two cars _____ with each other when they both tried to pass on the highway.

10. The Indians made a drinking cup from the rind of a plant, which they call a(n) _____ .

11. After Uncle Ralph had been drinking, he looked ill and _____ .

12. Uncle Ralph had a(n) _____ voice when he sang Pawnee songs.

13. We left the restaurant in _____ because the service was so bad.

14. Nobody should listen to _____ , which are seldom based on fact.

15. The _____ news greatly disturbed us.

3. Grammar: Commas

As you read "The Warriors," you probably noticed sentences like this: "He told us his version of the story of Pahukatawa, a Skidi Pawnee warrior." Why does the author place a comma after the word *Pahukatawa?* Immediately following Pahukatawa is the identification of the name, "a Skidi Pawnee warrior." This construction is called an **appositive** – it identifies or describes the word preceding it.

You must use a comma to separate the identification from the noun or pronoun it describes. Otherwise, the meaning would be obscure. For example, suppose the author wrote:

Uncle Ralph our Pawnee relative is here.

The reader could interpret this sentence in either of two ways:

1. Uncle Ralph is being told that a Pawnee relative has arrived. If so, the proper punctuation is: Uncle Ralph, our Pawnee relative is here. This is called **direct address** because the speaker is talking *to* Uncle Ralph, not *about* him.
2. Uncle Ralph *is* the Pawnee relative. In this instance, the sentence must be written with commas before and after "our Pawnee relative": Uncle Ralph, our Pawnee relative, is here. This construction shows an appositive.

You have now learned two uses of the comma: before or after direct address, and to separate an appositive from the word it modifies. Let's look at two more examples:

Have you written this letter, Maria?   (direct address)
Maria, our secretary, has written the letter.   (appositive)

The comma is also used to separate items in a series. Suppose you go to the store to buy groceries. You must separate one item from another with a comma:

I bought coffee, tea, peaches, pears, and a dozen eggs.   (series)

Another use of the comma is after an introductory clause. This means the clause must come at the beginning of the sentence, as shown here:

Because Uncle Ralph was proud of his heritage, he told the children Pawnee
   stories.   (introductory clause)

The clause in boldface introduces the main part of the sentence and thus is followed by a comma. If the clause comes after the main part of the sentence, do not use a comma. Let's reverse the sentence:

Uncle Ralph told the children Pawnee stories because he was proud of his heritage.

The conjunction *because* directly connects the two clauses into one sentence, and no comma is used.

Commas separate parenthetical expressions from the rest of the sentence. A **parenthetical expression** is extra information that could be omitted. If a parenthetical expression is left out, the sentence still makes sense:

The narrator of the story, **as well as her sister,** listened attentively to Uncle
   Ralph's tales of the Pawnees.   (parenthetical expression)

The expression, "as well as her sister," adds information. It is separated by commas because it could be lifted out of the sentence. The narrator is the subject, not her sister. Phrases like *as well as, together with,* and *including* introduce parenthetical expressions.

If you look at the dialogue in the story "The Warriors," you will see that commas are used before or after direct quotations. The sentences are punctuated as follows:

Uncle Ralph was a large man. He took Sister and put her on one knee. "You see,
   Sister," he said, "hobos are a different kind. They see things in a different way."

Notice that the comma goes inside the quotation marks except when the quotation resumes after the word *said*. Then the comma comes after the word *said* and before the quotation.

For each change of speaker the author begins a new paragraph, as shown in the following sentences. In the last sentence, note that a question mark is used **instead of** a comma.

Sister whispered, "Hi," to the black man. Her voice was barely audible.
"Boy, it's sure hot," he said. His voice was big and he smiled.
"Where are you going?" Sister asked.

Commas are also used to set off addresses and complete dates:

Chicago, Illinois   June 5, 1995

Do not use a comma to separate a partial date, such as June 5.

Commas often set off transitional or introductory words from the rest of the sentence. These words include *of course, for instance, however, therefore, indeed, yes,* and *no.* Note the following examples:

You are, **of course,** going to the meeting.   (transitional words)
Yes, we are thoroughly prepared to make the report.   (introductory word)

Finally, commas may be used to separate a nonrestrictive clause from the rest of the sentence. **Nonrestrictive** simply means **not necessary.** Look at the following sentence:

Helen Smith, **who is my sister,** is the president of our club.   (nonrestrictive)

The clause "who is my sister" is not necessary to identify or describe Helen Smith. Like a parenthetical expression, it is used to give extra information. Therefore, you can omit it if you choose. In the following sentence, however, you need the clause to complete the meaning:

The woman who is wearing a blue suit is Helen Smith.   (restrictive)

The clause "who is wearing a blue suit" is essential to the meaning of the sentence. This is a restrictive clause (necessary) and it cannot be omitted; therefore, no commas are used.

■ *Application*
For this exercise, insert the necessary commas, question marks, and quotation marks in each of the following sentences:

1. Uncle Ralph asked Do you know what hobos are.

2. Because Indians live on reservations they often are isolated from townspeople.

3. Phoenix Arizona is located in the West.

4. On July 4 1776 the Declaration of Independence was signed.

5. The narrator as well as her sister was fascinated with hobos.

6. Uncle Ralph who was a Pawnee told his nieces many Indian stories.

7. Since many immigrants come to New York the city is called a melting pot.

8. Have you read asked the teacher many stories about Indian tribes.

9. George Washington the first president of the United States is called the father of our country.

10. My dog an Irish setter likes to run through the woods.

11. When you go to the market please buy some pears apples and grapes.

12. Indeed I shall come to your party on Thursday.

13. We are of course expecting you.

14. Anna Lee Walters the author of this story is a Native American.

15. Although we had planned for twenty guests more than thirty people arrived.

4. *Grammar: Semicolons*

The comma, which you have just studied, could be called a half-stop. It does not, by itself, join complete sentences. If you wish to join two short sentences, you should use either a conjunction or a semicolon [;], which is a full stop:

It was the best of times *but* it was the worst of times.
It was the best of times; it was the worst of times.
Mary is a physician *and* her brother studies law.
Mary is a physician; her brother studies law.

The semicolon is also used to separate complicated items in a series:

On our trip we visited London, England; Paris, France; Vienna, Austria; and Rome, Italy.

If you used only commas, the same sentence would look like this:

On our trip we visited London, England, Paris, France, Vienna, Austria, and Rome, Italy.

Unless you use the semicolon, the same sentence looks as if the travelers visited eight places, not four.

The semicolon is also used before the following words in a compound sentence: *however, therefore, nevertheless,* and *whereas.* Remember: These words are not conjunctions; their sole function is to introduce an idea. Look at the following examples:

We received your order for twelve laser printers; **however,** we do not carry the model you requested.   (two complete sentences)

I am going home for the holidays; **therefore,** I must pack my luggage.   (two complete sentences)

5. *Grammar: Colons*

The colon [:] is used before a long quotation or a long list of items, especially after the word *following* or the expression *as follows.* Here are some examples:

John Adams, the second president of the United States, wrote: "Yesterday the greatest question was decided whichever was debated in America; and a greater perhaps never was nor will be, decided among men. A resolution was passed without one dissenting colony that these United Colonies are free and independent states."

Please send the **following** school supplies: 10 packages of 8 × 11 lined notebook paper, 100 number 2 pencils, 5 loose-leaf notebooks with soft covers, and 6 boxes of white chalk.

The colon is also used to express the exact time; for example, We are leaving at 8:20 P.M.

6. *Editing*

Punctuate the following paragraph (note the use of the colon here):

After we came to the United States we decided to plan a trip to the West. We want to visit the following places Denver Colorado Phoenix Arizona Santa Fe New Mexico Salt Lake City Utah and the national parks. We also want to see the Indian reservations particularly the Pawnees. We read about them in the stories of Anna Lee Walters a Native-American author. She is a writer she is an educator As a Native American she knows many interesting tales.

My friend Fran told me Don't miss the Grand Canyon it is an incredible sight. Indeed we look forward to our trip across the United States.

D THINKING ABOUT THE STORY

1. *Sharing Ideas*

Discuss the following questions with a partner, in a small group, or with the whole class:

1. What did the word *warrior* mean to Uncle Ralph? In what way was he a warrior? What was his battle?
2. What did the word *warrior* mean to the narrator and her sister when they were children? How did their concept of the term change when they grew up?
3. Why does the author introduce hobos into the story? Is there any foreshadowing in the seemingly unrelated incidents with hobos? Explain.
4. Uncle Ralph's sense of values seemed to be summed up in his statement, "For beauty is why we live." Do you agree? Or do you have a different belief about the purpose of life? Discuss.
5. Do you think that Ralph's sister was not supportive of her brother? Debate this with a partner.
6. What was Uncle Ralph's legacy to his nieces?

2. *Writing*

Read the writing ideas that follow. Your instructor may make specific assignments, or ask you to choose one of these.

1. There are many Native-American legends from various tribes like the Pawnees or Navajos. Look up an Indian legend and retell it in an essay.
2. Write a myth, legend, or fable from your own native culture.
3. Make up an original legend and write it as though you were Uncle Ralph telling it to his nieces.
4. The narrator says of her uncle, "Uncle Ralph had been born into the wrong time." If you are familiar with the story *Don Quixote* by Cervantes, compare Uncle Ralph to Don Quixote as tragic figures living in the past.
5. Why do you suppose alcoholism afflicts some Native Americans? Do some research on the social conditions of Native Americans living on reservations and write a report of your findings.

Chapter 18
Talking to the Dead SYLVIA WATANABE

A | PRE-READING

1. *Think Before You Read*

Answer the following questions before you read the story:

1. What does a mortician do? Why do most people not want to talk about this occupation?
2. Do you have any fears that you can't overcome?
3. Think of some superstitions that are connected with the dead.
4. This story is set in a small village in Hawaii. What do you know about Hawaii? See if the story conflicts with your perceptions of this state.

2. Literary Term: Theme

A **theme** is the message or central idea that an author wishes to stress in a story. In "The Last Leaf," for example, the theme might be stated as: An artist's masterpiece is the sacrifice of his life. See if you can determine the theme of "Talking to the Dead."

3. Idioms and Expressions

Note the following idioms and expressions that appear in the story:

six feet under to be dead (Graves are usually dug to a depth of six feet.)	**small talk** conversation that is not on a serious topic
go-between a person who arranges something between two parties	**come to no good** end in a bad way
laughingstock a ridiculous person whom everyone laughs at	**nothing but a bag of bones** a person who is too thin
laid out displayed in a coffin	**have another helping** eat more food
breathed his last died	**till you're blue in the face** trying hard to do something without success

B | THE STORY

ABOUT THE AUTHOR

Sylvia Watanabe was born in Hawaii on the island of Maui. She received a Japanese-American Citizen's League National Literary Award and a creative writing fellowship from the National Endowment for the Arts. In 1989 she was coeditor of an anthology of Asian-American women's fiction entitled *Home to Stay.* Her own collection of short stories, *Talking to the Dead,* was published in 1992. In her title story, the one you are going to read, the author fulfills her ambition of recording as she says, "a way of life which I loved and which seemed in danger of dying away altogether. . . . I wanted to save the stories that my parents and grandparents and aunts and uncles told whenever they got together around the dinner table."

Talking to the Dead

WE SPOKE OF her in whispers as Aunty Talking to the Dead, the half-Hawaiian kahuna lady. But whenever there was a death in the village, she was the first to be sent for; the priest came second. For it was she who understood the wholeness of things – the significance of directions and colors. Prayers to appease the hungry ghosts. Elixirs for grief. Most times, she'd be out on her front porch, already waiting – her boy, Clinton, standing behind with her basket of spells – when the messenger arrived. People said she could smell a death from clear on the other side of the island, even as the dying person breathed his last. And if she fixed her eyes on you and named a day, you were already as good as six feet under.

I went to work as her apprentice when I was eighteen. That was in '48, the year Clinton graduated from mortician school on the GI bill. It was the talk for weeks – how he'd returned to open the Paradise Mortuary in the heart of the village and had brought the scientific spirit of free enterprise to the doorstep of the hereafter. I remember the advertisements for the Grand Opening, promising to modernize the funeral trade with Lifelike Artistic Techniques and Stringent Standards of Sanitation. The old woman, who had waited out the war for her son's return, stoically took his defection in stride and began looking for someone else to help out with her business.

At the time, I didn't have many prospects – more schooling didn't interest me, and my mother's attempts at marrying me off inevitably failed when I stood to shake hands with a prospective bridegroom and ended up towering a foot above him. "It would be bad enough if she just looked like a horse," I heard one of them complain, "but she's as big as one, too."

My mother dressed me in navy blue, on the theory that dark colors make things look less conspicuous. "Yuri, sit down," she'd hiss, tugging at my skirt as the decisive moment approached. I'd nod, sip my tea, smile through the introductions and small talk, till the time came for sealing the bargain with handshakes. Then, nothing on earth could keep me from getting to my feet. The go-between finally suggested that I consider taking up a trade. "After all, marriage isn't for everyone," she said. My mother said that that was a fact which remained to be proven, but meanwhile it wouldn't hurt if I took in sewing or learned to cut hair. I made up my mind to apprentice myself to Aunty Talking to the Dead.

The old woman's house was on the hill behind the village, just off the road to Chicken Fight Camp. She lived in an old plantation worker's bungalow with peeling green and white paint and a large, well-tended garden – mostly of flowering bushes and strong-smelling herbs.

"Aren't you a big one," a voice behind me said.

I started, then turned. It was the first time I had ever seen her up close.

"Hello, uh, Mrs. Dead," I stammered.

She was little, way under five feet, and wrinkled. Everything about her seemed the same color – her skin, her lips, her dress. Everything was just a slightly different shade of the same brown-gray, except her hair, which was absolutely white, and her tiny eyes, which glinted like metal. For a minute those eyes looked me up and down.

"Here," she said finally, thrusting an empty rice sack into my hands. "For collecting salt." Then she started down the road to the beach.

In the next few months we walked every inch of the hills and beaches around the village, and then some. I struggled behind, laden with strips of bark and leafy twigs, while Aunty marched three steps ahead, chanting. "This is *a'ali'i* to bring sleep – it must be dried in the shade on a hot day. This is *noni* for the heart, and *awa* for every kind of grief. This is *uhaloa* with the deep roots. If you are like that, death cannot easily take you."

"This is where you gather salt to preserve a corpse," I hear her still. "This is where you cut to insert the salt." Her words marked the places on my body, one by one.

That whole first year, not a day passed when I didn't think of quitting. I tried to figure out a way of moving back home without making it seem like I was admitting anything.

"You know what people are saying, don't you?" my mother said, lifting the lid of the bamboo steamer and setting a tray of freshly steamed meat buns on the already crowded table before me. It was one of my few visits since my apprenticeship, though I'd never been more than a couple of miles away, and she had stayed up the whole night before, cooking. She'd prepared a canned ham with yellow sweet potatoes, wing beans with pork, sweet and sour mustard cabbage, fresh raw yellowfin, pickled eggplant, and rice with red beans. I had not seen so much food since the night she tried to persuade Uncle Mongoose not to volunteer for the army. He went anyway, and on the last day of training, just before he was to be shipped to Italy, he shot himself in the head while cleaning his gun. "I always knew that boy would come to no good," was all Mama said when she heard the news.

"What do you mean you can't eat another bite?" she fussed now. "Look at you, nothing but a bag of bones."

The truth was, there didn't seem to be much of a future in my apprenticeship. In eleven and a half months I had memorized most of the minor rituals of mourning and learned to identify a couple of dozen herbs and all their medicinal uses, but I had not seen, much less gotten to practice on, a single honest-to-goodness corpse. "People live longer these days," Aunty claimed.

But I knew it was because everyone, even from villages across the bay, had begun taking their business to the Paradise Mortuary. The single event that had established Clinton's monopoly was the untimely death of old Mrs. Parmeter, the plantation owner's mother-in-law, who'd choked on a fishbone in the salmon mousse during a fund-raising luncheon for Famine Relief. Clinton had been chosen to be in charge of the funeral. After that, he'd taken to wearing three-piece suits, as a symbol of his new respectability, and was nominated as a Republican candidate for the village council.

"So, what are people saying?" I asked, finally pushing my plate away.

This was the cue that Mama had been waiting for. "They're saying that That Woman has gotten herself a pet donkey, though that's not the word they're using, of course." She paused dramatically; the implication was clear.

I began remembering things about living in my mother's house. The navy-blue dresses. The humiliating weekly tea ceremony lessons at the Buddhist temple.

"Give up this foolishness," she wheedled. "Mrs. Koyama tells me the Barber Shop Lady is looking for help."

"I think I'll stay right where I am," I said.

My mother fell silent. Then she jabbed a meat bun with her serving fork and lifted it onto my plate. "Here, have another helping," she said.

A few weeks later Aunty and I were called outside the village to perform a laying-out. It was early afternoon when Sheriff Kanoi came by to tell us that the body of Mustard Hayashi, the eldest of the Hayashi boys, had just been pulled from an irrigation ditch by a team of field workers. He had apparently fallen in the night before, stone drunk, on his way home from the La Hula Rhumba Bar and Grill.

I began hurrying around, assembling Aunty's tools and potions, and checking that everything was in working order, but the old woman didn't turn a hair; she just sat calmly rocking back and forth and puffing on her skinny, long-stemmed pipe.

"Yuri, you stop that rattling around back there," she snapped, then turned to the sheriff. "My son Clinton could probably handle this. Why don't you ask him?"

Sheriff Kanoi hesitated before replying, "This looks like a tough case that's going to need some real expertise."

Aunty stopped rocking. "That's true, it was a bad death," she mused.

"Very bad," the sheriff agreed.

"The spirit is going to require some talking to," she continued. "You know, so it doesn't linger."

"And the family asked especially for you," he added.

No doubt because they didn't have any other choice, I thought. That morning, I'd run into Chinky Malloy, the assistant mortician at the Paradise, so I happened to know that Clinton was at a morticians' conference in Los Angeles and wouldn't be back for several days. But I didn't say a word.

When we arrived at the Hayashis', Mustard's body was lying on the green Formica table in the kitchen. It was the only room in the house with a door that faced north. Aunty claimed that a proper laying-out required a room with a north-facing door, so the spirit could find its way home to the land of the dead without getting lost.

Mustard's mother was leaning over his corpse, wailing, and her husband stood behind her, looking white-faced, and absently patting her on the back. The tiny kitchen was jammed with sobbing, nose-blowing mourners, and the air was thick with the smells of grief – perspiration, ladies' cologne, the previous night's cooking, and the faintest whiff of putrefying flesh. Aunty gripped me by the wrist and pushed her way to the front. The air pressed close, like someone's hot, wet breath on my face. My head reeled, and the room broke apart into dots of color. From far away I heard somebody say, "It's Aunty Talking to the Dead."

"Make room, make room," another voice called.

I looked down at Mustard, lying on the table in front of me, his eyes half open in that swollen, purple face. The smell was much stronger close up, and there were flies everywhere.

"We'll have to get rid of some of this bloat," Aunty said, thrusting a metal object into my hand.

People were leaving the room.

She went around to the other side of the table. "I'll start here," she said. "You work over there. Do just like I told you."

I nodded. This was the long-awaited moment. My moment. But it was already the beginning of the end. My knees buckled, and everything went dark.

Aunty performed the laying-out alone and never mentioned the episode again. But it was the talk of the village for weeks – how Yuri Shimabukuro, assistant to Aunty Talking to the Dead, passed out under the Hayashis' kitchen table and had to be tended by the grief-stricken mother of the dead boy.

My mother took to catching the bus to the plantation store three villages away whenever she needed to stock up on necessaries. "You're my daughter – how could I *not* be on your side?" was the way she put it, but the air buzzed with her unspoken recriminations. And whenever I went into the village, I was aware of the sly laughter behind my back, and Chinky Malloy smirking at me from behind the shutters of the Paradise Mortuary.

"She's giving the business a bad name," Clinton said, carefully removing his jacket and draping it across the back of the rickety wooden chair. He dusted the seat, looked at his hand with distaste before wiping it off on his handkerchief, then drew up the legs of his trousers, and sat.

Aunty retrieved her pipe from the smoking tray next to her rocker and filled the tiny brass bowl from a pouch of Bull Durham. "I'm glad you found time to drop by," she said. "You still going out with that skinny white girl?"

"You mean Marsha?" Clinton sounded defensive. "Sure, I see her sometimes. But I didn't come here to talk about that." He glanced over at where I was sitting on the sofa. "You think we could have some privacy?"

Aunty lit her pipe and puffed.

"Yuri's my right-hand girl. Couldn't do without her."

"The Hayashis probably have their own opinion about that."

Aunty dismissed his insinuation with a wave of her hand. "There's no pleasing some people," she said. "Yuri's just young; she'll learn." She reached over and patted me on the knee, then looked him straight in the face. "Like we all did."

Clinton turned red. "Damn it, Mama," he sputtered, "this is no time to bring up the past. What counts is now, and right now your right-hand girl is turning you into a laughingstock!" His voice became soft, persuasive. "Look, you've worked hard all your life, and you deserve to retire. Now that my business is taking off, I can help you out. You know I'm only thinking about you."

"About the election to village council, you mean." I couldn't help it; the words just burst out of my mouth.

Aunty said, "You considering going into politics, son?"

"Mama, wake up!" Clinton hollered, like he'd wanted to all along. "You can talk to the dead till you're blue in the face, but *ain't no one listening*. The old ghosts have had it. You either get on the wheel of progress or you get run over."

For a long time after he left, Aunty sat in her rocking chair next to the window, rocking and smoking, without saying a word, just rocking and smoking, as the afternoon shadows spread beneath the trees and turned to night.

Then she began to sing – quietly, at first, but very sure. She sang the naming chants and the healing chants. She sang the stones, and trees, and stars back into their rightful places. Louder and louder she sang, making whole what had been broken.

Everything changed for me after Clinton's visit. I stopped going into the village and began spending all my time with Aunty Talking to the Dead. I followed her everywhere, carried her loads without complaint, memorized remedies, and mixed potions till my head spun and I went near blind. I wanted to know what *she* knew; I wanted to make what had happened at the Hayashis' go away. Not just in other people's minds. Not just because I'd become a laughingstock, like Clinton said. But because I knew that I had to redeem myself for that one thing, or my moment – the single instant of glory for which I had lived my entire life – would be snatched beyond my reach forever.

Meanwhile, there were other layings-out. The kitemaker who hanged himself. The crippled boy from Chicken Fight Camp. The Vagrant. The Blindman. The Blindman's dog.

"Do like I told you," Aunty would

> *Louder and louder she sang, making whole what had been broken.*

say before each one. Then, "Give it time," when it was done.

But it was like living the same nightmare over and over – just one look at a body and I was done for. For twenty-five years, people in the village joked about my "indisposition." Last fall, my mother's funeral was held at the Paradise Mortuary. While the service was going on, I stood outside on the cement walk for a long time, but I never made it through the door. Little by little, I'd begun to give up hope that my moment would ever arrive.

Then, a week ago, Aunty caught a chill, gathering *awa* in the rain. The chill developed into a fever, and for the first time since I'd known her, she took to her bed. I nursed her with the remedies she'd taught me – sweat baths; eucalyptus steam; tea made from *ko'oko'olau* – but the fever worsened. Her breathing became labored, and she grew weaker. My few hours of sleep were filled with bad dreams. Finally, aware of my betrayal, I walked to a house up the road and telephoned for an ambulance.

"I'm sorry, Aunty," I kept saying, as the flashing red light swept across the porch. The attendants had her on a stretcher and were carrying her out the front door.

She reached up and grasped my arm, her grip still strong. "You'll do okay, Yuri," the old woman whispered hoarsely. "Clinton used to get so scared, he messed his pants." She chuckled, then began to cough. One of the attendants put an oxygen mask over her face. "Hush," he said.

"There'll be plenty of time for talking later."

On the day of Aunty's wake, the entrance to the Paradise Mortuary was blocked. Workmen had dug up the front walk and carted the old concrete tiles away. They'd left a mound of gravel on the grass, stacked some bags of concrete next to it, and covered the bags with black tarps. There was an empty wheelbarrow parked to one side of the gravel mound. The entire front lawn had been roped off and a sign had been put up that said, "Please follow the arrows around to the back. We are making improvements in Paradise. The Management."

My stomach was beginning to play tricks, and I was feeling shaky. The old panic was mingled with an uneasiness which had not left me ever since I'd decided to call the ambulance. I kept thinking that it had been useless to call it since she'd gone and died anyway. Or maybe I had waited too long. I almost turned back, but I thought of what Aunty had told me about Clinton and pressed ahead. Numbly, I followed the two women in front of me.

"So, old Aunty Talking to the Dead has finally passed on," one of them, whom I recognized as Emi McAllister, said. She was with Pearlie Woo. Both were old classmates of mine.

I was having difficulty seeing – it was getting dark, and my head was spinning so.

"How old do you suppose she was?" Pearlie asked.

"Gosh, even when we were kids it

seemed like she was at least a
hundred," Emi said.

Pearlie laughed. "'The Undead,' my
brother used to call her."

"When we misbehaved," Emi said,
"our mother always threatened to
abandon us on the hill where Aunty
lived. Mama would be beating us with
a wooden spoon and hollering, 'This is
gonna seem like nothing then.'"

Aunty had been laid out in a room
near the center of the mortuary. The
heavy, wine-colored drapes had been
drawn across the windows and all the
wall lamps turned very low, so it was
darker indoors than it had been
outside. Pearlie and
Emi moved off into
the front row. I
headed for the back.

There were about
thirty of us at the
viewing, mostly from
the old days – those
who had grown up on
stories about Aunty,
or who remembered
her from before the Paradise Mortuary.
People got up and began filing past the
casket. For a moment I felt dizzy again,
but I glanced over at Clinton, looking
prosperous and self-assured, accepting
condolences, and I got into line.

The room was air conditioned and
smelled of floor disinfectant and roses.
Soft music came from speakers
mounted on the walls. I drew nearer
and nearer to the casket. Now there
were four people ahead. Now three. I
looked down at my feet, and I thought
I would faint.

Then Pearlie Woo shrieked, "Her

*I was the only one
there who knew.
Aunty was talking
to* me.

eyes!" People behind me began to
murmur. "What – whose eyes?" Emi
demanded. Pearlie pointed to the body
in the casket. Emi cried, "My God,
they're open!"

My heart turned to ice.

"What?" voices behind me were
asking. "What about her eyes?"

"She said they're open," someone
said.

"Aunty Talking to the Dead's eyes
are open," someone else said.

Now Clinton was hurrying over.

"That's because she's not dead," still
another voice added.

Clinton looked into the coffin, and
his face went white.
He turned quickly
around and waved to
his assistants across
the room.

"I've heard about
cases like this,"
someone was saying.
"It's because she's
looking for someone."

"I've heard that
too! The old woman is trying to tell us
something."

I was the only one there who knew.
Aunty was talking to *me*. I clasped my
hands together, hard, but they
wouldn't stop shaking.

People began leaving the line.
Others pressed in, trying to get a better
look at the body, but a couple of
Clinton's assistants had stationed
themselves in front of the coffin,
preventing anyone from getting too
close. They had shut the lid, and
Chinky Malloy was directing people
out of the room.

"I'd like to take this opportunity to thank you all for coming here this evening," Clinton was saying. "I hope you will join us at the reception down the hall."

While everyone was eating, I stole back into the parlor and quietly – ever so quietly – went up to the casket, lifted the lid, and looked in.

At first I thought they had switched bodies on me and exchanged Aunty for some powdered and painted old grandmother, all pink and white, in a pink dress, and clutching a white rose to her chest. But there they were. Open. Aunty's eyes staring up at me.

Then I knew. This was *it:* my moment had arrived. Aunty Talking to the Dead had come awake to bear me witness.

I walked through the deserted front rooms of the mortuary and out the front door. It was night. I got the wheelbarrow, loaded it with one of the tarps covering the bags of cement, and wheeled it back to the room where Aunty was. It squeaked terribly, and I stopped often to make sure no one had heard. From the back of the building came the clink of glassware and the buzz of voices. I had to work quickly – people would be leaving soon.

But this was the hardest part. Small as she was, it was very hard to lift her out of the coffin. She was horribly heavy, and unyielding as a bag of cement. I finally got her out and wrapped her in the tarp. I loaded her in the tray of the wheelbarrow – most of her, anyway; there was nothing I could do about her feet sticking out the front end. Then I wheeled her out of the mortuary, across the village square, and up the road, home.

Now, in the dark, the old woman is singing.

I have washed her with my own hands and worked the salt into the hollows of her body. I have dressed her in white and laid her in flowers.

Aunty, here are the beads you like to wear. Your favorite cakes. A quilt to keep away the chill. Here is *noni* for the heart and *awa* for every kind of grief.

Down the road a dog howls, and the sound of hammering echoes through the still air. "Looks like a burying tomorrow," the sleepers murmur, turning in their warm beds.

I bind the sandals to her feet and put the torch to the pyre.

The sky turns to light. The smoke climbs. Her ashes scatter, filling the wind.

And she sings, she sings, she sings.

AFTER READING

1. Comprehension

Answer these questions to determine how well you understood the story.

1. Why was the narrator, Yuri, considered an unsuitable prospect for marriage?
2. Why did she decide to become an apprentice to a mortician?
3. Describe Aunty Talking to the Dead. How did she get that name?
4. In what ways was Yuri helpful to Aunty? What was Yuri's problem?
5. Why did Yuri become a laughingstock?
6. What decision did Yuri make after viewing Aunty's body?

2. Vocabulary

The following vocabulary words appear in Watanabe's story. Write the appropriate word in each sentence.

appease	towered	wheedled	self-assured
elixir	conspicuous	redeemed	unyielding
stoically	reticent	indisposition	retrieve
defection	recriminations	rituals	

1. Because she was very tall, Yuri _____ over all the men in the village.

2. The cute little girl _____ many gifts and privileges from her parents.

3. Big women, like Yuri, are _____ among a group of short people.

4. After the Hutchensons planted corn, they _____ bore the news of their son's death.

5. The _____ of many ballet dancers during the Cold War caused the Soviet government much concern.

6. We felt _____ about going to a large party where we did not know anyone except the host.

7. Our dog likes to _____ a ball when we throw it to him.

8. Most religious services are conducted according to the _____ of the particular sect.

9. He had a bad reputation, but his one act of bravery _____ him.

10. When applying for a job, we must appear to be _____.

11. The soprano's _____ prevented her from singing in the opera last night.

12. The ancient Greeks believed that human sacrifice would _____ the angry gods.

13. Since the days of Ponce de Leon, many people are still looking for a(n) _____ for eternal youth.

14. Despite the pleas of the attorneys, the judge was _____ in his decision.

15. After many _____ and accusations, the two motorists finally agreed to settle their dispute.

3. Grammar: The Topic Sentence

Whenever you want to get information quickly, whether it's from a business letter, a set of directions, or a class assignment, you look for the one sentence that will give you the basic facts. This sentence is called the **topic sentence** because it tells you what the rest of the letter or paragraph will contain. If, for example, you ask someone how to reach a particular destination, you will first be told to go right, left, or straight ahead. Then you listen for the other details.

In fiction, the reader is also pointed in the right direction with one sentence (sometimes two) that leads to the unfolding of the events in the story. Often the topic sentence begins the story, as in "Talking to the Dead":

We spoke of her in whispers as Aunty Talking to the Dead, the half-Hawaiian kahuna lady.

In this sentence, the author arouses the reader's curiosity; she makes us wonder exactly what Aunty did to earn this title.

In some stories, the topic sentence may come later. At the end of the fourth paragraph of "The Warriors," for example, the author delineates Uncle Ralph's passion for Pawnee history and hints at the conflicts he faces:

He knew intimate details of every battle the Pawnees ever fought since Pawnee time began, and Sister and I knew even then that Uncle Ralph had a great battlefield of his own.

A topic sentence is a springboard to the events that unfold in a story or essay. It gives the writer a focal point to develop a composition through various methods – details, examples, narration, or description.

■ Application

Look for other topic sentences in the stories you have read so far, and note how the author has developed the sentences into one or more paragraphs. Then try your own hand at writing topic sentences. For each of the following subjects, write a strong topic sentence:

1. the role of machinery in our lives

_____

2. a busy airport

_____

3. victims

_____

4. the significance of dreams

_____

5. more adventures into space

_____

6. body language

_____

Remember: A good topic sentence contains enough ideas that it can be developed into an entire paragraph. Prove this by developing one of the sentences you have just written into a short essay or story.

1. Sharing Ideas

Discuss the following questions with a partner, in a small group, or with the whole class:

1. Discuss how Clinton's professional ideas are different from those of his mother. What is his opinion of Yuri?
2. How does Yuri overcome her fear?
3. Even though this story is about death, there are touches of humor. Find passages and situations in the story that are funny.
4. Why do you agree (or disagree) with Yuri's decision to remove Aunty from her coffin and perform the rituals herself?
5. Explain the last sentence of the story.

2. Writing

Read the writing ideas that follow. Your instructor may make specific assignments, or ask you to choose one of these.

1. Take Clinton's viewpoint and write a defense of his behavior toward his mother and Yuri.
2. Aunty is what we may call "a character," an eccentric person who amuses or fascinates her neighbors. In your hometown or neighborhood, was there such a character who amused or frightened you as a child? Write a description of this person and include your reaction to his or her peculiarities.
3. Compare the beliefs of the people in Yuri's village to those in your native country. Write about the similarities or differences.
4. In some countries, marriages are still arranged by "go-betweens." In today's society, we may have another kind of go-between – computer dating. Compare the two practices and give your opinion of each.
5. The main theme in this story is overcoming fear. Write an essay in which you compare this theme to another story in which a character overcomes an inner conflict. Make specific references to plot situations and other characters in each story.

Summing Up

A | TAKE A CLOSER LOOK

1. Analyzing and Comparing

In each of the following sections, you are asked to think about and compare two of the stories in Part Five.

"A Rice Sandwich" and "The Circus"

- Compare Joey and Aram to Esperanza. How are their personalities different?
- Imagine that they are all in the same class. What would Esperanza learn from them? What would Joey and Aram learn from Esperanza?

"Talking to the Dead" and "A Rice Sandwich"

- Create a conversation between Aunty Talking to the Dead and Esperanza. What advice would Aunty give to Esperanza?
- Compare Esperanza's mother with Yuri's. How does each girl handle her mother?

"The Warriors" and "Talking to the Dead"

- Compare the endings of the two stories. Did the two sisters and Yuri learn something similar? Explain.
- How are Yuri and Uncle Ralph alike? How are they different?

2. Freewriting

What was the biggest challenge you ever had to face? How did you meet this challenge? Were you successful? When you encounter new challenges, do you remember previous successes? Write for fifteen minutes about challenges in your own life.

Look up the meanings of the following groups of words. After you have found the meanings of these words, make up a story using at least fifteen words from this list.

Words that have similar spellings, meanings, or pronunciations are often confused with one another.

From "The Rice Sandwich"

wear (verb), ware (noun), where (adverb)

one (pronoun), won (verb)

ate (verb), eight (adjective), eighth (adverb, adjective, or noun)

tired (adjective), tried (verb)

made (verb), maid (noun)

From "The Circus"

need (noun or verb), knead (verb)

whole (adjective), hole (noun)

tear (noun), tear (verb)

fair (adjective or noun), fare (noun)

pole (noun), poll (noun or verb)

seem (verb), seam (noun)

real (adjective), reel (noun or verb)

From "The Warriors"

wary (adjective), weary (adjective)

stars (noun), stairs (noun)

brought (verb), bought (verb)

tape (noun or verb), tap (noun or verb)

From "Talking to the Dead"

past (adjective or noun), passed (verb)

blue (adjective), blew (verb)

potion (noun), portion (noun or verb)

morning (noun), mourning (noun)

grip (noun or verb), gripe (noun or verb)

C SPELLING

Plurals of Nouns Ending in o

The children in "The Warriors" regarded Uncle Ralph as a *hero.* How do we make this noun plural? Nouns that end in *o* form their plurals by adding *-es* if the *o* is preceded by a consonant. Since the letter *r* is a consonant, *hero* becomes *heroes;* and *echo* is pluralized as *echoes.*

However, if a noun ending in *o* is preceded by a vowel, its plural is formed by just adding *-s.* Thus, *radio* becomes *radios; shampoo* becomes *shampoos.*

This pattern does *not* apply to musical terms, such as *solo.* Regardless of the letter preceding the *o,* the plural of a musical term is always formed with an *s.* Therefore, *solo* becomes *solos* in the plural, and *soprano* becomes *sopranos.*

To review these patterns, form the plural of each of the following nouns:

patio _____	basso _____
potato _____	tomato _____
studio _____	trio _____
kangaroo _____	zoo _____
stereo _____	piano _____

D FINAL REVIEW TEST

Some of the following sentences are correct; in others, there are errors in grammar or usage. If you think the sentence is correct, write the letter *C* in the space below each sentence. If the sentence is incorrect, underline the error(s) and rewrite the sentence correctly. In some instances, you may just be improving awkward constructions.

1. I like the fruit very much. I always keep it at my refrigerator.

---

2. Store is closed. We should have went earlier.

_____

3. Not one of these stories is boring.

_____

4. We're always interesting in reading new fiction.

_____

5. Let's keep the secret between you and I.

_____

6. We enjoy reading short stories by American authors.

_____

7. I dislike to go to the dentist.

_____

8. Jane and myself are going to the game.

_____

9. The teacher objected to me talking in class.

_____

10. We go never to the beach on weekends. It's too crowded.

_____

11. I don't want to go with John. He drives too quick.

_____

12. That leather nice black Italian handbag is on sale.

_____

13. You look tired. Don't you feel well today?

_____

14. Not one of them write a clear memo.

_____

15. There were a novel and a biography on her desk.

_____

16. Their house is the most prettiest one on our street.

_____

17. It's too bad our dog hurt it's paw.

_____

18. If I was you, I would rent a house instead of buying one.

_____

19. We were so thirsty that we could have drank a pitcher of water.

_____

20. It was Mr. Behrman who Johnsy owed her life to.

_____

21. Ted sent flowers to my mother and I.

_____

22. The life on a farm is very difficult, especially in winter.

_____

23. Hal went on the farm to tell the Hutchensons the tragic news.

_____

24. Please put the milk in the refrigerator on the top shelf.

_____

25. We read often articles about life in various parts of United States.

_____

Appendix

The list on the left shows common errors many students make.
Correct versions are on the right.

STOP: DON'T USE THESE	GO: DO USE THESE
almost people	most people
an all piece	a whole piece
arrive to New York	arrive in New York
between you and I	between you and me
enjoy to go	enjoy going
explain me	explain to me
fell off of the bus	fell off the bus
he wish, she wish	he wishes, she wishes
how you say	how do you say
if I was	if I were
I see never him	I never see him
make my homework	do my homework
more prettier	prettier
one of my friend	one of my friends
people is	people are
some persons	some people
the life is funny	life is funny
to talked	to talk
United States	the United States
want shopping	want to shop

LITERARY TERMS

Allegory a story with characters and actions that symbolize ideas and morals, e.g., "The Lottery"

Antagonist a character or force of nature that opposes the main character, e.g., the storm in "The Ambitious Guest"

Atmosphere the mood of a story created by its setting, e.g., "All Summer in a Day"

Characterization a technique the author uses to create a believable character, e.g., Mary in "Too Soon a Woman"

Climax the high point or turning point of a story, e.g., when Sue lifts the shade in "The Last Leaf"

Conflict the struggle between opposing forces, e.g., "A Visit to Grandmother"

Dialect the manner of speech used by characters to reflect their ethnic or regional background, e.g., "Thank You, Ma'm" and "The Warriors"

Dialogue the conversation carried on by characters, e.g., "The Circus"

Fable a short story that uses animals as characters to teach a lesson or moral, e.g., the story Uncle Ralph began to tell about the rats in "The Warriors"

Fantasy a story that is deliberately unreal, like a fairy tale or science fiction, e.g., "All Summer in a Day"

Flashback a device in which the author interrupts the sequence of events to relate an earlier scene, e.g., the beginning of "Désirée's Baby"

Foreshadowing hints or clues that indicate something is about to happen, e.g., "The Lottery"

Imagery descriptive language used to paint a vivid picture of a scene, e.g., "The Corn Planting"

Interior monologue (stream of consciousness) the revealing of events through the thoughts and impressions of a character, e.g., "My Father Sits in the Dark"

Irony the opposite of what was intended; a cruel twist of fate, e.g., "All Summer in a Day"

Local color details of dress, speech, or customs that give the time and place of a story, e.g., "The Warriors"

Metaphor a comparison between two unlike objects to create an image, e.g., "The inside of Woolworth's is swimming-pool green." (from "The Quickening")

Narrative a series of events that make up a plot

Personification giving human characteristics to an inanimate object, e.g., "Pneumonia stalked about the colony touching one here and there with his icy fingers." (from "The Last Leaf")

Plot the plan or arrangement of events that make up a story

Poetic justice the rewarding or punishing of characters in an ironic way, e.g., when Yuri gets rewarded for her perserverance in "Talking to the Dead"

Point of view seeing the events of a story through the eyes of one or more characters, e.g., "A Day's Wait"

Protagonist the main character, the hero or heroine of a story, e.g., Charley in "The Third Level"

Realism life presented as it really is, e.g., "The Corn Planting"

Romanticism life presented as one would like it to be, as in stories with a happy ending, e.g., "The Circus"

Satire the use of ridicule or sarcasm to expose a social evil, e.g., "The One Day War"

Sense impressions a form of imagery in which the author uses language to appeal to the five senses, e.g., "The Quickening"

Setting the time or place in which a story takes place, e.g., nineteenth century Creole society in "Désirée's Baby"

Simile a comparison between unlike objects using the words *like* or *as*, e.g., "I feel my face heating up like a warm bath." (from "The Quickening")

Suspense a series of events that create tension or excitement leading to a climax, e.g., "The Ambitious Guest"

Symbolism a person, place, or object that represents an idea, e.g., planting corn representing new life in "The Corn Planting"

Theme the general message or idea that the author wishes to convey, e.g., the importance of Native American heritage in "The Warriors"

Tragedy the final defeat of the protagonist by the opposing forces, e.g., "Désirée's Baby"

IRREGULAR VERBS

VERB	PAST TENSE	PAST PARTICIPLE (use with *has*, *have*, and *had*)
awake	awoke, awaked	awoken, awoke
be (am, is, are)	was (were)	been
bear	bore	borne
beat	beat	beaten, beat
become	became	become
begin	began	begun
bet	bet	bet
bite	bit	bitten
blow	blew	blown
break	broke	broken
bring	brought	brought
build	built	built
burst	burst	burst
catch	caught	caught
choose	chose	chosen
cling	clung	clung
come	came	come
cost	cost	cost
creep	crept	crept
cut	cut	cut
dive	dived, dove	dived, dove
do	did	done
draw	drew	drawn
dream	dreamt, dreamed	dreamt, dreamed
drink	drank	drunk
drive	drove	driven
eat	ate	eaten
fall	fell	fallen
feel	felt	felt
fight	fought	fought
fling	flung	flung
fly	flew	flown
forget	forgot	forgotten
freeze	froze	frozen
get	got	got, gotten
give	gave	given
go	went	gone

VERB	PAST TENSE	PAST PARTICIPLE (use with *has*, *have*, and *had*)
grow	grew	grown
hang	hung	hung
hang (a person, kill)	hanged, hung	hanged, hung
hear	heard	heard
hit	hit	hit
hurt	hurt	hurt
keep	kept	kept
know	knew	known
lay	laid	laid
lead	led	led
leave	left	left
let	let	let
lie (position)	lay	lain
lose	lost	lost
make	made	made
pay	paid	paid
put	put	put
read	read (pronounced *red*)	read (pronounced *red*)
ride	rode	ridden
ring	rang	rung
rise	rose	risen
run	ran	run
say	said	said
see	saw	seen
send	sent	sent
set	set	set
shake	shook	shaken
shine	shone	shone
show	showed	shown, showed
sing	sang	sung
sink	sank	sunk
sit	sat	sat
sleep	slept	slept
slide	slid	slid
speak	spoke	spoken
spring	sprang	sprung
steal	stole	stolen
swear	swore	sworn
swim	swam	swum

Verb	Past Tense	Past Participle (use with *has*, *have*, and *had*)
swing	swung	swung
take	took	taken
teach	taught	taught
tear	tore	torn
tell	told	told
think	thought	thought
throw	threw	thrown
wake	woke	woken
wear	wore	worn
win	won	won
write	wrote	written

Acknowledgments

Ernest Hemingway, "A Day's Wait," From *Winner Take Nothing* by Ernest Hemingway. Reprinted with permission of Scribner, a Division of Simon & Schuster, from *Winner Take Nothing* by Ernest Hemingway. Copyright 1933 Charles Scribner's Sons. Copyright renewed by Mary Hemingway. Also © Hemingway Foreign Rights Trust. Reprinted by permission.

Langston Hughes, "Thank You, M'am," from *Short Stories* by Langston Hughes. Copyright © 1996 by Ramona Bass and Arnold Rampersad. Compilation and editorial contribution copyright © 1996 by Akiba Sullivan Harper. Reprinted by permission of Hill and Wang, a division of Farrar, Straus and Giroux, LLC. and Harold Ober Associates Incorporated.

Sherwood Anderson, "The Corn Planting," from *The Sherwood Anderson Reader* by Sherwood Anderson. Copyright © 1934 by Crowell Publishing Company. Copyright renewed 1961 by Eleanor Copenhaver Anderson. Reprinted by permission of Harold Ober Associates Incorporated.

Lisa Interollo, "The Quickening," by Lisa Interollo. Copyright © 1984 by Lisa Interollo. Published by arrangement with the author.

O. Henry, "The Last Leaf," from *The Complete Works of O. Henry* by O. Henry published by Garden City Books, a division of Bantam Doubleday Dell, Inc.

Nathaniel Hawthorne, "The Ambitious Guest" from *Twice Told Tales Vol. II* by Nathaniel Hawthorne. Published by the Riverside Press, Houghton Mifflin & Co., 1903.

Shirley Jackson, "The Lottery," from *The Lottery* by Shirley Jackson. Copyright © 1948, 1949 by Shirley Jackson. Copyright renewed 1976, 1977 by Laurence Hyman, Barry Hyman, Mrs. Sarah Webster and Mrs. Joanne Schnurer. Reprinted by permission of Farrar, Straus and Giroux, LLC.

Judith Soloway, "The One Day War," by Judith Soloway. Copyright © 1985 by Judith Soloway. Reprinted by permission of the author.

Jack Finney, "The Third Level," by Jack Finney. Reprinted by permission of Don Congdon Associates, Inc. Copyright © 1950 by the Crowell-Collier Publishing Co., renewed 1977 by Jack Finney.

Ray Bradbury, "All Summer in a Day," by Ray Bradbury. Originally published in

The Magazine of Fantasy and Science Fiction by The Mercury Press. Reprinted by permission of Don Congdon Associates, Inc. Copyright © 1954, renewed 1982 by Ray Bradbury.

Kate Chopin, "Désirée's Baby," by Kate Chopin from *The Awakening and Selected Stories* of Kate Chopin by Barbara H. Solomon, editor, New American Library, a division of Penguin USA, 1976.

William M. Kelley, "A Visit to Grandmother," from *Dancers on the Shore* by William Melvin Kelley. Copyright © 1964 by William Melvin Kelley. Used by permission of the William Morris Agency Inc., on behalf of the author.

Dorothy M. Johnson, "Too Soon a Woman," by Dorothy M. Johnson. Copyright © 1953, renewed 1981 by Dorothy M. Johnson. Originally published in *Cosmopolitan*, March 1953 by The Hearst Corporation. Reprinted by permission of McIntosh and Otis, Inc.

Jerome Weidman, "My Father Sits in the Dark," from *My Father Sits in the Dark and Other Stories* by Jerome Weidman. Copyright © 1961 by Jerome Weidman. Copyright renewed © 1989 by Jerome Weidman. Reprinted by permission of Brandt & Brandt Literary Agents, Inc.

Sandra Cisneros, "A Rice Sandwich," from *The House on Mango Street* by Sandra Cisneros. Copyright © 1984 by Sandra Cisneros. Published by Vintage Books, a division of Random House, Inc., and in hardcover by Alfred A. Knopf in 1994. Reprinted by permission of Susan Bergholz Literary Services, New York. All rights reserved.

William Saroyan, "The Circus," from *My Name is Aram* by William Saroyan. Reprinted by permission of the Trustees of Leland Stanford Junior University.

Anna Lee Walters, "The Warriors," from *The Sun is Not Merciful* by Anna Lee Walters. Copyright © 1985 by Anna Lee Walters. Reprinted by permission of Firebrand Books, Ithaca, New York.

Sylvia Watanabe, from *Talking to the Dead* by Sylvia Watanabe, copyright © 1992 by Sylvia Watanabe. Used by permission of Doubleday, a division of Random House, Inc.

Index